Becoming a Reflective Mathematics Teacher

A Guide for Observations and Self-Assessment

SECOND EDITION

STUDIES IN MATHEMATICAL THINKING AND LEARNING

Alan H. Schoenfeld, Series Editor

Wilcox/Lanier (Eds.) • *Using Assessment to Reshape Mathematics Teaching: A Casebook for Teachers and Teacher Educators, Curriculum and Staff Development Specialists*

Wood/Nelson/Warfield (Eds.) • *Beyond Classical Pedagogy: Teaching Elementary School Mathematics*

Zaskis/Campbell (Eds.) • *Number Theory in Mathematics Education: Perspectives and Prospects*

For additional information on titles in the Studies in Mathematical Thinking and Learning series visit **www.routledge.com**

Becoming a Reflective Mathematics Teacher

A Guide for Observations and Self-Assessment

SECOND EDITION

Alice F. Artzt
Queens College, City University of New York

Eleanor Armour-Thomas
Queens College, City University of New York

Frances R. Curcio
Queens College, City University of New York

LEA Lawrence Erlbaum Associates
Taylor & Francis Group

New York London

Lawrence Erlbaum Associates
Taylor & Francis Group
270 Madison Avenue
New York, NY 10016

Lawrence Erlbaum Associates
Taylor & Francis Group
2 Park Square
Milton Park, Abingdon
Oxon OX14 4RN

Printed in the United States of America on acid-free paper
10 9 8 7 6 5 4 3 2 1

International Standard Book Number-13: 978-0-8058-6194-5 (Softcover) 978-0-8058-6193-8 (Hardcover)

Library of Congress Cataloging-in-Publication Data

Artzt, Alice F.
  Becoming a reflective mathematics teacher : a guide for observations and self-assessment / Alice F. Artzt, Eleanor Armour-Thomas, and Frances R. Curcio.
-- 2nd ed.
      p. cm. -- (Studies in mathematical thinking and learning)
  Includes bibliographical references and index.
  ISBN 978-0-8058-6193-8 (hardback : alk. paper) -- ISBN 978-0-8058-6194-5 (pbk. : alk. paper)
  1. Mathematics--Study and teaching--Evaluation. 2. Mathematics teachers--Psychology. I. Armour-Thomas, Eleanor. II. Curcio, Frances R. III. Title. IV. Series.

QA11.A784 2008
510.71--dc22   2007017211

Visit the Taylor & Francis Web site at
http://www.taylorandfrancis.com

Dedication

This book is dedicated to our immediate families and our family of students.

Contents

List of Figures and Tables

Figure

Tables

Preface to the Second Edition

Welcome to the revised and expanded edition of *Becoming a Reflective Mathematics Teacher*. Similar to the first edition, this book provides preservice and in-service mathematics teachers with practical ideas for developing and honing reflective and self-analytical skills needed to advance and improve instruction.

On the basis of the advice and recommendations from colleagues to demonstrate the application of the model for elementary mathematics teacher preparation, we included examples of observations of elementary mathematics lessons in chapters 5 and 6. We eliminated the repetition of text in Appendix B and chapter 5. We also updated the references and provided rubrics for the observation report and items included in the portfolio that we developed with our students (see Appendixes B.11 and E).

We want to thank Naomi Silverman, Alan Schoenfeld, and the staff at LEA, Taylor & Francis Group for the opportunity to revise and extend this work. We hope that it continues to be a viable supplemental resource for the professional development of preservice and in-service elementary and secondary mathematics teachers.

Alice F. Artzt
Eleanor Armour-Thomas
Frances R. Curcio

Preface to the First Edition

Congratulations on your decision to become a mathematics teacher—a profession suited for a very select group of people. But keep in mind that great teachers are not born, they are made. Just as the most talented musicians or artists become great by reflecting on their art, beginning teachers become accomplished teachers, and skilled teachers become great teachers, by thinking hard about their teaching and finding ways to improve it. This book, based on over 20 years of research and teaching, will prepare you for your work in the mathematics classroom and for developing the thoughtfulness and reflectiveness you need to become a great teacher.

A few obvious prerequisites are that you must be a good mathematician and a lover of mathematics. You must enjoy relating to young people and recognize the importance of their learning mathematics well. A less obvious prerequisite is your willingness and ability to be a reflective, self-critical thinker. As any experienced mathematics teacher will affirm, there is no such thing as a perfect lesson. There is always room for improvement. But whether you improve, or how well or how quickly you improve, depends on what you reflect on and assess before, during, and after your instructional practice. The key to developing into the type of mathematics teacher who can empower students with the love and understanding of mathematics is to continually question your teaching in ways that lead to sustainable changes in both your thinking and your classroom practice.

This process of reflection and self-assessment must be approached in a knowledgeable and systematic way. Toward this end, we have created activities based on a model grounded in a cognitive perspective of student-centered teaching.

Part I provides background, giving you the big picture regarding mathematics teaching. In chapter 1, you will learn about student-centered teaching—an approach to teaching that focuses not on flashy presentations but on what really counts: what your students come to understand and how you help them learn. There's more to teaching than meets the eye, and we will help you understand what it means to teach effectively. Chapter 2 takes a closer look at the image of teaching and learning discussed in chapter 1 and describes a framework for examining the teaching process. That framework looks at two aspects of a lesson: phases and dimensions. In chapter 3, we delve beneath the surface to find out what makes the classroom work. It is what the teacher knows and thinks that shapes what happens in the classroom. We'll present a framework for examining teacher cognitions and discuss the ways that those cognitions shape what the teacher does. Understanding this framework will help you make sense of lessons you see other people teach. And, more important, it will help you think about your own teaching. Before you learn how to use the frameworks presented in chapters 2 and 3, you have a right to ask, "Does this approach make sense?" Chapter 4 shows that it does. We report on the research we have on the relationship between classroom teaching and teachers' underlying cognitions. After documenting the validity of the model and thus rounding out the theoretical frame, we are ready to turn to the "how-to."

In part II, we'll show you how to use the model to observe other teachers' classroom work and then to use it to reflect on your own teaching. In chapter 5, we give you detailed guidelines and instruments to use when observing other teachers' lessons. There are so many things to watch when observing someone else's classroom that if you are not focused, you will gain little from the experience. The techniques suggested in this chapter ensure that you will learn something different and worthwhile from each lesson you observe. The techniques you learned in chapter 5 prepare you for the most important observations you will do in your career as a mathematics teacher—your observations of yourself. Chapter 6, possibly the most important chapter in the book, presents a detailed process for objectively examining both your own teaching of mathematics and your goals, knowledge, and beliefs that underlie everything you do in your classroom. You will learn how to prepare for lesson observations and postlesson conferences with your cooperating teacher or college supervisor in ways that will help them better understand your teaching. You want to be sure that during your postlesson conference, you share all that you thought about and learned from having taught the lesson. In this chapter, we give you specific techniques to help you analyze your lessons and your related thoughts in a detailed and comprehensive manner. Videotaping yourself and having your peers observe you can also be powerful tools for self-improvement, especially when done in the structured manner we discuss in this chapter. Finally in chapter 6, we explain the value of expressing your thoughts and feelings in a written journal. We show you how rethinking the decisions you make during the course of instruction can help you improve your teaching. By examining your own and others' teaching in the way we outline in part II, you can produce much written evidence of your growth as a teacher. In chapter 7, we show you how you can organize these materials into a portfolio that will document your growth as a teacher. This portfolio can be used as part of the requirements for National Board Certification.

If you are still wondering if or how the model works, you will want to read the case studies that we have included in part III. You will see how we used the method to help five of our student teachers improve specific aspects of their instruction. Finally, in our conclusion, we summarize our feelings about and experiences with the model as well as the reactions of our student teachers.

Throughout the text, you will see examples of the work of our student teachers. In addition, you can find the forms you need to apply the model in Appendixes B, C, and D.

Acknowledgments

Behind every book is a cast of characters making a unique and essential contribution. Our cast ranges from supportive family members, to hardworking students, to encouraging colleagues, to wise and insightful experts in the field. Although it is impossible to mention all of the people who directly or indirectly contributed to this book, we will do our best to mention the main cast and the roles that they played.

The book originated with the time-consuming work we did with our students. Our devoted husbands, Russ and Bernard, and our loving children, Michele, Kurt, Julie, and Greg, and Renate and Bianca, were understanding, encouraging, and supportive of the time we gave to these students and to the writing of the book. Our dear students who worked so hard to become the best mathematics teachers they could be played the starring roles. Several students deserve special mention as they contributed to this book in major ways: Sara Lamm helped do the videotaping and coding for the research project. Cindy Phillips, Alison Wank, and Dahlia Sacks wrote many of the insightful observation reports, self-reflective comments, and journal and portfolio entries included in the book.

The original model could not have taken form without feedback from many people. Carol Tittle and the late Zita Cantwell were our mentors in the early stages of the research. We will always be indebted to them for the endless hours they spent advising us. The precursor to the teaching model presented here was a cognitive–metacognitive framework that we developed to examine problem solving in small groups. That framework was based on earlier ones designed by George Pólya, Frank Lester, Joe Garofalo, and Alan Schoenfeld. The specific input given to us by Frank Lester and Alan Schoenfeld regarding the development of that framework was invaluable. It set the stage for how we would later consider teaching as problem solving.

When the first research reports were written, Elizabeth Fennema lent us her support, confidence, and advice. She was the first to plant the idea of turning our ideas and experiences into a book. Frank Lester later gave generously of his time and expertise in helping us shape the research articles for publication. Having his vote of confidence was what we needed to continue our efforts in this work.

Implementation of the model was made possible through the tireless efforts of Naomi Weinman. Not only did she work with the students but she also helped shape the final versions of the activities used for self-reflection. She also spent endless hours identifying the most exemplary pieces of student work for inclusion in the book. Her role in this book cannot be overestimated. And thanks go to our dear friend and colleague Frances Curcio, who lent us her support by using the model with her students and providing us feedback as well as her vote of confidence. She was the one who gave us the idea to submit our proposal for this book to Alan Schoenfeld's editorial series.

We also express our deepest appreciation to Naomi Silverman, senior editor at Lawrence Erlbaum Associates, for her encouragement, wise advice, and patience. We are indebted to both her and Lori Hawver, assistant editor, for their editorial expertise. Our gratitude extends to Sandra K. Wilcox, Michigan State University, and Mary Lynn Raith, Pittsburgh Public Schools, for their painstaking efforts in reviewing the manuscript for this book. Other thanks go to the production editor, Barbara Wieghaus, the cover designer, Kathryn Houghtaling Lacey, and the production manager, Lesley Rock, for their high-quality and prompt work in putting the manuscript into its finished form.

Finally, thanks go to Alan Schoenfeld. From our beginning work on problem solving in small groups to the present work, he has given generously of his time, his wisdom, and his hands-on help. We feel comfortable in saying that through our entire research career in this area, he has been our main guiding light. When we presented this new work to him, Alan had the vision to turn this document into a "user-friendly" book. His editorial flair is evident throughout the pages of this book, so if it manages to contribute to the improvement of mathematics education, the main credit goes to him.

We are privileged to have stood on the shoulders of so many giants!

Alice F. Artzt
Eleanor Armour-Thomas

A Note to Professors

This book can be used in various ways. The authors and others have used it as a secondary text for a mathematics teaching methods course. The structured observation activities are designed to help students relate the concepts they learn in their methods course to the instructional practice they observe in actual mathematics classrooms. This book has also been used to support the activities preservice teachers engage in as they student teach. The reflective activities provide a structure through which beginning teachers can think about their teaching in an insightful, thorough, and productive manner.

Students can work through the activities described in this book over the period of a year. The structured observations and reflective activities are modular, and the model applies to all observations of teaching, no matter what the instructional context. Thus the ideas and activities in this book can be of value when used as a supplement to a course that is already in place.

Part I

Philosophical Basis for the Model

1 Toward an Understanding of Student-Centered Teaching

You have decided to join the teaching profession at a time when there is a great need for highly qualified, well-prepared mathematics teachers. Expectations of teachers in the 21st century are very different from what they were as little as a generation ago. The purpose of this chapter is to give you a vision of what high-quality teaching looks like and the issues you must consider to teach that way. A description of instructional practice in mathematics, the complexities of teaching, the challenges of facilitating student-centered teaching, reflective practice, and professional development sets the stage for the remaining chapters in this book.

Instructional Practice in Mathematics

What does it mean to be a competent mathematics teacher? What do you envision when you think of a good mathematics lesson? Picture two lessons involving probability. In the first lesson, the teacher presents a clear lecture providing all the definitions and rules. The students take copious notes, and then, after watching the teacher model how to do a few problems, they do some practice problems at their seats. The teacher then brings the class together and answers questions about how to do the problems. In the second lesson, the teacher engages the students in an unfair game of dice. The students must make conjectures regarding the fairness of the game. They work in pairs to figure out why the game is unfair and then have a class discussion during which they inadvertently construct the concepts of probability underlying the game. The teacher helps the students organize and formalize their ideas.

As you may notice, student involvement is maximized in the second lesson. In contrast to the first lesson where the students are passive recipients of information, in the second lesson the students are actively engaged with one another in the problem-solving process. In such a lesson, the teacher oversees, guides, and facilitates the students' construction of new knowledge. Endorsement for this latter type of teaching comes from the literature on how students learn mathematics; that is, research suggests that learning is an active problem-solving process in which social interaction plays a critical role (Cobb, 1986; Vygotsky, 1978). Learning is facilitated when learners are encouraged to link new information to their prior knowledge and thereby generate new understandings (Fennema, Carpenter, & Peterson, 1989; Greeno, 1989; Lampert, 1986; Noddings, 1990; von Glasersfeld, 1987).

In line with this research, the *Professional Standards for Teaching Mathematics* (National Council of Teachers of Mathematics [NCTM], 1991) and the *Principles and Standards for School Mathematics* (NCTM, 2000) suggest that teachers must create opportunities that stimulate, guide, and encourage students to make connections among mathematics concepts, construct mathematical ideas, solve problems through reasoning, and take responsibility for their own learning. The research supportive of student-centered teaching is also consistent with standards for beginning teachers that were developed by the Interstate New Teacher Assessment and Support Consortium (INTASC, 1990).

Teaching Is More Than Meets the Eye

Although it is true that a competent teacher must engage in classroom behaviors that are likely to promote student learning of mathematics, this is not the full story of professional competence. There is growing recognition that teaching involves more than what teachers actually do in the classroom and extends to the driving forces behind the teachers' actions: their cognitions. For example, if you were to interview the two teachers described in the previous section about their lessons, what differences would you expect to find? What issues do you think they would discuss? For example, which teacher would be more apt to focus on covering the content? Which teacher would be more apt to focus on student understanding?

For almost two decades, researchers have been building frameworks and models that seek to understand the mind and related actions of a teacher (e.g., Artzt & Armour-Thomas, 1998; Fennema & Franke, 1992; Schoenfeld, 1998; Simon, 1997). Our conceptualization on this issue is that teacher knowledge, beliefs, and goals directly influence decision making across three stages of teaching: *preactive* (i.e., planning), *interactive* (i.e., monitoring and regulating), and *postactive* (i.e., evaluating and revising). These components form a network of overarching cognition that directs and controls the instructional behaviors of teachers in the classroom. To examine both areas of teaching (i.e., instructional practice and cognitions), we developed a model of two interrelated frameworks grounded in a student-centered perspective of teaching. The first framework, which we call the phase-dimension framework (PDF), consists of indicators of instructional practice and is described in detail in chapter 2. The other framework, the teacher cognitions framework (TCF), consists of indicators of teacher cognitions and is elaborated on in chapter 3.

The Challenge of Facilitating Student-Centered Teaching

Although there is broad agreement in the mathematics education and research communities concerning the cognitive view of learning and its implications for teaching, it is not yet well understood how to help teachers develop student-centered practices in the classroom and the cognitions that guide and shape such practices.

One difficulty is that not enough is yet known about how to change the deeply entrenched beliefs about mathematics learning and teaching that are based largely on our own experiences as students. For example, one widely held belief about teaching is that the role of the teacher is to transmit mathematical content, demonstrate procedures for solving problems, and explain the process of solving sample problems. Although there may be some instances when such an approach may be appropriate, there is much more to teaching for student understanding.

A commonly held belief about learning is that students learn the content by listening well to the teacher and remembering what they are told. In this rather narrow view, students show that learning has occurred by applying the demonstrated procedures and working problems similar to the ones introduced earlier by the teacher.

Another difficulty involves the unpredictability of change, even among teachers given the same learning experiences intended to transform their teaching. Predicting change can be inaccurate because each prospective teacher comes to a learning situation with an existing cognitive structure that includes certain personal beliefs, knowledge, and goals. Although a group of teachers might be exposed to the same learning experiences, what one teacher notices and acts on depends on how the experiences filter through her or his unique existing cognitive structure. Consequently, different interpretations of the same experiences could lead to differential patterns of change. In short, understanding new teachers' trajectories is still an inexact science.

Despite these difficulties, cognitive models of teacher change maintain that teachers move through pathways that culminate in student-centered practice (e.g., Cooney, 1993; Cooney & Shealy, 1997; Fennema et al., 1996; Franke, Fennema, & Carpenter, 1997). In reviewing these studies, Goldsmith and Schifter (1997) identified three stages of teaching. The *initial stage* is characterized by traditional instruction, where the teacher is driven by the belief that students learn best by receiving clear information transmitted by a knowledgeable teacher. In *subsequent stages* of instruction, the teacher is more focused on helping students build on what they understand and less focused on helping them in the sole acquisition of facts. The instruction is founded on the teacher's belief that students should take greater responsibility in their own learning. In what Goldsmith and Schifter call the *final stage,* instruction is in line with high-quality teaching. (We prefer to refer to this stage as an *advanced stage* of teaching to indicate that there is always potential for future growth.) At this advanced stage, the teacher arranges experiences for students in which they actively explore mathematical topics, learning both the hows and whys of mathematical concepts and processes. The teacher is motivated by the belief that, given appropriate settings, students are capable of constructing deep and connected mathematical understanding.

We address the question of teacher change in our mathematics education program by requiring prospective teachers to use a reflection and self-assessment procedure. We believe that if teachers are to become truly student centered in their teaching, they must view themselves as agents in their own learning and development. They must be willing and able to take responsibility for their actions in the classroom by giving careful consideration to what they intend to do not only before and during the lesson but after the lesson as well. To recognize that one must be committed to thinking deeply about various aspects of one's teaching is to climb to the first step on the ladder of change. More than 70 years ago, Dewey (1933) defined this type of thinking as reflective thinking: *"Active, persistent, and careful consideration of any belief or supposed form of knowledge in the light of the grounds that support it"* (p. 9; italics in original).

Reflection, though necessary, is not sufficient for transformative teaching. Teachers must also be willing and able to *acknowledge* problems that may be revealed as a result of the reflective process. Moreover, they must explore the reasons for the acknowledged problem, consider more plausible alternatives, and eventually *change* their thinking and subsequent action in the classroom. We argue that over time, the habitual use of reflective and self-assessment processes about learning experiences leads to transformation in teaching.

Definition of Reflection and Self-Assessment

Reflection is defined as thinking about teaching. It involves the thoughts teachers have before, during, and after the actual enactment of a lesson. Although there are many definitions of *reflection* (e.g., Dewey, 1933; Schon, 1983; Van Manen, 1977; von Glasersfeld, 1991), the construct resembles several of the thinking processes identified by Pólya (1945) in his conception of mathematical problem solving: understanding, planning, and looking back. In Pólya's model of problem solving, expert problem solvers think about the problem to be solved by using thinking processes indicative of understanding and planning. We contend that teachers must engage in similar types of thinking before the actual enactment of a lesson. For example, they must think about their goals for the students and thereby activate their knowledge and beliefs about the students, pedagogy, and content. Teachers also must think about the difficulties students are likely to encounter in their efforts to attain the goals; consequently, teachers must think about the strategies they will need to consider in conducting the anticipated lesson.

Continuing with the problem-solving analogy, we view Pólya's "looking back" as another type of reflective thinking that teachers engage in after conducting a lesson. In other words, just as an expert problem solver reexamines the steps taken to solve a problem, a teacher, on completing a lesson, must rethink lesson goals and reconsider what the teacher and the students said, did, and felt during the lesson. This reflective phase is likely to uncover difficulties or problems that, if the teacher does not address them, may impede progress toward self-improvement in teaching. How do teachers increase the likelihood that problematic aspects of their teaching are indeed revealed during this reflective process? And, as important, what conjectures or judgments do they make about such difficulties?

The second strand in our procedure is self-assessment. Self-assessment describes the kinds of evaluative questions teachers ask themselves as they reflect on their teaching after completing lessons.

Taking personal responsibility and control of one's learning is a hallmark of academic excellence. A critical factor in this type of learning that researchers define as self-regulated (e.g., Harris, 1979; Paris & Newman, 1990; Zimmerman, 1990) is self-assessment. When students are in the habit of asking themselves such questions as "What do I need to do?" "How am I doing?" and "How well did I do?" in relation to academic goals, their learning is more proficient than that of students who do not habitually ask themselves these questions. Indeed, most contemporary models of human cognition consider self-assessment an important dimension of good thinking (A.L. Brown, 1978; Flavell, 1981; Schoenfeld, 1987; Sternberg, 1986). Likewise, we believe that self-assessment plays a pivotal role in enabling teachers to become student centered. The focus of teachers' self-assessment may be quite varied, ranging from prelesson thoughts, lesson plans, and classroom practices to specific pedagogical actions taken during the actual teaching of lessons.

In our teacher education program, we use procedures of reflection and self-assessment to enable preservice teachers to examine the relationship between their cognitions and instructional practice. Our integrative model of teaching (i.e., PDF and TCF) provides the conceptual guidance for their reflections and self-assessment.

Learning Experiences for Promoting Teacher Growth

As a prospective teacher, you need to engage in specific learning experiences that put you on the road to having a successful profession as a mathematics teacher. Specifically, you need to participate in structured activities that get you in the habit of reflecting on and assessing your cognitions and your instructional practice.

During the beginning of your teacher preparatory program, it is important to observe other mathematics teachers. This experience helps sensitize you to some of the major areas of teachers' work in the classroom. Structured observation assignments encourage you to make conjectures about the cognitions of the teachers you observe and to consider the role of cognition in teaching.

During your student-teaching experiences, you should be provided with supervision that encourages you to engage in structured reflection and self-assessment that are based on the model described in this book. This guidance is based on Vygotsky's (1978) idea that certain kinds of assistance influence growth in thinking. The first type of assistance, which some researchers (P. Wood, Bruner, & Ross, 1976) call "scaffolding," is given when a knowledgeable adult or capable peer interacts with a novice learner. These individuals listen, prompt, ask questions, and give feedback and in so doing give just the right amount of assistance to advance the learner's understanding. As the learner's understanding develops, the adult or capable peer gradually reduces instructional assistance and allows the learner to assume greater independence for her or his learning. The second type of assistance occurs when an individual uses tools to support thinking and learning. Goldsmith and Schifter (1997) gave an example of writing as a tool for facilitating intellectual growth: "Writing allows us to stop, reflect, think, reflect again, and struggle to articulate further. Having a physical record of the thinking process also broadens the opportunities for sharing ideas and engaging in dialogue with a wide variety of others (as well as with self), thus expanding the possibilities for developing further understanding" (p. 43).

By observing teachers in the field, you can begin to examine classroom practices and speculate about the cognitions that may undergird such classroom behavior. During student teaching, your supervisor, cooperating teacher, and peers perform the conceptual scaffolding function. Tools such as journals, videotapes, written comments about thoughts before and after the lesson, and portfolios can help you to reflect on and assess your cognitions and classroom practice. The integrative model (i.e., PDF and TCF) provides the conceptual basis for your observations in the field and the scaffolding activities. And finally, the reflection and self-assessment procedures help you to gain a more insightful understanding of the relationship between your cognitions and instructional practice.

2 A Framework for the Examination of Instructional Practice

In this chapter, we demonstrate how to dissect a lesson, looking at its pieces and how they fit together. This approach orients your examination of others' teaching and helps you focus on important aspects of your own lessons. The first decomposition of a lesson is temporal and straightforward; we describe the parts of a lesson as it unfolds. The second decomposition is more complex; we discuss lesson dimensions and dimension indicators—the material of the lesson and how to think about it.

One challenge facing teacher educators today is how to prepare their students to teach in a manner consistent with new ideas about learning and the nature of mathematics. In the previous chapter, we identified a number of propositions about student learning that suggest new roles and responsibilities for teachers. We have developed a phase-dimension framework (PDF) to help teachers better understand and appreciate these roles and responsibilities from a new cognitive perspective that has student learning as its focus.

Teaching for student learning with understanding is at the heart of the framework. We believe it is the essence of student-centered teaching and provides focus and direction for teachers' energies in the classroom. Two issues guided us in this belief. First, with others in the mathematics education and research communities, we share the view that a primary goal of instruction is to promote student learning of mathematics with understanding (Hiebert & Carpenter, 1992). Second, theoretical and empirical research on learning from psychology, mathematics education, and cognitive science suggests positive consequences for students who learn with understanding. For example, some researchers claim that initial understanding enables children to construct relationships and create productive inventions (Hiebert & Carpenter, 1992). Others have shown that learning with understanding promotes remembering (Bartlett, 1932; Rumelhart, 1975) and enhances transfer (J.S. Brown, Collins, & Duguid, 1989; Perkins & Salomon, 1989). As suggested by the standards of the Interstate New Teacher Assessment and Support Consortium (INTASC, 1990), the teacher must know how to use instructional strategies that foster student development of critical thinking, problem solving, and performance skills.

What would classroom practice look like if the goal of teaching were to enable student learning of mathematics with understanding? To be more specific, how would teachers help students to relate new ideas of mathematics to what they already know and can do, use their prior knowledge and skill to construct new meaning through reasoning and problem solving, and extend their learning to new contexts? We created two classifications to answer these questions: lesson phases and lesson dimensions.

Lesson Phases

Lesson phases describe a temporal sequence of teaching–learning experiences that occur over the duration of a lesson. The concept of lesson phases is derived from the cognitive instruction literature that suggests that the ways teachers initiate, develop, and close instructional episodes have important implications for student learning (e.g., Jones, Palincsar, Ogle, & Carr, 1987). Lesson phases function as transition markers that indicate different segments of an enacted lesson. For example, when designing instruction, teachers must ensure that they set aside time in which they (a) establish students' readiness for learning, (b) build new concepts by enabling learners to recognize relationships and construct new meanings, and (c) enable learners to integrate and extend their learning to new contexts. It is important to note that although each of these phases is essential for effective instruction, they need not all occur in one class period. For example, an interesting problem might have different components that the class needs to work on for several days before the main ideas are developed. However, for the purpose of clarity, it is helpful to students for the teacher to identify the specific phase of instruction in which they are engaged. For example, before a summarizing activity takes place, the teacher might make it clear to the students that it is now time to tie up all the ideas that they have learned thus far.

We adopted the descriptors for these temporal phases of a lesson from the Connecticut Competency Instrument for Beginning Teachers: initiation, development, and closure. (For further discussion of the use of these terms, see Armour-Thomas and Szczesiul [1989].)

Lesson Dimensions

Table 2.1 provides a bird's eye view of a lesson, focusing on its most important dimensions. The major categories described in Table 2.1—tasks, learning environment, and discourse—are fundamental components of a lesson. In this section, we describe the characteristics of each component and explore how they work.

Tasks

Tasks provide opportunities for learners to connect their knowledge to new information and to build on their knowledge and interest through active engagement in meaningful problem solving. According to the general literature, to foster student involvement, tasks must be motivational, at an appropriate level of difficulty, and sequenced in a meaningful way so that different representations are available to help students clarify and connect their ideas. A further elaboration of these ideas follows.

Table 2.1   Lesson Dimensions and Dimension Indicators

Dimensions	Description of Dimension Indicators
Tasks	
Modes of representation	Uses such representations as symbols, diagrams, manipulatives, and computer or calculator representations to accurately facilitate content clarity. Provides multiple representations that enable students to connect their prior knowledge and skills to the new mathematical situation.
Motivational strategies	Uses tasks that capture students' curiosity and inspires them to speculate on and to pursue their conjectures. Takes into account the diversity of student interests and experiences. The substance of the motivation is aligned with the goals and purposes of instruction.
Sequencing and difficulty levels	Sequences tasks so that students can progress in their cumulative understanding of a particular content area and can make connections between ideas learned in the past and those they will learn in the future. Uses tasks that are suitable to what the students already know and can do and what they need to learn or improve on.
Learning environment	
Social and intellectual climate	Establishes and maintains a positive rapport with and among students by showing respect for and valuing students' ideas and ways of thinking. Enforces classroom rules and procedures to ensure appropriate classroom behavior.
Modes of instruction and pacing	Uses instructional strategies that encourage and support student involvement as well as facilitate goal attainment. Provides and structures the time necessary for students to express themselves and explore mathematical ideas and problems.
Administrative routines	Uses effective procedures for organization and management of the classroom so that time is maximized for students' active involvement in the discourse and tasks.

(*continued*)

Table 2.1   (continued)

Dimensions	Description of Dimension Indicators
Discourse	
Teacher–student interaction	Communicates with students in a nonjudgmental manner and encourages the participation of each student. Requires students to give full explanations and justifications or demonstrations orally and/or in writing. Listens carefully to students' ideas and makes appropriate decisions regarding when to offer information, provide clarification, model, lead, and let students grapple with difficulties.
Student–student interaction	Encourages students to listen to, respond to, and question each other so that they can evaluate and, if necessary, discard or revise ideas and take full responsibility for arriving at mathematical conjectures and/or conclusions.
Questioning	Poses a variety of levels and types of questions using appropriate wait times that elicit, engage, and challenge students' thinking.

Source: From "A Cognitive Model for Examining Teachers' Instructional Practice in Mathematics: A Guide for Facilitating Teacher Reflection," by A.F. Artzt and E. Armour-Thomas, 1999, *Educational Studies in Mathematics, 40*(3), p. 217. Copyright © 1999 by Kluwer Academic Publishers. Adapted with kind permission from Kluwer Academic Publishers.

Modes of Representation

Modes of representation are the forms for representing mathematical concepts or principles externally through the use of oral or written language, diagrams, manipulatives, computers, or calculators. Research suggests that how individuals represent information in memory is partly influenced by the form of the content represented (C.A. Brown & Baird, 1993; Hiebert & Carpenter, 1992). In creating opportunities for children to learn with understanding, teachers must figure out what modes of representing mathematics concepts and principles are likely to help them make connections with these ideas.

Motivation

Motivation is a key concept in learning. According to Good and Brophy (1995), "Motivation is a hypothetical construct used to explain the initiation, direction, intensity, and persistence of goal-directed behavior" (p. 343).

This means that the tasks that students engage in must possess attributes that attract and sustain their attention and emotional investment over time. In applying this construct to mathematical tasks, teachers must consider three basic questions:

- Are the tasks in alignment with the lesson goal of learning with understanding?
- Will the tasks arouse students' curiosity and interest and inspire them to speculate and pursue conjectures?
- Will the tasks be sufficiently challenging to sustain students' interest until completion?

Difficulty Level and Sequencing

The level of difficulty of a task is its complexity, and sequencing is the order in which students attend to and work on features of the task and/or the order in which the teacher makes the task salient for them. Teachers must decide how and when to sequence tasks and how to select tasks with appropriate levels of difficulty. On one hand, if a task is too easy, students will lose interest, become bored, and apply minimal effort. On the other hand, if the tasks are so difficult that students cannot succeed, many will become frustrated and give up trying. Therefore, the difficulty level and sequencing of a task must allow students to use their past knowledge and experience to help them understand the requirements of the task. Yet, the task must be challenging enough that students create new connections to deepen their understanding and extend their learning. These attributes of tasks are consistent with the suggestion of the National Council of Teachers of Mathematics (NCTM, 1991) that tasks must "engage all students in formulating and solving a wide variety of problems, making conjectures and constructing arguments, validating solutions, and evaluating the reasonableness of mathematical claims" (p. 21).

Learning Environment

The term *learning environment* describes the conditions under which the teaching–learning process unfolds in the classroom. It defines the tone and patterns of interpersonal interactions between student and teacher as well as the terms for such engagement. It also refers to the circumstances that affect the flow of action in the classroom and the mechanisms by which time is allocated for learning. This definition of *learning environment* is similar to the concept of *context* as it has been used in the educational and psychological literature for many years. For example, some researchers assert that the context in which cognitive activity is undertaken shapes not only the perceived nature of the problem but the solution as well (Rogoff & Lave, 1984; Vygotsky, 1978). The psychological significance of the context is consistent with the NCTM's (1991) vision of a learning environment as one that promotes the development of students' conceptual and procedural understanding.

In making decisions about learning environments, teachers can consider several categories of attributes. The first category, and perhaps the one most directly related to the promotion of student learning with understanding, has to do with the social and intellectual climate of the classroom. The question is whether the environment is conducive to the discourse and whether task engagement is likely to foster the development of mathematical understanding among all students. The second category of attributes concerns the modes of instruction and amount of class time allotted for them. The third category has to do with practical or technical issues related to classroom organization and management, such as the classroom furniture arrangement, routines, rules for student deportment, and allocation of time for administrative activities. A further elaboration of these attributes follows.

Social and Intellectual Climate

The social and intellectual climate defines the tone, style, and manner of the interpersonal interactions in the classroom. Research in the humanistic tradition (Bossert, 1977; Rogers, 1983) has emphasized the importance of affective and emotional elements in interpersonal relationships and their implications for student social and cognitive growth and development. When the interpersonal chemistry in a classroom is positive, students are encouraged to activate and use their prior knowledge in relation to the problem at hand and to engage in the process of knowledge consolidation and construction. When the social and intellectual climate is positive, it supports a feeling of mutual respect among and between students and teacher, and all have patience for one another and value diverse ideas and ways of thinking. It creates a safe haven for students to engage in challenging tasks without the fear of failure or threat of punishment.

Modes of Instruction and Pacing

Modes of instruction are the activities that teachers use in the classroom to help students attain the objectives of the lesson. Activities include seatwork, discussions, recitation, pair work, lab work, guided discovery, and small-group work, to name a few. To facilitate student learning with understanding, instructional activities must encourage students' active exploration of mathematical ideas and stimulate their thinking in ways that build and deepen mathematical understanding. Moreover, teachers must properly pace activities so that students are provided enough time in which to express themselves freely, make and test conjectures, debate ideas with one another, and construct new knowledge.

Administrative Routines

Administrative routines are predictable or ritualized procedures or activities in classroom organization and management. Saphier and Gower (1987) identified three types of routines of importance in the classroom: those that are concerned with housekeeping (e.g., distribution of materials and equipment, attendance, and cleanup); those that are related to class business (e.g., taking turns, collecting homework); and those that pertain to work procedures (e.g., use of equipment and tools, and procedures for doing assignments). Kounin and Gump (1974) asserted that routines provide an ongoing signal of organizational and interpersonal behavior in the classroom. The less time teachers spend on these technical administrative aspects of the learning environment, the more time they have for engaging students in activities more directly related to learning mathematics with understanding.

Discourse

Discourse describes the verbal exchange among members of the community in the classroom, both teachers and students. Discourse can facilitate task engagement for learning with understanding. There are many critical features of discourse that define the nature and quality of interactions among members: the kinds of questions posed, the responses elicited, and the time allowed for responding. Let us examine these attributes of discourse further.

Teacher–Student Interactions

Some researchers studying mathematics from a constructivist perspective call attention to the importance of social relationships in teaching. They conceive of the classroom as a potential learning community in which students experience a sense of efficacy as learners and thus show a willingness to take risks for learning in a public forum (Richards, 1991; T. Wood, Cobb, & Yackel, 1995). This means that teachers should interact as mathematical learners on an equal basis with students, always in search of more in-depth mathematical understanding and discovery. Through questions, comments, and feedback, the teacher may press the students to reflect on what they or their classmates have asked or proposed to build and extend their own understandings. Furthermore, the teacher may encourage students to attend to and stay engaged in the task at hand and solicit contributions from everyone. The teacher plays a critical role in orchestrating discourse. According to the *Professional Standards for Teaching Mathematics* (NCTM, 1991), teachers must think very carefully about *"when to provide information, when to clarify an issue, when to model, when to lead, and when to let a student struggle with a difficulty"* (p. 35; italics in original). This means that teachers must also know how to use verbal and nonverbal strategies to communicate effectively, that is, to promote inquiry, collaboration, and supportive interaction in the classroom (INTASC, 1990).

Student–Student Interactions

For students to build their own mathematical constructions, they need to interact with each other in ways that reinforce and support yet challenge each other's ideas.

Within the classroom environment as a community of learners, students should be encouraged to listen to, respond to, and question each other and to debate and give explanations and justifications for their ideas and feedback to their peers' ideas. The nature and quality of these student–student interactions, though, must encourage students to make connections of their prior knowledge to new information, to make new connections between mathematical ideas, and to integrate and extend these new understandings into their existing knowledge structures.

Questioning

Questioning in teacher–student interactions is an important medium through which students build on their preexisting knowledge. The level and type of questioning and the time for student responses vary in the classroom because this medium serves many purposes. Research suggests that both the cognitive level of questions (Klinzing, Klinzing-Eurich, & Tisher, 1985; Samson, Strykowski, Weinstein, & Walberg, 1987) and the time for responding to teacher questions (Rowe, 1986; Tobin, 1983) have had positive consequences for students in terms of their quality of participation and achievement. Through questioning, the teacher encourages students to make public their knowledge, skills, and attitudes in relation to the problem under consideration. Teacher questioning may also seek to determine how well students are making connections or what kinds of connections are being made among mathematical ideas. Confrey (1990) suggested that the following types of questions promote student learning with understanding: "'What are we doing?' 'What is the problem?' or 'What does this problem say?' ... 'Why? What does that tell you? What can you tell me? Why not?' and 'What do you mean it doesn't work?'" (pp. 116–117). Depending on the cognitive demands of the questions and the student's level of understanding, the teacher determines how much time to allow for student responses. When students respond to the questions, the teacher may decide to adjust the pace of teaching, reteach, or reinforce the concepts. The *Professional Standards for Teaching Mathematics* (NCTM, 1991) acknowledges the critical role of teacher questioning and suggests that the teacher's role begins to shift from telling and describing to listening, questioning, and probing for understanding.

In our work with teachers, we have found that these attributes allow us to understand better variation among instructional practice. The next chapter describes the framework we used to examine the cognitions underlying these areas of instructional practice.

3 A Framework for the Examination of Teacher Cognitions

In this chapter, we suggest ways to examine the aspects of teaching that are the driving force behind every lesson: teacher cognitions. This approach allows you to understand better your own and others' teaching and provides the mechanism with which you can engage in self-reflection and improvement. As we have argued, what counts is the teacher's cognition and how it comes into play at different times. Table 3.1 provides an overview of the nature of teacher cognitions and when it gets applied. The overarching aspects of teacher cognitions are teachers' *goals, knowledge,* and *beliefs.* Other cognitions come into play at different times and in different ways: planning prior to the lesson, monitoring and regulating during the lesson, and evaluating and revising after the lesson.

Student-centered instruction must be backed by mental activities and thought processes of teachers who have a student-centered philosophy of instruction. On the basis of our position that teacher cognitions drive teachers' actions in the classroom, we developed a teacher cognitions framework (TCF), using the same conceptual orientation as the phase-dimension framework (PDF): teaching for student learning with understanding. We used Jackson's (1968) conceptual distinction of preactive, interactive, and postactive stages of teaching to examine teacher cognitions before, during, and after teaching a lesson. We identified two broad components of cognition: overarching cognitions and cognitive processes. A brief description of these aspects of teachers' mental activities follows, along with examples of their potential impact on the dimensions of instructional practice discussed in chapter 2: tasks, learning environment, and discourse.

Overarching Cognitions

There are three components of overarching cognitions: goals, knowledge, and beliefs. The centrality of these components to teaching is supported by extensive research (e.g., Schoenfeld, 1998). We use the term *overarching* because we think that these cognitions comprise a dynamic network that functions as a control center for all our thoughts and actions about teaching. It is these overarching cognitions that influence the decisions teachers make before (i.e., *planning*), during (i.e., *monitoring* and *regulating*), and after (i.e., *evaluating* and *revising*) a lesson.

Table 3.1   Components of Teacher Cognitions and Description of Indicators

Cognitions	Description of Indicators of Cognition
Overarching Cognitions	
Goals	The teacher desires to help students construct their own meaning so that they will develop conceptual and procedural understanding and will value mathematics and feel confident in their abilities.
Knowledge	
Pupils	The teacher has specific knowledge of pupils' prior knowledge and experiences, abilities, attitudes, and interests.
Content	The teacher has conceptual and procedural understandings of the content and is aware of and appreciates the connections between it and past and future areas of study.
Pedagogy	The teacher understands how students learn mathematics and knows how to develop suitable teaching strategies and anticipates and prepares for areas of difficulty based on that understanding.
Beliefs	
Pupils	The teacher views the role of students as active participants in their own learning, and believes students should make conjectures, propose approaches and solutions to problems, debate the validity of one another's claims, and verify, revise, and discard ideas on the basis of their own and other students' mathematical reasoning.
Content	The teacher views mathematics as a "dynamic and expanding system of connected principles and ideas constructed through exploration and investigation" (NCTM, 1991, p. 133).
Pedagogy	The teacher views the teacher's role as a facilitator of student learning through selections of problem-solving tasks and the leading and orchestration of communication in which students are challenged to think for themselves through mathematical reasoning.
Cognitive Processes	
Preactive	
Planning	The teacher focuses the lesson on building conceptual understanding based on what the students already know and focuses on mathematical processes underlying the procedures to be developed and the skill development required by the content specifications. The teacher sequences tasks logically to build on previous student understanding and to clarify new concepts and arouse students' interest and curiosity and makes obvious how much time is allowed for each segment of the lesson (i.e., initiation, development, closure).

(continued)

Table 3.1 (continued)

Cognitions	Description of Indicators of Cognition
Interactive	
Monitoring	The teacher observes, listens to, and elicits participation of students on an ongoing basis to assess student learning and disposition toward mathematics.
Regulating	The teacher adapts or changes plans while teaching based on the information received through monitoring student learning and interest.
Postactive	
Evaluating	The teacher describes and comments on students' understanding of concepts and procedures and dispositions toward mathematics as well as the effects of instruction on these outcomes.
Revising	The teacher uses information from evaluations of student learning and instructional practices to revise and adapt subsequent plans for instruction.

Goals

We define *goals* as expectations about the intellectual, social, and emotional outcomes for students as a consequence of their classroom experiences. In the *Curriculum and Evaluation Standards for School Mathematics,* the National Council of Teachers of Mathematics (NCTM, 1989) sets forth its vision of mathematical power through the articulation of five general goals for all students: that they value mathematics, become confident in their ability to do mathematics, become mathematical problem solvers, learn to communicate mathematically, and learn to reason mathematically (p. 5). More recently, in its *Principles and Standards for School Mathematics,* the NCTM (2000) reiterated the importance of these processes and expressed the expectation that teachers reflect these goals in their instructional practice. Furthermore, researchers (Hiebert, 1986; Silver, 1986) and reform initiatives (Mathematical Sciences Education Board & National Research Council, 1991) have begun to give more attention to goals that emphasize the importance of teaching for conceptual and procedural understanding.

Teachers' goals (often implicit) become apparent through observations of their instructional practices. For example, a teacher whose goal is that students learn to value mathematics tends to design meaningful and worthwhile tasks. A teacher whose goal is to have students communicate mathematically tends to include such instructional routines as small-group work that facilitates such communication. Finally, a teacher whose goal is that students engage in mathematical reasoning tends to orchestrate the classroom discourse in such a way that the burden of explanation and justification is placed on the students.

Knowledge

We define *teacher knowledge* as an integrated system of internalized information acquired over time about pupils, content, and pedagogy. This definition is based in part on Shulman's (1986) conception of teacher knowledge as a multidimensional and interrelated construct that includes content knowledge, pedagogical content knowledge, and curricular knowledge. More recently, other researchers have concurred that these categories of knowledge are important for teaching (Ball, 1990; Borko & Putman, 1996; C. A. Brown & Borko, 1992; Grossman, Schoenfeld, & Lee, 2005; Schoenfeld, 1998, 2002) and can make a difference in instructional practice and student learning (Fennema & Franke, 1992; Peterson, 1988).

Although it is not yet clear how these categories of knowledge are organized and structured in memory in ways to inform lesson planning and classroom practice, we do know that teacher knowledge reveals itself in different ways throughout classroom instruction. For example, in an exploratory study (Artzt & Armour-Thomas, 1999), we found that teachers who seemed to know their students well (i.e., their prior knowledge and experiences, their interests and attitudes, and their learning styles and abilities) created tasks that were motivational and at an appropriate level of difficulty. Teachers who seemed to have a broad knowledge of pedagogical approaches and knew how these approaches fit the needs of different students and different content areas tended to use a wide range of instructional strategies that could enhance the learning opportunities for their students. Teachers who seemed to have a deep knowledge of the content and were aware of and appreciated its connections with past and future areas of study tended to ask a variety of questions of different levels that focused on both procedural and conceptual issues. The type of questions they asked helped students make the connections necessary for them to construct new understandings.

Beliefs

We define *beliefs* as an integrated system of personalized assumptions about the nature of the subject, the students, learning, and teaching. Beliefs function as an interpretative filter for teachers' goals and knowledge and strongly affect classroom practice (Cooney, 1985; Ernest, 1989; Schoenfeld, 1998; Swafford, 1995; Thompson, 1992). For example, to provide classroom opportunities for students to understand mathematics as a "dynamic and expanding system of connected principles and ideas constructed through exploration and investigation" (NCTM, 1991, p. 133), teachers must believe it is such. Only then can they design tasks that provide opportunities for students to act like real mathematicians who engage in authentic mathematical inquiry. Furthermore, teachers who consider themselves facilitators of student learning tend to use instructional strategies that foster communication among students and challenge students to think for themselves and engage in mathematical reasoning. Finally, teachers who believe that the role of *all* students in the classroom is to be active participants in their own learning tend to create social and intellectual climates that set the stage for discourse that can offer every student an equal opportunity to participate.

Although beliefs are undoubtedly a driving force behind the nature of a teacher's instructional practice, teachers' stated beliefs are not always consistent with their behaviors. In research on this issue, Artzt and Armour-Thomas (1998) found that several teachers professed beliefs about how to teach mathematics consistent with ideas espoused by the NCTM (1989), yet their classroom practice suggested otherwise. A possible reason for this may have to do with the readiness of the preservice teachers' existing cognitive structures to accommodate experiences with perplexities. As we earlier surmised, the receptivity of one's cognitive structure to new experiences plays a key role in influencing what is learned.

Other researchers have found similar contradictions between teachers' professed beliefs and their actions in the classroom (Cohen, 1990; Cooney, 1985; Cooney, Shealy, & Arvold, 1998; Franke, Fennema, & Carpenter, 1997). Therefore, in our work with student teachers, we talk about beliefs only after they have taught their lessons. By trying to justify their instructional practice, they can get a better insight into their own beliefs.

Teacher Cognitive Processes

We selected three classes of thinking processes that affect instructional practice in important ways: planning, monitoring and regulating, and evaluating and revising. These processes are involved in teacher decision making and judgments before, during, and after classroom instruction. A brief description of each of these thinking processes follows, with a commentary on their potential impact on classroom instruction.

Preactive Stage: Planning

Planning is the thinking that teachers do as they prepare to teach lessons. According to the standards of the Interstate New Teacher Assessment and Support Consortium (1990), teachers' instructional planning must be based on knowledge of subject matter, students, the community, and curricula goals. A lesson plan is a concrete embodiment of the teacher's thinking regarding the instructional activities to be enacted in the classroom. Research has demonstrated that teachers' plans are reflected in the tasks, learning environment, and, indirectly, discourse that takes place during their instructional practice (Hill, Yinger, & Robbins, 1981; Peterson, Marx, & Clark, 1978). Thus, the planning teachers engage in before instruction has the potential to affect the nature and quality of their lessons. In an exploratory study (Artzt & Armour-Thomas, 1999), teachers whose lesson objective was building students' conceptual and procedural understanding tended to design tasks at an appropriate level of difficulty and sequenced them so as to facilitate the students' ability to extend their own learning. They tended to design lessons that incorporated the types of instructional strategies that maximize the chances for student involvement and learning with understanding. They also allotted enough time for these activities so that a comfortable environment was set within which rich interactive discourse among students occurred.

Interactive Stage: Monitoring and Regulating

Monitoring and regulating are the metacognitive strategies used to check and modify one's actions during problem solving. Research studies show that these decision-making processes play a pivotal role not only in the efficacy of the problem-solving process but also in the ultimate solution of the problem (Artzt & Armour-Thomas, 1992, 2001; Garofalo & Lester, 1985; Schoenfeld, 1987). Just as monitoring and regulating influence problem solving in critical ways, they also affect instructional practice.

Teachers who observe, listen to, and elicit the participation of students on an ongoing basis to assess student learning and disposition toward mathematics are more likely to meet the needs of their students. They do this by adapting or changing their plans based on the information they receive. For example, in an exploratory study (Artzt & Armour-Thomas, 1999), teachers who noticed that some students were confused during instruction often suggested the use of more concrete modes of representation to improve clarity. A teacher who noticed that students were getting too talkative during a cooperative learning session realized that the task needed more structure and decided to bring the group together for spontaneous group presentations. Another teacher, while monitoring students' comments to one another during a classroom discourse and noting that the conversation was digressing too far from the objectives of the lesson, decided to change the course of the discussion by steering the students back to the initial question.

Postactive Stage: Evaluating and Revising

Evaluating and revising are two decision-making processes teachers use after their instructional practice. Teachers reexamine recently enacted lessons to determine whether the goals of instruction were achieved. This process enables teachers to become aware of the strengths and weaknesses of their teaching and revise classroom practices. We agree with Leiva (1995) that "teacher self-evaluation and the analysis of teaching are central to improving mathematics teaching within the framework of the Standards document" (p. 44). Examples of how teachers' postlesson thoughts can affect their subsequent instructional practice follow.

Teachers who evaluate their lessons in terms of students' understanding of concepts and procedures and dispositions toward mathematics, as well as the effects of their instruction on these outcomes, are likely to revise their lessons in ways that will enhance student learning. For example, in an exploratory study (Artzt & Amour-Thomas, 1999), one teacher conducted a lesson in which she felt the contextual setting for a problem would motivate the students. After evaluating the low level of student involvement in the lesson, she suggested the use of a different setting that might be of greater interest to the students. Another teacher allotted too little time for an activity and noticed that students were not asking enough questions or debating enough issues. After evaluating the student behavior in light of the pacing, she decided to change the structure of the lesson so as to allot more time for that particular activity. After evaluating the nature of the students' questions and the students' in-class work, and believing that they revealed a lack of conceptual understanding, another teacher decided to probe deeper into the reasons for this lack of understanding. She decided to use a writing assignment in which students would explain what they did and did not understand.

To indicate how teacher knowledge, beliefs, goals, and thinking processes influence what teachers do in classrooms, the next chapter describes an exploratory research study that was conducted using the TCF presented thus far. This study revealed empirical evidence for some specific ways that the components of teacher cognitions influence teachers' instructional practice.

4　Putting It All Together

This is, for the most part, a practical book. Starting in the next chapter, we will suggest how to observe lessons (including your own), reflect on them, and improve them. But you have a right to ask whether this is a valid model for examining teaching, and we have an obligation to show that it is. This chapter provides the evidence. It describes research results in which we documented the specific relationships of teachers' cognitions and their instructional practices. We also present evidence of the usefulness of the model.

In an effort to understand better the relationship between teachers' thoughts and actions in the classroom, we combined the phase-dimension framework (PDF) and the teacher cognitions framework (TCF) into an integrative model of teaching. The model is based on the assumption that what teachers do in the classroom is influenced by the goals they set for students, what they believe and know about teaching and learning mathematics, and the decisions they make about these matters before, during, and after classroom practice. Figure 4.1 illustrates the components of the model and the suggested interrelationships among them.

In an exploratory study of teachers of secondary school mathematics, we demonstrated how the model allowed us to determine some specific relationships between cognitions and instructional practices of teachers with varying levels of experience (Artzt, 1999; Artzt & Armour-Thomas, 1998). Seven experienced and seven first-year teachers of secondary school mathematics voluntarily participated in the study. The experienced teachers had taught from 7 to 25 years. The beginning teachers were student teachers from local public middle schools and high schools in the New York metropolitan area. Teachers were asked to choose any lesson that would allow for an examination of both their classroom practice and their thoughts underlying that practice.

One author and a research assistant observed the lessons, wrote notes as they observed the lessons, and videotaped each of the teachers teaching a mathematics lesson of their own design. The observation notes provided information about classroom occurrences that might not have been visible on the videotape. Transcriptions were made of the audio part of the videotapes for analysis.

The PDF was used to observe the lessons of these teachers. A descriptive analysis of the data allowed us to distinguish three groups of lessons. That is, specific patterns of instruction seemed to emerge and fall into two distinct groups, with a third group consisting of lessons that resembled a combination of the two other groups. For ease of discussion, we labeled these groups SC (student centered), TC (teacher centered), and M (mixed).

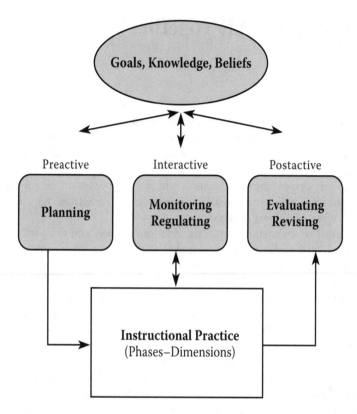

Figure 4.1　Components of the model for teaching. Adapted from "A Structure to Enable Pre-Service Teachers of Mathematics to Reflect on Their Teaching," by A. F. Artzt, 1999, *Journal of Mathematics Teacher Education, 2*(2), p. 145. Copyright © 1999 by Kluwer Academic Publishers. Also adapted from "Mathematics Teaching as Problem Solving," by A. F. Artzt and E. Armour-Thomas, 1998, *Instructional Science, 26*(1–2), p. 8. Copyright © 1998 by Kluwer Academic Publishers. Adapted with kind permission from Kluwer Academic Publishers.

We used the TCF to examine the cognitions of teachers whose lessons we observed using the PDF. Following the enactment of a lesson, we asked each teacher questions about her or his cognitive processes: preactive cognitions (i.e., lesson planning), interactive cognitions (i.e., monitoring and regulating), and postactive cognitions (i.e., evaluating and suggesting; Artzt & Armour-Thomas, 1998). We used these data to describe the patterns of cognitions associated with each of the three categories of lessons (i.e., SC, TC, M) that were derived from the PDF analysis.

The results are presented according to lesson groups. That is, for each group, we give a description of the most interesting characteristics of the lessons and the related cognitions underlying these lessons. (See Appendix A for summary statements of all characteristics of the lessons and related cognitions.) Woven throughout these descriptions are an example of one lesson from the group and the related cognitions of the teacher of that lesson. To exemplify the ideas clearly, we chose to highlight the most extreme cases.

Instructional Practices and Underlying Cognitions of Teachers in the Student-Centered (SC) Group

The SC group conducted five lessons: Four were taught by experienced teachers, and one was taught by a first-year teacher. The descriptive analysis revealed that the instructional practices in these lessons consistently promoted student learning with understanding across all dimensions and phases of the lessons. The teachers' expressed cognitions revealed a similar focus. That is, their articulated knowledge, beliefs, and goals centered on student learning with understanding, as did their thought processes before, during, and after the lesson.

A more detailed description of the results follows, with specific examples and quotations taken from Gina's lesson and cognitions. Gina was in her 10th year of teaching high school mathematics and was observed teaching a geometry lesson on proving overlapping triangles congruent to a class of 33 tenth graders in an urban high school.

Preactive

In their preactive interviews, teachers in the SC group revealed goals for their students to attain both procedural and conceptual understandings of the content. Gina said, "I wanted to focus in on a plan that we needed to have. Lots of times in the past, they don't know what they're doing. They don't know how to think about it, where they're going. So they have to have a definite plan." Gina demonstrated knowledge of the content, pedagogical techniques, and students. She knew that students had difficulty visualizing overlapping triangles and was prepared to use colored chalk as an aid. She also prepared problems that, instead of requiring proofs, required only the recognition of the overlapping sections.

Interactive

The instructional practices of the teachers in the SC group were consistent with their preactive cognitions. For example, the tasks appeared to be interesting to students, logically sequenced, and at a suitable level of difficulty. Gina started with triangles that were not overlapping, went to triangles with one full overlapping part, and then moved to the more difficult case where the triangles had segments of parts overlapping. Also, most of the students in the SC group appeared to be actively involved in the tasks. Gina had the students work in pairs on several problems.

During their stimulated-recall interviews, these teachers made specific comments regarding their beliefs about the necessity of a student-centered approach for student learning. Gina said, "I would like them to talk more, listen to each other, because that's how you learn." Furthermore, teachers in the SC group gave descriptions of how they used student participation and feedback as a means of monitoring student understanding, which they used for subsequent regulation of instruction. The discourse during the instructional practice was consistent with these cognitions. That is, the teachers encouraged all the students to think and reason, give full explanations of their thoughts, and listen to and respond to one another's ideas. Gina said, "There are a few good students who always have their hands up. They would, if I let them, dominate the class, and nobody else would ever have time to think."

Postactive

In their debriefing interviews, the teachers in the SC group showed a consistency with their preactive goals, in that they rated their lessons primarily in terms of their evaluation of how much their students understood. Gina said, "I would have liked to have finished more. But I felt pretty good about how it went. There were a lot of hands raised. I thought they understood." Finally, the teachers gave detailed suggestions for improving their instructional techniques aimed at increasing clarity and interest for students. Gina said, "Next time, I would try using transparencies maybe. Move it around a little bit. Maybe have some cut-outs and take two overlapping triangles and put them different ways."

Instructional Practices and Underlying Cognitions of Teachers in the Teacher-Centered (TC) Group

The TC group conducted four lessons, all taught by first-year teachers. In contrast to the lessons for the SC group, the instructional practices in these lessons consistently seemed less likely to promote student learning with understanding across all dimensions and all phases of the lessons. Similarly, the expressed cognitions of these teachers were consistently focused on their own practices rather than on student learning with understanding. That is, their articulated knowledge, beliefs, and goals centered on content coverage for skill development and management concerns, as were their thought processes before, during, and after the lesson.

A more detailed description of the results follows, with specific examples taken from the lesson and cognitions of Ellen, a student teacher in an urban middle school. She was observed teaching a first lesson on graphing linear equations to a class of 26 seventh graders.

Preactive

In their preactive interviews, the teachers in the TC group expressed only procedural goals for their students and desires to cover the content. They revealed a general and vague knowledge of their students, the mathematical content, and related pedagogy. Ellen said, "The students are of average ability. Some of them have had this before, so I don't want them to get bored." The teachers spoke about the content in isolation and focused mainly on time-saving management strategies to cover the content. Ellen said, "I want my students to learn how to plot a line. I just wanted to do one example and to just get right into the graphing."

Interactive

The instructional practices of the TC group involved tasks that were illogically sequenced and either too easy or too difficult for the students. For homework, Ellen gave the students the tedious and simple task of plotting 14 pairs of points on a coordinate grid. During the lesson, she made a large leap to the idea of solving equations in two variables and gave a misleading example. Both the organization of the content and the tools used by these teachers masked the clarity of the concepts. The instructional routines, combined with pacing that was either too fast or too slow, contributed to a tense and awkward classroom atmosphere in which many of the students appeared to be off task. In Ellen's class, one by one, in a time-consuming manner, 14 different students were requested to plot their points on a small, hard-to-read coordinate grid that was placed on an overhead projector. The students at their seats were inattentive and noisy.

The verbal interactions during the TC group's lessons reflected these teachers' cognitions. The absence of monitoring for student understanding during the lessons was evidenced in the nature of the discourse. The teachers asked low-level, leading questions with wait times that were mostly too short but sometimes too long. They did not require students to give explanations of their responses or encourage interactions between students. They passed judgment on student responses and often resolved questions without student input. Throughout the lesson, Ellen asked all low-level questions, accepted responses from students who called out, and told them whether their answers were right or wrong. When a response was incorrect, she made such derogatory comments as "How could you forget that?" and then engaged in a one-on-one conversation with the student, further losing the class' attention.

During the stimulated-recall interviews, the TC group made no statements regarding their beliefs about how students learn best, unlike the SC group. They gave descriptions of how they monitored student behaviors as a means for improving classroom management but made no mention of monitoring for student understanding. In fact, none of these teachers described or made any deviations from the original plans, despite feedback from students during the course of the lesson that indicated they were confused. Ellen seemed bewildered by the students' incorrect responses and explained it by saying, "I think he wasn't thinking" and "They don't think."

Postactive

In their debriefing interviews, the teachers in the TC group showed a consistency with their preactive goals in that their primary focus was on their insufficient content coverage and the behavior of the students. Ellen said, "I didn't get to cover as much as I thought. I thought it would go quicker. There wasn't enough time to summarize, to put it all together at the end. I think the kids were very good today. But some kids were still not paying as much attention as I'd like." Several gave suggestions for improvement of the pacing of their lessons to achieve more efficient content coverage. Ellen said, "Next time I would not require the students to organize the data pairs in a table since it took so long."

Instructional Practices and Underlying Cognitions of Teachers in the Mixed (M) Group

The M group conducted five lessons: Three were taught by experienced teachers, and two were taught by first-year teachers. These lessons were assigned to the M group because each lesson had components that resembled those of both the SC and TC groups. In each lesson, the nature of the instructional practice was fairly inconsistent. A descriptive analysis revealed a similar inconsistency in the focus of the expressed cognitions of these teachers. In some essential characteristics, to be explained subsequently, the lessons and cognitions of three of the teachers, two experienced and one beginning (to be referred to as the M1 group), were similar, and the lessons and cognitions of two of the teachers, one experienced and one beginning (to be referred to as the M2 group), were similar.

M1 Group

The tasks and learning environments of the lessons for the M1 group were similar to those of the lessons in the SC group, but the discourse was more similar to the lessons in the TC group. To be more specific, a teacher-dominated style of discourse prevailed in which little monitoring for student understanding occurred during any phase of the lesson. Similarity among the beliefs of these teachers shed light on their instructional practices.

A more detailed description of the results follows, with specific examples taken from Betty's lesson and cognitions. Betty was in her 17th year of teaching secondary school mathematics. She was observed teaching a geometry lesson on proving the properties of isosceles triangles to a class of 22 tenth graders in a suburban high school.

Preactive

In their preactive interviews, the three teachers from the M1 group revealed goals for their students similar to those of the SC group. That is, they wanted students to develop conceptual and procedural understanding of the content. Betty said, "I wanted to reinforce previous concepts and to get the students to realize what does happen in an isosceles triangle." Teachers in the M1 group exhibited detailed knowledge about their pupils, the content, and related pedagogy. Betty stated, "I know the speed at which to go with this class." She said that, in fact, she was not in a rush, because "we're right on target with time."

Interactive

With respect to the tasks and most aspects of the learning environments, the instructional practices of each of the three teachers from the M1 group resembled the instructional practices of the SC group. That is, throughout all lesson phases, the tasks were logically sequenced and at a suitable level of difficulty. The tools used and the organization of tasks contributed to the clarity of the lessons. Betty had handouts prepared for the students that contained accurately drawn triangles with problems of increasing difficulty. Teachers in the M1 group handled administrative routines effectively without disrupting their students, who were doing their assigned work. While students completed the handout, Betty checked attendance, walked around checking homework, and also checked their progress on the handout to select students to put their work on the board.

With respect to discourse, however, the instructional practices of the M1 group resembled those of the TC group. That is, discourse was normally fast paced and not conducive to student input. Betty's overriding questioning technique was to ask a student a question, allow a very short wait time, accept a one-word answer from the student, and then give the explanation for the student's answer herself.

During their stimulated-recall interviews, the teachers in the M1 group revealed beliefs quite different from those expressed by the teachers in the SC group, who valued the student-centered approach to teaching. Both of the experienced M1 group teachers stated that a more teacher-centered approach was desirable to cover the content efficiently. That is, they believed it was best to tell students the information rather than spend the time getting them to discover it for themselves. Betty stated, "Sometimes I let students explain their work. But because of time factors, I took charge. It works well when the teacher stands in front of the room and answers student questions." Note that this view seemed inconsistent with her preactive assertion that time was not a problem. The first-year teacher expressed her uncertainty regarding how much to elicit from students and how much to tell them, in light of the time constraints of a class period and her concerns about covering the content. Similar to the TC group teachers, all three M1 group teachers explained that the primary reason they called on students was to keep them on task.

Postactive

In their debriefing interviews, the teachers in the M1 group evaluated their lessons as the TC group had, in terms of content coverage (e.g., "I accomplished what I wanted to"), and gave suggestions for improvement that focused on ways to accomplish more efficient pacing. This was inconsistent with their preactive cognitions that, similar to those in the SC group, focused on helping students to attain procedural and conceptual understandings.

M2 Group

During the initiation phases of the two lessons conducted by the M2 group, the tasks, learning environments, and discourse were all similar to the SC group's lessons. However, during the development and closure phases, the discourse was similar to the TC group's lessons. Similarity in the extent of the knowledge they revealed shed light on this instructional practice.

A more detailed description of the results follows, with specific examples taken from the lesson and cognitions of John, a student teacher in an urban middle school. He was observed teaching a lesson on plotting points on a rectangular coordinate system to a class of 30 seventh-grade students.

Preactive

Similar to the SC group, in their preactive interviews, the two teachers in the M2 group revealed goals for their students to develop conceptual and procedural understandings of the content. John said, "My main objective is to get the students to plot the points, to connect them, and review geometric concepts and understand the relations." The M2 group also expressed beliefs about the importance of having students play an active role in their own learning by asking them questions and challenging them to think for themselves and interact with one another. John said, "If a kid can do it, I prefer if he explains. It helps him." However, unlike the teachers in the SC group, the teachers in the M2 group either admitted to or demonstrated that they had inadequate or superficial knowledge about some aspects of the content, students, and pedagogy. John revealed only a general and vague knowledge of his students by anticipating that "it would be an easy lesson and [he] wouldn't have any difficulty." To accomplish his goals, John said, "I plan to help them to do it instead of to do it myself. I'm going to send them to the board."

Interactive

During the initiation phase of the lessons given by the M2 group, the tasks, learning environments, and discourse resembled those of the SC group's lessons. However, during the development and closure phases of their lessons, the tasks and discourse resembled those of the TC group's lessons. That is, the tasks were either too difficult or confusing for students, the discourse was teacher centered, and the instructional routines and pacing were teacher dominated and not conducive to student input. After students explained their work on plotting pairs of points to one another at the board, John assigned a complex problem that required students to plot four given points, join them, and find the perimeter and area of the resulting figure. The students showed a lack of familiarity with the concepts of perimeter and area. Therefore, John was unable to elicit the responses he wanted in the short time remaining. He resorted to telling the students how to do the problem and gave them the answers as the bell rang. Because the students did not have the prerequisite understanding of the concepts of perimeter and area, the quick telling did not seem to help them understand.

As they watched the videotape of the initiation phase of their lessons, the teachers in the M2 group, similar to the SC group, claimed that they called on students to check for understanding and determine how to proceed. John said, "I was trying to see if they were able to do the Do Now, because if they couldn't do it, forget it. And I saw that some of them had some difficulty." However, as they watched the development and closure phases of their lessons, the teachers in the M2 group remarked that the tasks they introduced caused confusion, which required them to tell the students the information. John said, "I was thinking how long this part is going to take me since the students didn't understand, but I have to do it since it's on the homework so I just had to tell them."

Postactive

In their debriefing interviews, both teachers in the M2 group, similar to those in the SC group, evaluated student understanding and gave appropriate suggestions for how to improve the design of the tasks in their lessons. John admitted, "I was too ambitious. I'm not sure that many knew what was going on. I should have just focused on plotting points and not include area and perimeter." Both teachers claimed that their inadequate knowledge of the content, students, and pedagogy impeded their efforts to teach in a way that was consistent with their goals and beliefs.

Through the application of our model, we were able to discern differences in instructional practices and use teacher cognitions as a way of better understanding the nature of these differences. That is, patterns of cognitions paralleled differences in the nature of instructional practices.

Conclusion

The purpose of this exploratory study was to use a "teaching for understanding" perspective to develop a model to examine teachers' instructional practices in secondary school mathematics in relationship to their underlying cognitions. We used the PDF to differentiate 14 mathematics lessons. We then engaged in a systematic examination of the cognitions of the teachers of these lessons.

We used the PDF to partition lessons into three categories based on the dimensions of teaching (i.e., tasks, learning environment, discourse) across the three phases of instruction (i.e., initiation, development, closure). By examining teachers' cognitions, we gained some insights regarding the variations in the nature of the instructional practice of these lessons. In many ways, the results presented here are in alignment with the results found by researchers who have studied changes in mathematics teachers' beliefs and practices (e.g., Cooney, Shealy, & Arvold, 1998; Fennema et al., 1996; Schifter & Simon, 1992; Schram, Wilcox, Lappan, & Lanier, 1989; Thompson, 1991). These researchers all agree that there appear to be several developmental stages of teaching. These stages are somewhat evident in the cognitions and instructional practices of the teachers of the lessons grouped in this study.

The instructional practices and cognitions of the teachers in the SC group in many ways exemplified those of teachers who have developed beyond the initial stage of teaching. In these classes, there were rich verbal exchanges among the students and between the students and the teachers. The teachers engaged in extensive monitoring of the verbal interactions and behaviors of students throughout their class sessions. This close monitoring may have accounted for their subsequent accurate postlesson judgments regarding whether they had accomplished their goals of teaching for student understanding. These teachers' monitoring behaviors were similar to those of expert teachers (Leinhardt & Greeno, 1986; Livingston & Borko, 1990) and good problem solvers (Schoenfeld, 1987; Silver, 1985). It was encouraging to note that these competencies, usually associated with expertise, were exhibited by one of the beginning teachers. This has positive implications for preservice teachers. That is, although experience plays an important role in the development of a teacher, it is possible for a beginning teacher to think and teach in ways that place students at the center of instruction.

In contrast, the instructional practices and cognitions of the teachers in the TC group at best resembled those of initial stage teachers. Initial stage teaching has been characterized as traditional instruction by teachers driven by the belief that students learn best by receiving clear information transmitted by a knowledgeable teacher (Goldsmith & Shifter, 1997). For example, there were relatively no verbal interactions between students, and those that occurred between the teacher and students were minimal. Providing little room for the expression of student ideas prevented these teachers from being able to monitor the level or quality of their students' understanding of the mathematical ideas. This lack of monitoring may have accounted for the inaccurate postlesson judgments these teachers made that their lesson went well or that their students understood. In many ways, the four first-year teachers in the TC group exhibited behaviors similar to those of other novice teachers (Borko & Livingston, 1989; Livingston & Borko, 1990) and naïve problem solvers (Hinsley, Hayes, & Simon, 1977). For preservice teachers, these findings indicate that if the goal of instruction is student understanding, then one way to assess whether this goal has been accomplished is by consistently monitoring student understanding throughout the lesson.

The teachers in the M group revealed a lack of consistency within or among components of their cognitions. For some lessons, the teachers expressed knowledge and goals consistent with teaching to promote student understanding. However, their lack of monitoring for student understanding during the interactive stage of teaching was inconsistent with these preactive cognitions. Furthermore, they showed an unawareness of the lack of coherence between their postlesson cognitions, which focused only on content coverage and more efficient pacing in subsequent lessons, and their preactive cognitions, which focused on student understanding. Teachers' beliefs about the value of "teacher telling" on a regular basis may have accounted for the persistent use of teacher-dominated strategies for discourse, which resulted in the absence of monitoring for student understanding across all phases of their lessons. During their debriefing interviews, they expressed the belief that when they have limited time, covering the content efficiently must take precedence over student learning with understanding. Similar to the teachers in Lampert's work (1985), these teachers were unable to maintain the tension between simultaneously covering the content and attending to student understanding. Coping effectively with this apparent paradox of teaching remains an important challenge for teachers.

Other teachers in the M group revealed beliefs and goals that suggested the importance of student learning with understanding. However, because of their inadequate or superficial knowledge about the content, students, and pedagogy, in the development and closure phases of their lessons, they were unable to monitor and regulate their classroom teaching in a manner consistent with their preactive cognitions. For teachers of these lessons, regardless of experience, their major source of difficulties seems to have been weaknesses in different aspects of their knowledge. Research suggests that teacher knowledge plays a prominent role in the nature of instructional practice (cf. Peterson, 1988; Shulman, 1986). To be specific, after the initial phase of their lessons, when they realized that they had introduced tasks that were causing confusion for themselves or for their students and did not know how to adjust the tasks, the M group resorted to teacher-centered lessons. One might say that a teacher-directed style of teaching can serve as a mask for teachers who do not possess full knowledge of the content, students, and pedagogy. That is, without the demands that arise from student input, teachers are free to impose the material on the students even when they do not fully understand it or have inappropriately sequenced the material. With the present emphasis on the critical role of discourse for the teaching of mathematics with understanding, it is ever more important that teachers develop a thorough and integrated knowledge system.

The absence of monitoring for student understanding was a common weakness in the lessons conducted by the TC group and in all or parts of the lessons in the M group. A greater weakness may be these teachers' apparent unawareness of the importance of monitoring for student understanding as a way to make accurate postlesson judgments of student understanding. This has important implications for beginning teachers because accurate postlesson assessments of student understanding are an important means of obtaining more information about students for subsequent planning and classroom practice. Monitoring student understanding and appropriately regulating instruction are key factors in the nature of teachers' instructional practice and their potential for professional growth. Researchers on problem solving support this notion of the critical role of cognitive monitoring and subsequent regulation in the efficacy of the problem-solving process and in the ultimate solution of the problem (Artzt & Armour-Thomas, 1992; Garofalo & Lester, 1985; Schoenfeld, 1987).

Although we are excited by the promising nature of our work, it is only an exploratory study, and we are aware of its limitations. Nevertheless, through the use of the model, we were able to examine the teaching of mathematics as an integrated whole and obtain a better understanding of instructional practices and associated teacher cognitions. We have used the model in our teacher education program as a vehicle through which our student teachers systematically reflect on their mathematics teaching and their underlying cognitions (Artzt, 1999).[1] According to the research on teacher change, such systematic reflection and self-assessment can be a powerful facilitator of teacher improvement (Jaworski, 1994; Kemmis, 1985; Schon, 1983).

This model linking teachers' cognitions with their instructional practices serves as the conceptual basis for the reflective and self-assessment activities you will engage in during your year of teacher preparation. The model will be the foundation for your observations of other teachers, for observations you and others do of your own teaching, and for the portfolio you will create. Part II of this book describes the structure for each of these activities in detail and in some cases provides samples of the work of our student teachers.

Note

1. In particular, preservice teachers enrolled in the innovative, comprehensive, four-year undergraduate TIME 2000 program (i.e., Teaching Improvements through Mathematics Education) have been reaping the benefits of using the model (Artzt & Curcio, 2003).

Part II

How to Use the Model

5 Using the Model to Examine Teachers' Instructional Practice and Cognitions

One of the most valuable experiences that should precede teaching and continue throughout a teaching career is observing other teachers. Observations can sensitize you to some of the critical aspects of instructional practice and their relationship to teachers' cognitions. Because teaching is such a complex endeavor, observations must be done with a specific focus grounded in a theoretical framework. This chapter describes 10 structured observations with examples from reports of actual lessons observed in elementary, middle, and secondary schools. Each of the first 9 observations focuses on a critical aspect of instructional practice in mathematics: the nature of the mathematical content, questioning, motivation and teaching strategies, homework, use of class time, verbal behavior of students, task orientation of students, assessment, and teacher expectations and stereotyping. The observations have been arranged so that they first focus primarily on the content, then focus on the teacher, and then focus on the individual students. However, because all aspects of instruction are deeply interrelated, these observations can certainly be sequenced differently.

Each of the critical aspects of instruction is identified by elements within the model. For example, for the observation on questioning, the specific dimension of instructional practice to be examined is discourse. Although each of these aspects of instructional practice concern all the dimensions of teaching (i.e., tasks, learning environment, and discourse), the preactive (i.e., planning) and interactive (i.e., monitoring and regulating) stages of teaching, and the phases of teaching (i.e., initiation, development, closure), some are directly related more to one dimension, phase, or stage than to another. Therefore, although the observation focus might be on discourse, other areas such as monitoring and regulating, and possibly the learning environment, come into play as well. Each observation also considers the probable teacher cognitions that accompanied the observed practice. The 10th observation uses the entire model and encompasses all the dimensions, phases, and stages of the lesson and conjectures for the teacher's cognitions that drive the lesson.

Each observation assignment includes a rationale for the assignment, an overview of the observation, and elementary and secondary examples based on actual observed lessons. Appendix B presents detailed guidelines for all the observations presented in this chapter. Before you read each observation, it is important for you to read about the related topic in your methods text (e.g., Posamentier, Smith, & Stepelman, 2006; Van de Walle, 2007), so that you can bring a more informed understanding to your interpretation of what you are viewing. For example, if you are doing an observation that asks you to evaluate discourse, you should read the section in your text that discusses questioning.

Observation 1: Nature of the Content (Tasks)

Mathematics is an exciting and dynamic area of study that offers students the chance to use the power of their minds. It is essential that teachers engage students in tasks that exemplify the beauty and usefulness of mathematics. What teachers know and believe about mathematics strongly influence what they do in their classrooms and, ultimately, what students learn about mathematics. Furthermore, teachers' knowledge and beliefs about mathematics shape their goals for student learning.

Observation Overview

The purpose of this first observation is to sensitize you to the messages students receive about what mathematics is and what is of importance to learn. You are encouraged to use the mathematical tasks you observe as a basis for making conjectures about the cognitions of the teacher. The guidelines provided in Appendix B.1 will help you to focus on the mathematical content of the lesson.

Observation Examples

The first example supporting this initial observation was prepared by Jaime, a preservice elementary teacher who observed a Grade 6 bilingual lesson on collecting, organizing, and analyzing data. The second example was prepared by Elise, a preservice secondary teacher who observed a Grade 9 lesson on logic.

Grade 6 Bilingual Lesson on Data Analysis

Jaime did not report any mathematical errors or misconceptions as the teacher guided students in determining the best buy among several brands of chocolate chip cookies. However, he did notice that similar to all learners of mathematics, bilingual students need to read, write, hear, and speak the language of mathematics:

> Although there were no mathematical errors, misconceptions, or misrepresentations, the teacher should have spent time writing important mathematical vocabulary on the chalkboard in English and Spanish for students to copy into their notebooks. Then, he should have had the students pronounce the words to help them learn the mathematical terms in English.

Since mathematical misunderstandings can be detected through the (mis)use of language, Jaime's suggestions are well taken.

Inherent in the tasks assigned is a message about the usefulness of mathematics. Jaime recognized how the value of the content was revealed in the task and how the teacher engaged the students:

> Being presented with a real-world problem, the students were aware of the value of the mathematics they were learning and applying as they worked together to collect, organize, and analyze data to determine the best buy. I heard some children comment that they look for the best buy when they go to the supermarket with their parents. Students suggested that they find the unit price by dividing the total cost of the package by the number of cookies in the package. To stress the meaningfulness of the task, throughout the lesson the teacher kept asking the class, "Does that make sense to you?" "Is there another way to think about that?" His enthusiasm and energy generated wonder and curiosity among the children.

Jaime was able to infer the teacher's expectations for his students:

> Based on the student-centered, second-language-learning techniques the teacher used (i.e., oral repetition, manipulatives, and cooperative learning), it is clear that the teacher believes that all students have the potential to learn and that they should be active participants in their own learning.

These comments indicate that Jaime was attentive to the content embedded in the task and how the teacher's design of the task revealed his beliefs about the usefulness and value of learning mathematics.

Grade 9 Lesson on Logic

Although Elise reported that there were no mathematical errors, she found the lesson lacking because it did not point out the value of learning the logical rules. The lesson required students to determine whether certain arguments were valid by transliterating them into symbols and then comparing them to the Laws of Modus Tollens and the Law of Detachment that were written symbolically on the board.

> I was almost shocked at how neglected the mentioning of any values was. I was especially surprised because I felt that a lesson on logic lends itself most easily and naturally to stating explicitly the value of the material. After all, logical thinking and decoding of statements to determine truth values and necessary consequences is something everyone does a hundred times a day. How invigorating to see that a mathematical transliteration of everyday occurrences into a precise symbolic representation can make us able to analyze clearly our everyday environment, interactions, patterns of thought, and more!

Clearly, Elise has a genuine appreciation for the value of learning logic.

Elise pointed out that the teacher made reference to the usefulness of what they were learning but did not make it come alive when they discussed the sample problem:

> The most I can say is that the teacher once told the students that if they learn how to do this, they will be able to analyze whether what a friend is telling them is the truth or not. However, he didn't demonstrate how, or give an example, or show how the examples they were discussing was an instance of that opportunity. It was clear that the students did not understand that what they were doing would in fact make them able to do such a thing. For example, one word problem asked the students to state whether the following argument was valid, and if so, which law was being illustrated. The argument was:
>
> > If you're voted MVP, you win a trophy.
> > Cathy won a trophy.
> > Therefore, Cathy was voted MVP.
>
> Rather than discussing the situation and leading the students to get the answer intuitively and then showing how the system of transliteration and the fact that there is no such law that corresponds because the argument is not valid, the teacher had them robotically transliterate the incorrect argument, then compare it to the laws on the board, and conclude that the argument isn't valid because the symbols don't match. It was clear to me that the majority of the students had no connection between the actual argument and the symbols on the board!

Elise was sensitive to the strict, abstract procedural approach the teacher took and had good ideas for improving on this approach in a way that would help students appreciate the value of the mathematical concepts they were learning:

> Throughout the period I was thinking of ways to make the students understand and appreciate what they were learning to do. For example, before having them transliterate into symbols, I'd have tried to lead them to the conclusion that the argument was invalid. For example, I'd ask them things like: Is it true that just because Cathy won a trophy, it means she must have been voted MVP? Is it possible that she got a trophy but wasn't voted MVP? Can you think of such a situation? OK, now let's see how our systematic representation and mathematical logical argumentation leads us straight to what your intuition is telling you. At that point we would transliterate it, and seeing that it wasn't one of the laws, we see that you can't conclude for sure that Cathy was voted MVP.

At this point I would show them how this was an example of how mathematics helps us to understand our environment. You see, if Cathy had come up to you and said, "If you're voted MVP, you win a trophy. See, here's my trophy—I was voted MVP!" You'll know she's not necessarily telling you the truth! She could've gotten the trophy for something else! On the other hand, you'll know she's not necessarily lying either. This is a perfect opportunity to express to the students how amazing it is that this system of mathematical logic aids us in our societal interactions.

Elise's suggestions show that she has a deep understanding of and appreciation for the laws of logic. Regarding the teacher's level of appreciation, Elise said, "Judging from this lesson, I feel that this teacher thinks about mathematics as an arbitrary set of rules disconnected from experience. His goals seem to be to make sure that his students know how to apply this set of rules." Elise not only revealed her awareness of how devoid of meaning this lesson was but also gave specific ways to make it more meaningful to students. Of course, one lesson cannot reveal a teacher's entire knowledge of or beliefs about mathematics. However, Elise has begun to think about this teacher's cognitions and how they may have contributed to the nature of this particular lesson.

The next observation assignment focuses on a teacher's use and style of questioning. The teacher's questioning strategies can promote or impede the discourse that occurs within the mathematics class.

Observation 2: Questioning (Discourse)

Discourse is a critical aspect of mathematics instruction, central to the current vision of desirable mathematics teaching (National Council of Teachers of Mathematics [NCTM], 1989, 1991, 2000). The teacher's role today is to create a mathematical "discourse community" (Silver & Smith, 1996). Specifically, according to the Professional Teaching Standards (NCTM, 1991), the teacher should

- pose questions that elicit, engage, and challenge each student's thinking;
- listen carefully to students' ideas and ask them to clarify and justify their ideas; and
- encourage students to listen to, respond to, and question the teacher and one another.

Student teachers generally find discourse to be the most critical ingredient for satisfying teaching experiences but also the most difficult part of their work. Discourse happens in unique ways in each class, partly planned and most often involving instantaneous decision making. A teacher's style of discourse is a reflection of her or his knowledge, beliefs, and goals. A good start in learning how to orchestrate discourse for maximum student understanding is to examine the discourse that takes place in other teachers' classes.

Observation Overview

The purpose of this observation, divided into two parts, is to help you to analyze the effect that teachers' questioning strategies have on students' responses and the influence these interactions have on the discourse throughout the lesson. The first part of this assignment requires that you observe the questioning style of the teacher. The second part focuses more closely on the discourse structure of the lesson, research about which has been reported by Cazden (1986).

In preparation for this observation, read about "discourse" and "questioning strategies" in your methods text. The guidelines provided in Appendix B.2 will help you to focus on teacher–student discourse.

Observation Examples

Observing two kindergarten teachers who use cognitively guided instruction (CGI) to formulate mathematics word problems (Carpenter, Fennema, Franke, Levi, & Empson, 1999), Tanica prepared the two parts for the elementary example. Observing two different teachers in 11th-grade honors classes, Olive prepared the two parts for the secondary example.

CGI Kindergarten Lessons

In the first class she observed, Tanica noted that the teacher directed questions related to join-result unknown word problems to specific children:

> During the eighteen-minute lesson occurring during snack time, the teacher asked 24 questions, 21 of which were formulated especially for specific children. As children responded, the rest of the class listened. In three instances, the teacher called on volunteers to assist children having difficulty responding to her questions.
>
> Of the 24 questions asked, 1 was factual (i.e., "What shape is this snack?"), 10 were convergent (e.g., "Tiffany, there are three children sitting at your table and two children standing at your table. How many napkins will you need to bring to the children at your table?"), and 13 were divergent (e.g., "How did this problem change?"). It was truly amazing to observe kindergarten children applying their number facts in a meaningful context as they distributed the napkins, cups, and crackers.

Although Tanica noted a mean wait time of 3.5 seconds as "adequate," she indicated that the teacher's rapid-fire follow-up after answers yielded a mean of 1.5 seconds. Tanica conjectured that this rapid-fire approach reveals that the teacher was aware not only of which students she intended to call on but also of the number range and structure of the word problem she wanted to present to each student:

> The teacher definitely knows her students. She framed the problems in the form of questions (e.g., join-result unknown, partitive division) and employed numbers (e.g., doubles vs. one more than a double) based on her knowledge of her students. The majority of the responses (i.e., 21 out of 24; 87.5%) were from students who were teacher selected. The children tried to solve the problem directed to them by the teacher. When a child had difficulty, the teacher asked whether she or he needed a classmate to help, and then called on another child to help solve or explain an answer to the problem.

Tanica identified several difficulties that the children might have had as they attempted to solve the problems presented by the teacher:

> It was not clear whether the children knew to include themselves in the total. That is, were the helpers included in the original count? The teacher could have asked the children to count the number of classmates at their respective table, including herself or himself to determine the number of items needed for all of the children at the table.

Tanica was able to apply her knowledge of CGI to the observation by focusing on the teacher's knowledge of her students, the design of the problems to tap into students' levels of understanding, and her perceived goals of the lesson:

> The teacher knows her students very well—so well that she can formulate problems to target levels of numerical skills and computational understandings. By posing problems and asking how the children solved the problems, the teacher clearly believes that children construct their understandings. The teacher's goals for the lesson supported how she believes children learn mathematics—in the context of solving real-world problems that were designed for snack time. The children in this diverse, multiethnic class were being instructed in an environment supportive of their differences.

Tanica contrasted the approach taken by the second teacher with the teaching style of the first teacher she observed:

> The teacher attempted to apply the principles of CGI, but, unlike the first lesson I observed, the teacher's approach led to a very teacher-centered lesson.
> The lesson was dominated by the teacher asking questions and the children responding. One hundred percent of the answers and explanations requested

were initiated by the teacher. One hundred percent of the answers stated were from the children.

Tanica recognized that the teacher's language could be used to infer the teacher's beliefs about her and her students' roles in discourse:

> Her teacher-centered language and teaching style leads me to say that she believes her role as the teacher is to "be in charge" of asking all the questions, dominating and directing everyone and everything. She believes that the students are to answer her questions and follow her orders.

As Tanica suggested, giving the children the opportunity to become autonomous learners can begin as early as kindergarten:

> To increase student learning, I think that after having the students describe what they notice about a graph, they should be asked to formulate questions related to the graph, identifying which questions can be answered using the data in the graph and which questions cannot be answered.

Grade 11 Honors Lessons

Regarding the first class she observed, Olive made the following comments in the first part of her observation:

> While observing in the classroom, I noticed that the teacher primarily asked questions that required a chorus response. The teacher asked over thirty questions and only three were addressed to specific students. The teacher generally had his back toward the students when asking questions. This caused him primarily to ask chorus response questions because he could not see whether a student was volunteering to answer a question.

Olive saw the connection between the teacher's position in the classroom and the nature of his questioning. She also detected the factual nature of the questions and the form in which they were asked:

> The teacher's questions were over 80% factual and convergent and consisted mainly of whiplash and leading questions. These are examples of the type of questions that occurred frequently: "And the what?" "Which would be what?" "And all this really does is what?" "Wouldn't you say they are equal?" He usually expected a chorus response to these questions and gave students about half a second to respond to the question. I did not hear any questions that required the students to think beyond recalling past information learned.

Olive expressed her thoughts about the beliefs that she felt contributed to the teacher's "poor" questioning style:

> I suppose, because of the fact that it is an honors math course, the speed in which the material has to be covered must be fast. The teacher probably believes that the best way to cover all the material and at the same time involve the kids a little bit is to use the chorus-response type of question. By keeping the questions straightforward he can get most of the kids to respond quickly and then just move along. He probably thinks that because they are smart kids they can learn it this way.

Olive had some insightful comments regarding both suggestions for ways to improve the questioning and her beliefs about how to teach honors classes:

> Before suggesting my ideas for improving the questioning, I want to say that I think that more than other kids, bright students need to be given a chance to think about hard questions. They should be challenged more and not just be given a fast set of procedures to follow. If they are so smart, they can practice more of the examples on their own time and discuss interesting concepts during the lesson. At the very least the teacher should turn away from the board and ask more interesting questions directed at individual students. Rather than him reviewing an assigned problem, he could allow the students to explain their own work.

Even if Olive's conjectures about this teacher's beliefs were faulty, the important thing is that she recognized the connections between a teacher's style of questioning, how it meets the needs of the individual learners, the thoughts of the teacher, and the dilemma teachers face when presented with a crowded curriculum.

Olive completed the second part of her report on the second class she observed. Again, she noticed a very teacher-centered style of discourse:

> In this lesson the conversation was mostly like this: The teacher requested an answer and one of the students gave the answer, or a student requested an explanation and the teacher gave the explanation. Only twice did students give an explanation of anything and only once did the teacher request an explanation. So most of the time, the teacher was explaining and explaining, and the students were either giving short answers or asking questions. I was disappointed that in such a bright class, the students were not given the chance to do some of the explaining. I'm sure many of them could have done it and would have learned something in the process. Also, never were students given the chance to answer another student's question. The teacher always took it upon himself to answer all of the students' questions.

Olive's ideas for changing the discourse conformed to a more student-centered approach. She said, "I think that after a student gave an answer, the teacher should have asked the student to explain it better. I also think that when a student asked the teacher for an explanation, sometimes the teacher should have asked the other students if any of them could explain it."

Olive had strong ideas about what this teacher's beliefs might have been:

> I think this teacher believed that he alone could give the best explanation of the material and that the students would learn it better if he explained it. I think he really cared about the students and made them feel comfortable enough to ask him lots of questions. But he did not give them enough credit for being able to contribute worthwhile ideas or good explanations. I also don't think that he believed, or maybe he just never thought about, the fact that it would help the students learn if they gave an explanation. Or maybe he believed it would take longer to let the students explain anything and he was in a rush to cover the content.

Olive sees the relationship between a teacher-dominated style of discourse and the teacher's belief about his role in the classroom. Often secondary school students share the belief that it is the teacher's role to be the explainer. After being taught this way in the past, students believe their role is to sit quietly in the class, acting as passive receivers of information. Getting students to become active participants in their own learning involves addressing their beliefs about the role of their teachers and their role as students.

The next observation assignment concerns the motivational and teaching strategies that are used in the mathematics class. These strategies are connected with all three dimensions of classroom instruction: tasks, learning environment, and discourse.

Observation 3: Motivation and Teaching Strategies (Tasks, Learning Environment, Discourse)

Motivation is a key aspect of good instructional practice. Without motivation it is difficult, if not impossible, for student learning to occur. Although motivation is a complex area of study dealing with such topics as achievement motivation, social motivation, extrinsic motivation, and intrinsic motivation, the teacher still plays a pivotal role in motivating students to learn. That is, the teacher can design lessons that maximize the chances that students' interest and curiosity will be aroused and thus be motivated to learn a particular concept.

Through the use of effective teaching strategies and interesting questions, teachers can create powerful motivations for students. Of course, teachers can accomplish this only if they are convinced that it is their responsibility to do so. Teachers who believe that students should come to school motivated to learn and succeed usually believe that students are motivated by being given problems that will prepare them to do well on upcoming examinations. Unfortunately, such an attitude is accurate only for the small number of students who are high achievers. Furthermore, using the carrot of "doing well on an exam" as a reason for learning may prevent students from ever understanding or appreciating the real value of the material they are learning.

To accept the responsibility for motivation, teachers must have a deep knowledge of the content and related effective pedagogical strategies. They must also know their students' abilities and interests to be able to design motivational questions that will be both at an appropriate level of difficulty and of interest to them. A first step in learning about motivation is to observe it in others' classrooms.

Observation Overview

The purpose of this assignment is to sensitize you to the importance of capturing learners' interest and attention at the beginning of and throughout a lesson. Focus is also on how teachers' instructional strategies are influenced by their beliefs about motivation and their knowledge of students.

In preparation for this observation, read about "motivation" and "effective teaching strategies" in your methods text. The guidelines provided in Appendix B.3 will help you to focus on motivation and teaching strategies.

Observation Examples

What follows are excerpts from two observation reports. One is an observation prepared by Ji-Sun of a Grade 3 lesson on multiplication, and the second one is an observation prepared by Ellen of a Grade 9 lesson on factoring.

Grade 3 Multiplication

Ji-Sun recognized that the teacher used ideas that she had learned from participating in the Mathematics in the City (Fosnot & Dolk, 2001a) project:

> The teacher motivated the 20-minute lesson by presenting the third-grade children with a challenging multiplication example, revealing a void in their knowledge: 29 × 5. After the teacher wrote the example on the chalkboard, knowing that the children did not have formal knowledge of the multiplication algorithm, she asked the children to turn and talk to their partners to discuss how they would go about computing the product.

Ji-Sun used the children's enthusiasm, sustained throughout the lesson, as an indicator of how well the teacher motivated the children to explore and share their ideas:

> The children were very excited and animated as they discussed their ideas, building on their prior knowledge related to single-digit by single-digit

multiplication and number strings. After a few minutes, the teacher called the class together and asked selected children to share the ideas discussed with their partners. As the children explained their strategies, the teacher wrote their solutions on the chalkboard and asked other children to explain what they had heard in their own words. The children, representing many different ethnic groups, were very articulate in explaining their thinking, revealing that they have had a lot of experience sharing their mathematical ideas. After two other children shared their strategies, the teacher shared hers, not imposing her way to think about the example but rather offering an alternative strategy. Although the teacher wanted the children to think of multiple strategies, she wanted them to find the fastest and quickest way to compute each product. As the children sat on the rug listening to their peers responding when called upon by the teacher, they were always ready to offer assistance and commentary when asked either by a peer or by the teacher.

Ji-Sun recognized how the teacher's use of a diagram of an array to make a connection between geometric and numerical representations could have been used as a mathematical curiosity to motivate the discussion further:

> The teacher illustrated the two-digit by one-digit multiplication example (i.e., 29×5) by making a rectangular diagram on the chalkboard and pointing out the parts of the example, $(30 - 1) \times 5$. However, the partial products were not clearly identified. Although none of the children questioned the teacher about this, it could have been visually confusing for them. Instead of drawing the array and describing the parts of it, the teacher could have asked, "What does this diagram have to do with this problem?"

Ji-Sun's sophisticated interpretation of motivation based on her observation during this third-grade lesson and her conjectures about the teacher's beliefs are expressed very well:

> I think the teacher would define motivation as problems or examples that capture and sustain the children's interest at the beginning and throughout the lesson. I agree with this. By the way the teacher started and developed the lesson, I think the teacher believes that she has an important responsibility to formulate problems, examples, and questions to motivate learners. I think the teacher believes that the children are naturally inquisitive, and by tapping into this phenomenon, the children will provide the resources to help her to develop the lesson successfully.

Ji-Sun's analysis of the children's ability to respond to the teacher's challenging examples indicates that she understood the relationship between the teacher's knowledge of her students and the teacher's ability to design appropriate tasks to sustain the children's interest in the lesson:

> The teacher knew her students very well. She built on their prior knowledge, natural inquisitiveness, and interest in computing the products of challenging examples.

Grade 9 Factoring

Ellen described the class she observed:

> I observed a second-semester ninth-grade class consisting of those students who could not pass the course or the state exam last semester. When discussing the class and motivational techniques used by the teacher, I think it is important to keep in mind the size of the class (only 19 students are registered in the class; of those, only 12 came to class, and of those 12, 3 went to the nurse) and the aforementioned achievement level of the class.

Ellen recognized the importance of knowing the students in the class when considering issues of motivation. Ellen also noticed a level of motivation that was not requested in the observation report:

> The teacher started the class by having the students work on Do Now examples written on the board while she spot-checked the students' homework. Many of the students did not do their homework, and the teacher asked them why they had bothered coming to class at all. The students responded by asking where else could they be, and the teacher responded that they could be flipping burgers at McDonald's. Although this was not directly a motivation for learning mathematics, it did send a message that if the students did not take advantage of attending school, they may end up in a dissatisfying position in life.

Ellen described what she considered was the main motivation of the lesson:

> The main motivation of the class was the Do Now. It consisted of two examples of factoring polynomials followed by five examples of multiplying binomials together. Three of the latter examples were the difference of two squares, which the students had never before (or rather never this semester) encountered. Students were given some time to work on the examples and were then called on (involuntarily) to write their answers on the board. After all the answers were written and verified (by the teacher and the students), the teacher asked the class why some answers had two terms and others had three terms. She waited for an answer, but the class was quiet for a little while.

> I felt that this question was motivating because it presented a challenge to the students, as well as indicating a void in their knowledge.

It is clear that Ellen has a keen eye for motivation. She noticed that it was not the problems that were motivating but rather the question that the teacher posed regarding the solutions to these problems. That is, the students were being asked to engage in analysis of what seemed like a surprising situation. It is also interesting that Ellen connected the students' quietness with their being motivated. Perhaps the students also had thoughtful looks on their faces that made Ellen so convinced that they were indeed interested in the question.

Ellen explained how the teacher's questioning style sustained the motivation of this class:

> A few students made some random guesses, and the teacher did not evaluate these. Instead, she asked the class to create a problem multiplying two binomials to produce a two-termed product. This question again was motivating in that it presented a challenge. One student suggested $(x + 3)(x - 5)$. The teacher wrote this on the board and asked the class to check the product. When the students informed the teacher that the product was three-termed, the teacher asked why and what happened? That question went unanswered and instead a student said that the example had to be $(x + 3)(x - 3)$. This was verified by the students sitting at their desks who calculated the difference of two squares, a two-termed answer. This example was motivating because not only did it present a challenge but it also got the students actively involved in justifying mathematical curiosities.

Even though Ellen believed the motivation she observed was quite effective, she still had ideas for improvement:

> In general I felt that the questions asked in the Do Now were motivating for the aforementioned reasons, though they could have been even better if they had been asked in a different order. For example, the first few questions of the Do Now could have been multiplying binomials, including a few examples of differences of squares. Those questions could have then been followed by a few factoring problems, including one or two differences of squares. This would have more clearly pointed out a void in the students' knowledge.

Ellen also had suggestions for using teaching strategies that would have gotten more of the students actively involved and motivated to learn:

> Another way of approaching this lesson would have been to split the class into groups, and each person in the group could have been given a couple of multiplication [of binomials] examples, including one that resulted in a difference of two squares. The group assignment might be either to write down their observations (i.e., ask the question, "Why do some of these products

have two terms while others have three terms?") or try to factor a difference of two squares. Each group may then present its results. This would not only have gotten the students more actively involved in solving a problem but could also foster their motivation to learn the topic.

Ellen recognized the possibility that the teacher's knowledge of her own students and the class might have been the reason that she structured the lesson as she did and that in fact her own idea might not have worked as well:

> I don't know how well my suggestions could have worked considering this class' achievement level. Perhaps this teacher knew that it was necessary to guide them more, as she did. Perhaps this teacher knew the desires of her students and how they related to each other and felt the group format would not be effective for them. She probably knew that the small class size enabled her to give every student her attention and get every student involved.

Finally, Ellen appeared sensitive in her conjectures about this teacher's beliefs about motivation:

> I was impressed with how little the teacher had to do to motivate these students. I think this teacher really understood the fact that you don't need any gimmicks or toys to motivate even these low-achieving kids. This teacher probably believes that these kids, and probably all kids, are motivated by questions that they find curious and that are within their ability to figure out. Unlike many teachers of low-ability students, this teacher still believes in their ability and desire to think.

The next observation assignment concerns the homework procedures that are a part of every mathematics class. Because homework involves a selection of tasks, a method of review, and techniques of assessment, it cannot be discussed without addressing all three dimensions of classroom instruction—tasks, learning environment, and discourse, as well as lesson phases and monitoring and regulating.

Observation 4: Homework (Tasks, Learning Environment, Discourse, Phases, Monitoring, Regulating)

The tasks assigned to students to be completed in the privacy of their own homes play a critical role in mathematics instruction. Homework is one way of getting students actively involved in their learning of mathematics. Mathematics is not a spectator sport. Students need to practice doing many different types of problems if they are to gain proficiency and understanding of the content. Often students claim that they understand the material when it is discussed in class, but when they go home to try some problems on their own, they cannot do them. When the teacher carefully selects problems, the homework can be an effective vehicle for students to find out what they do and do not understand. If students can identify their areas of confusion to themselves, their peers, and their teachers, they are in a better position to be helped. It is a good time for them to practice what they have learned how to do, to find out what they do not understand, and to make discoveries on their own. The problems assigned for homework need not and should not be limited to practice of the day's lesson. They might include a review of past concepts; work that will set the stage for future learning; problems that will take time and last over the course of several days, weeks, or even months; or work that involves problem solving, research, and discovery.

Of course, creating an assignment is only the first part of the homework process. The teacher has the responsibility for allotting the time and means for students to discuss the work they have done on their own (i.e., discourse). The teacher also orchestrates what procedure is used (i.e., learning environment) and the phase of the lesson in which it is done. A review of homework can range from having students discuss their work in small groups to having different students present their work to the class as a whole to discussing only problems that are requested by students. Each method has its unique advantages and disadvantages, and the method chosen by the teacher is usually a reflection of her or his goals for student learning, beliefs about how students learn best, and knowledge of the students.

Another part of the homework process concerns assessment (i.e., monitoring and regulating). Does the teacher check whether each of the students has done her or his homework? If so, what criteria are used? Does the teacher collect the homework? If so, does the teacher collect all students' homework or just a subset of the students' homework? How often is homework collected? Is it checked for accuracy or for neatness? Is it graded? Does the teacher write comments on the homework or merely place check marks at the top? As with the procedures for reviewing homework, the different procedures used for assessing homework each have their own advantages and disadvantages, and the method that the teacher chooses is usually a reflection of her or his own overarching cognitions.

A first step in learning about the aspects of assigning, reviewing, and assessing homework is to observe the different procedures that other teachers use in their mathematics classrooms.

Observation Overview

The purpose of this assignment, which includes an interview with the teacher, is to sensitize you to the content of homework assignments and the procedures for reviewing, checking, and assessing homework. Prior to the observation, read about "homework" in your methods text. The guidelines provided in Appendix B.4 will help you to focus on aspects of the lesson related to homework.

Observation Examples

What follows are excerpts from two observation reports. One is an observation prepared by Brian of a Grade 5 homework review on measurement, and the second one is an observation prepared by Keith of a Grade 10 homework review on parabolas.

Grade 5 Homework Review

The teacher Brian observed tried to prepare the children for the forthcoming lesson by relating the assignment to the children's home environment by having them measure the windows and doors in their dwellings. However, Brian recognized several problems with the homework assignment and offered some suggestions for improving the task:

> Although the purpose of the assignment was to get the children thinking about measuring items in preparation for the day's lesson, the measurement assignment lacked a purpose and it was too vague. Why would anyone want to measure windows and doors? It would have been better if there were a reason for measuring. For example, "Your mom wants to buy new curtains for the kitchen window. Help her to find out the size of the window by measuring the length and the width." Or "Your dad needs to order blinds, shades, or shutters for the kitchen window. Help him to find out the size of the window by measuring the length and the width." It was not clear whether the children were to use metric or standard units of measure. Also it seemed as though some children did not have rulers or tape measures at home to do the assignment, and it is possible that some children did not know how to use the measurement tools (e.g., meterstick, yardstick, tape measure).

During the review, Brian noted that when the children do not actively participate in the homework review, their attention wanders. He also noted the importance of comparing the quality of the assignment with the quality of the work the children produce:

> The teacher started the lesson by asking the children what they measured and how they measured it. He called on four students who raised their hands to share their work. The review took about ten minutes. After the first child responded, the children started to fidget and lose interest. It became a teacher–student conversation with the rest of the class disengaged. It might be hard for fifth graders to maintain interest if they all have different answers to different situations. To improve the procedure for reviewing the homework, it is first necessary to improve the homework assignment. The children could have been asked to sketch the window or door that they had measured and label the dimensions with the measurements. Or the teacher could have given the class a diagram of a window or door and asked the children to measure the dimensions in the diagram. The homework review could have then focused

on the size, shape, and measurements recorded in their diagrams. There was very little mathematical substance, if any, in what the children described.

Brian was able to make several conjectures related to the teacher's beliefs about students and the purpose of homework:

> The teacher seems to assume that his students understand vaguely stated homework tasks. By assigning a task related to the day's lesson, he is trying to help the students prepare for the lesson, but he did not think through the task from a fifth grader's point of view. This indicates that he has a limited knowledge of his fifth graders.

The teacher's desire to improve his mathematical and pedagogical content knowledge was revealed in an interview conducted by Brian. The teacher's difficulty in creating meaningful and worthwhile homework tasks may be related to his limited knowledge base:

> In the postlesson interview, I learned that the teacher assigns math homework every night. He admitted that he has a lot to learn about the elementary mathematics curriculum, and he is working on improving his comfort level with the content. He does not like sticking to the textbook because the textbook has only computation exercises. He tries to create assignments that will interest the children. His assignments usually take no longer than 15 minutes. He checks the children's work during a whole class review. Homework is not graded. He sometimes assigns projects in social studies, but he has not assigned any projects in math.

Brian's report highlighted several critical features of effectively assigning, reviewing, and assessing homework: The tasks are to be meaningful and worthwhile and provide insight into student understanding, and the children are to be involved and interested in the review.

Grade 10 Homework Review

In his observation report, Keith showed his awareness that, on the basis of the nature of the homework assignment, the teacher he was observing did not expect enough of her students:

> The teacher's current homework assignment, as well as the past lesson's homework, was much too easy. I can tell by the number of chorus responses by the class that the class seemed bored and unenthused. For example, the previous lesson was on graphing parabolas. The homework consisted of a few very easy questions where the students were asked to move the parabola along the y-axis according to the equation shown.

Keith used the discourse to ascertain that the assignment was far too easy. By so doing, he showed his awareness of the close link that exists between tasks and discourse.

Keith also gave an appropriate suggestion for improvement:

> So much more could have been done. For example, she could have produced examples of leading coefficients with a negative sign that would change the concavity of the parabola. The students could have been challenged a lot more. They could have made discoveries about what happens when you change the coefficients, and this would have motivated them more for the upcoming lesson.

Judging from the nature of the teacher's assignment, Keith decided "the teacher used the homework assignment as a review of previous material learned." From the suggestion he gave for improving the assignment, it appears that Keith saw the potential for homework being used as an opportunity for students to make discoveries that can lead to a motivation for learning the next lesson. He also noted the missed opportunity to use homework as a review of material learned in the past. He wrote, "Spiraling was not evident in this assignment. It was too bad, because that could have been used to review throughout the semester rather than only before an exam." Keith also found fault with the procedure the teacher used to review the homework:

> The teacher went over the homework directly after the Do Now was presented at the beginning of the lesson. She selected a few homework questions to be put on the board and had the students (selected randomly) put up their answers. Although this seemed like a good tactic at first, it defeated its own purpose later on in that the teacher controlled most of the discussion. The students did not explain their work to the rest of the class. The teacher answered most of the questions that came from the classmates. The students should be able to reason and communicate mathematically, and this would have been a great opportunity to allow students to obtain confidence in math. Overall, the review was clear and concise and lasted only about 5 to 10 minutes. The only problem was that the teacher did not empower the students who did the homework problems.

Keith recognized the importance of giving students a more active role in the homework review. He then went on to describe the teacher's assessment procedure:

> She checked the homework by walking around the room during the Do Now portion of the class. I noticed that she was very strict when it came down to writing down the questions before writing an answer. She also insisted that the students frame their answers by either drawing boxes around them or underlining the correct responses.

Although Keith agreed with the teacher's insistence on proper form, he noticed again the teacher's disinterest in seeing students' thought processes:

> I strongly agree with the teacher's insistence on good format. Homework needs to be a tool for the student to use for review after completion, so neatness and clarity are important. However, I think the teacher should have placed a greater emphasis on noticing the quality of the mathematical work the students produced.

Underlying Keith's comments is his awareness that if the teacher does not assess the quality of the students' mathematical work, she cannot monitor student understanding and thus cannot regulate the instruction appropriately.

Based on homework procedures of this teacher, Keith was able to make conjectures about her view of homework, her beliefs about her role as the teacher, and her knowledge of the students:

> I think that this teacher thinks that homework is to be used for review of problems exactly like those learned in the previous day's lesson. I don't think this teacher really knows the ability of her students because she never asks them to explain their work at the board or answer other students' questions. Also, when she checks homework, she mainly looks at format and doesn't really study the mathematical thinking of the students. The problems are so simple that it leads me to believe that she doesn't think her students are capable of thinking beyond what she has shown them. I think she believes that her role is to show students exactly how to do certain problems and then to make sure that they do it exactly the way she has shown them.

Keith understood that without giving students the opportunity to explain themselves, teachers can never increase their knowledge of the understanding and abilities of their students.

The next observation assignment concerns an essential part of every mathematics lesson: the use of class time. The use of class time throughout the full period involves a discussion of lesson phases and all dimensions of instructional practice: tasks, learning environment, and discourse.

Observation 5: Use of Class Time (Phases, Tasks, Learning Environment, Discourse)

Instructional time is very precious, whether it is in elementary, middle level, or senior level mathematics classes. One of the main complaints of teachers is that they do not have enough time to work with the students. This is especially true in schools that have periods that have only 40 to 50 minutes of instructional time per day. It is therefore essential that teachers use their precious class time effectively and efficiently. To accomplish this, teachers must create a learning environment in which students cooperate with the teacher and with one another. Furthermore, teachers must create tasks that engage the students from the moment they enter the room until the moment they leave. Teachers also must orchestrate task-oriented, productive discourse. Finally, the phases of the lesson must allow for initiation, development, and closure of ideas. The way teachers make use of the limited time they have is largely an outgrowth of the priorities they have, which are a reflection of their cognitions. A first step in learning how to take maximum advantage of limited classroom time is to observe how others make use of their time.

Observation Overview

The purpose of this observation is to make you aware of and sensitive to the way each minute of class time is used in the class that you observe. You will need a watch with a second hand to record the time for each phase (i.e., initiation, development, closure) and activity. Because you will write a lesson plan that you believe best fits the lesson you observe, you will need to record the aim of the lesson and infer the main objectives. As you focus on the use of class time, you will make conjectures about the teacher's knowledge, beliefs, and goals.

In preparation for this observation, read about "use and organization of class time" in your methods text. The guidelines provided in Appendix B.5 will help you to focus on the use of class time.

Observation Examples

What follows are excerpts from two observation reports. The first excerpt is from a report prepared by Dimitri about a mixed second- and third-grade lesson on finding patterns in a 100s chart. The second excerpt is from a report prepared by Joshua about an algebra test review.

Grades 2–3 Lesson on the 100s Chart

The class that Dimitri observed started with a 15-minute warm-up activity in the meeting area of the classroom. The children sat on the rug as the teacher asked some children to pick number cards from a container and place them on a partially filled 100s chart posted on the chalkboard. Dimitri noted, "Throughout the activity, the teacher emphasized accountable talk as the children listened carefully to each other, asked each other questions, and rephrased responses to reveal their level of understanding." He reported that the 15-minute development phase of the lesson also occurred in the meeting area, where the children compared the placement of the numbers 75, 19, and 86 and the teacher unveiled at the appropriate time a completed 100s chart. Dimitri indicated, "For the last 15 minutes of the lesson, the children returned to their seats to complete a partially filled 100s chart, and then to find patterns in the 100s chart and write a description of the patterns. There was not enough time for the teacher to bring the lesson to closure."

Dimitri offered a suggestion related to differentiating the tasks to address one of the shortcomings of the lesson:

> Although there were minisummaries throughout the 15-minute development, there was no time for sharing or closure following the children's individual seat work. It seems as though there were two lessons packed into one. Perhaps the individual seat work could have focused on completing the partially filled 100s chart for the second graders. For the third graders for whom completing a 100s chart would be a review, they could have been directed to work on finding patterns for adding 10, adding 9, and adding 11 in the 100s chart.

Dimitri made several conjectures about the teacher's knowledge, beliefs, and goals:

> I think the teacher's knowledge of the content (i.e., number patterns) was adequate to conduct the lesson. However, if she had specific knowledge of her students' abilities, she could have targeted specific tasks to various groups of children (e.g., second graders vs. third graders; those who were "ready" to look for patterns vs. those who needed to review the 100s chart). She framed questions to help the children focus their attention on patterns related to adding 10, adding 9, and adding 11. On the basis of the teacher's instructional strategies, she is committed to developing children's accountable talk, helping them to construct their own meanings and making sense of the patterns being discussed, which were the broad goals reflected in her instruction.

Dimitri recognized that having second and third graders mixed together in one class could be problematic when trying to maximize meaningful instructional time for each group. He questioned how the teacher might provide adequate time to challenge all of the children without frustrating them.

Algebra Test Review

In the class that Joshua observed, students had taken an exam the day before, and the teacher focused the lesson on the types of problems that students found difficult. Joshua documented the time frames of this review lesson that incorporated the use of cooperative learning. It was a 45-minute lesson. During the first 6 minutes, students worked individually on two problems. During the next 4 minutes, students were divided into groups and given an assignment, followed by the next 18 minutes in which they worked in groups, and the next 12 minutes in which different students explained portions of the group work to the class. The teacher used the final 5 minutes to return test papers and assign homework. Joshua noted the way the teacher monitored and regulated the instruction during the group work section: "The groups worked well together, but they began to lose their focus after about

14 minutes. The teacher began to notice that the class was getting unruly, so he ended the group session and had the students return their desks to their normal position. I felt that the session lasted about 5 minutes too long, but I had the luxury of being an observer in the class and I was not busy helping the students as the teacher was." Joshua recognized the different perspectives one has as a teacher of a lesson versus an observer of a lesson and that careful orchestration of a lesson can be very tricky.

Joshua explained the instructional strategy as follows: "The main instructional strategy used was cooperative learning. The teacher had students go to the blackboard, do the problem and explain their work. The students explained the work to the teacher and the class as they wrote it on the board."

Joshua had a positive impression of the teacher's movement during the class: "The teacher was away from the board for the cooperative learning session. He moved around quite a bit and talked to each group. Before and after the group session, the teacher remained at the front of the room. All of the students were working during the group session. ... I think the students genuinely enjoyed having the teacher move around the room and work with them in small groups. It seemed to energize them through the rest of the class." Joshua saw the value of using diverse instructional strategies during the course of one lesson and the importance of the timing of these instructional strategies. That is, for this particular class, had the teacher allowed the students to work in small groups during the entire period, it would not have been effective.

Even though this was a review lesson, Joshua noticed the phases that existed during this lesson:

> At the start of the class, the teacher introduced the two types of problems that the students had trouble with on the previous day's test: algebraic fractions with division and the other subtraction with unlike denominators. He gave them different types of problems to do in the groups and asked them to notice the patterns. This was like the development of the lesson. At the end of the class, he had several students summarize how to do the two types of problems introduced at the beginning. This was the closure of the lesson.

Joshua made interesting conjectures regarding the teacher's beliefs about how students learn: "The fact that this teacher allotted 18 minutes for the students to work on the problems in groups and 12 minutes for students to explain their work to the class tells me that he believes in the value of having students learn from one another and communicate their ideas. He didn't feel that he had to explain it himself to get the students to understand it." Joshua made the connection between a teacher's beliefs and how he apportioned the time in his class.

The next observation assignment concerns the verbal behavior of individual students throughout the class period. No discussion of verbal behavior can take place without discussing the discourse that occurs within the class.

Observation 6: Verbal Behavior of Students (Discourse)

The value of having students communicate mathematically is undisputed. The vision of an effective mathematics class is one in which students are actively involved in worthwhile mathematical tasks, exploring and discussing ideas, much beyond a teacher's show-and-tell approach. In the mathematics class of the 21st century, at many points in the lesson students are usually expected to participate actively in their learning. They are expected to express themselves orally. That is, they should be engaged in a verbal exchange of mathematical concepts with their teacher and with their classmates. Although having every student in the class engaged in conversation about mathematics during some segment of the class time is an admirable goal, it is very difficult to accomplish. In most classes, some students do not speak at all, others monopolize the class discussion, and others veer away from the subject matter. In most cases, the teacher bears the responsibility for the nature of the verbal interactions that occur in the class. For example, if the teacher designs a well-structured cooperative learning activity, the probability will be high that each student will have the opportunity to speak about mathematics. If the teacher calls on only the students who raise their hands, probably only a small number of them will orally express their mathematical ideas. If the teacher does not design interesting tasks and has not created a productive and respectful learning environment, chances are the students will be talking to each other about topics other than mathematics.

It is clear then that the verbal interactions are largely dependent on the tasks teachers design, the learning environment they create, and the discourse they promote. Therefore, it seems reasonable to assume that teachers' cognitions (i.e., knowledge, beliefs, and goals) play a critical role in the verbal interactions that occur within a class. For example, a teacher who believes that it is essential to have all students explain their mathematical reasoning aloud and has the knowledge of instructional strategies that will engage all students in oral mathematical communication will not call on just a select group of students but give all of the students a chance to participate in the discussion.

Observation Overview

The purpose of this assignment is to sensitize you to the verbal interactions that occur during class so that when you teach, you will be more aware of the discourse that occurs within your class. During the observation, you will make a rough seating chart, and, referring to the Legend for Verbal Flow Observations in Appendix B.6, each time a student speaks the appropriate notation is to be entered on the seating chart.

Prior to the observation, read about "discourse" in your methods text. The guidelines provided in Appendix B.6 will help you to focus on students' verbal behaviors during a lesson and prepare the written report.

Observation Examples

What follows are excerpts from two observation reports. The first one was prepared by Karen about a Grade 7 lesson on graphical representations, and the second one was prepared by Elena about a Grade 10 lesson on geometric proofs. The Verbal Interaction Chart that accompanies the excerpts of Elena's report can be found in Appendix C.1.

Grade 7 Lesson on Graphical Representations

Only 11 out of the 24 students (i.e., about 46%) in the class that Karen observed had the opportunity to speak during the lesson. She noted the arrangement of the students and described the tasks:

> The students were arranged in pairs, all facing the front of the classroom with their eyes on the teacher. Students spoke only when called on. The entire 40 minutes were spent translating situations presented verbally by the teacher into graphical representations, with attention given to labeling axes, positioning a line on the coordinate plane, comparing and contrasting three students' graphs, and discussing the effects of the independent variable on the dependent variable, which were the goals of the lesson. It was unbelievable that there was absolutely no overt off-task conversations or off-task behaviors.

Karen was very sensitive to the ethnic diversity in the classroom and the teacher's seemingly biased attitude toward her students:

> All of the students who responded gave correct answers. Although two girls and four African American males participated occasionally by raising their hands and were called on by the teacher, all the students who were selected to go to the chalkboard to share their work were White males. Ian was called on most frequently, and he was one of the three boys invited to put his work on the chalkboard. Although the White female teacher welcomed and encouraged opinions and responses from all of the students, I wonder whether she realized that she was sending a message of bias and inequity to the students in the class. I found this disturbing.

Karen documented a teacher-centered approach and made a suggestion for maximizing individual students' participation:

> For the most part, the teacher posed open-ended questions, asking students to construct, interpret, and compare graphs of situations she presented verbally. These situations were appropriate and challenging for the students and kept them interested throughout the entire lesson. The teacher was like an orchestra conductor, leading the class, posing the questions, calling on

students, and asking for comments and opinions about individual students' responses. The teacher was the center from whom all questions and directions flowed. All classroom conversation emanated from and returned to the teacher. The approach was very teacher centered. It might have been more beneficial if the students were able to work on several situations in pairs or in small groups and then have the group work displayed on the chalkboard and compared.

By not hearing from more than 50% of the class, Karen noted that the teacher had a limited knowledge of the students' graph comprehension. She was able to infer the teacher's beliefs about how students learn:

The teacher seemed to know which students to call on and depend on to move the lesson along. I am not sure that she knew anything about the 54% of the students who did not say anything during the lesson but sat in the class quietly and respectfully. This teacher seems to believe that students learn from listening to and responding to her questions and expressing their agreement or disagreement with their peers. But all communication is directed to and from the teacher.

Although it is not fair to criticize the teacher based on one observation, Karen made some very astute and important observations related to classroom discourse that address the equity principle (NCTM, 2000). It will be interesting to observe how Karen transfers this experience to similar situations in her own classroom when she begins to teach. More attention to stereotyping, diversity, and equity is the focus of Observation 9.

Grade 10 Lesson on Geometric Proofs

Elena observed a class in which there was very little verbal behavior regarding the subject matter and too much regarding nonsubject matter. This is obvious from the seating chart she created (see Appendix C.1). Elena detected the relationship between the teacher's poor questioning style and the lack of subject-directed verbal behavior of the students:

A total of only 12 students (i.e., 40%) participated during the lesson. The teacher could increase this percentage by calling on particular students for responses, especially those who are not paying attention or do not participate at all. Besides, the class management should be less teacher centered. The few questions the teacher actually asked were directed to the whole class. Students' responses were choral responses. The teacher should let students come up with their own explanations instead of him explaining all the exercises.

Elena also noted how the teacher-dominated approach used in this lesson contributed to the verbal interactions that were not related to the subject:

> The right side of the classroom was involved in having irrelevant conversations. Students were talking about the color of a lipstick or about the party coming up this Saturday. They raised their hands to ask irrelevant questions such as whether they could go to the bathroom. This happened because the teacher talked for the whole period of class, and he did not let students participate. He did not use any challenging problems so students could be more interested in the lesson. He did not move from the board, and he completely ignored students who were not paying attention to his lecture.

Elena had an interesting conjecture regarding this teacher's knowledge of his students: "I believe that this teacher knows his students, and he knows who is doing well and who is repeating. However, I do not understand why he does not realize how boring a repeating lesson could be for some of his students." Elena raised an interesting question with regard to what is in the mind of this teacher. If he knows his students' abilities and past experiences, why isn't he tailoring his instruction to meet the needs of these students? Does he lack knowledge of ways to make it interesting, or doesn't he believe it is his responsibility to make it interesting? The important thing about this observation is that it caused Elena to make the link between the students' verbal behaviors and the cognitions of the teacher.

The next observation assignment concerns the task orientation of students throughout the class period. All three dimensions of instructional practice have a direct effect on the task orientation of students: tasks, learning environment, and discourse.

Observation 7: Task Orientation of Students (Tasks, Learning Environment, Discourse)

One of the critical concerns beginning teachers have is how to maintain discipline in their classes. The idea of losing control of students can be very frightening, especially for recent college graduates teaching in high schools where they are not much older than their students. Although discipline can be a great challenge in certain types of classes, the best prevention against such problems is to create well-designed tasks, a respectful learning environment, and active discourse during all phases of the lesson. A first step in learning how to do this is to observe firsthand the connection between the on-task and off-task behaviors of students and the dimensions of a lesson throughout each phase of the lesson.

Observation Overview

If possible, you are to revisit the class you observed for Observation 6. The purpose of this assignment is twofold: first, to focus your attention on the behavioral relationships among the students and on their level of involvement with each other and with the assigned task during each phase of the lesson (i.e., initiation, development, and closure), and second, to compare students' verbal interactions documented in Observation 6 with what you observe for this assignment. If you are able to revisit the class you observed for Observation 6, and there are no changes in the students' seating arrangement, you may use the same chart constructed for the previous assignment.

Prior to the observation, read about "developing tasks and activities" and "classroom management" in your methods text. The guidelines provided in Appendix B.7 will help you to focus on students' behaviors during the three phases of the lesson and prepare the written report.

Observation Examples

What follows are excerpts from two observation reports. One is from Karen's report, prepared after she revisited a Grade 7 class that she observed for the previous assignment. The seventh graders were involved in a lesson on scale factor using the Connected Mathematics (CMP) text *Stretching and Shrinking* (Lappan, Fey, Fitzgerald, Friel, & Phillips, 1998). Karen's line graph can be found in Appendix C.2.

The second excerpt, prepared by Dorothy, is of a Grade 11 lesson on the Law of Sines. The line graph and seating chart that accompany the excerpts of Dorothy's report can be found in Appendix C.3.

Grade 7 Lesson on Scale Factor

Corresponding to her line graph (see Appendix C.2), Karen recognized the critical importance of making sure that all students have the necessary tools to maximize their on-task behavior at the beginning of the lesson, and she made an appropriate suggestion for improving classroom management:

> At the initiation phase of the lesson, students who were unprepared were not on task because they did not have the proper tools (e.g., rulers and notebooks). Although the teacher was ready for them by having extra rulers and paper, distributing the tools to one third of the class took several precious minutes of class time at the start of the period. If the teacher had the rulers and paper on a table near the door when students entered the room, they could have just taken the tools they needed and immediately started to work without wasting time and waiting for the teacher to distribute the tools.

Karen noticed that for about half of the 1-hour period, 100% of the students were on task, attributing this to the selected CMP task, the teacher's expectations, and the learning environment established by the teacher:

> This was an amazing lesson. When the students were working in pairs to complete the exercises from the CMP book, 100% of the students demonstrated

their interest in the activity by being on task most of the time. The teacher was very task oriented and businesslike. She had high expectations for the students, calling on them to respond to her questions and to react to their classmates' responses. The class atmosphere was friendly and constructive. Students were permitted to ask each other questions and talk about the exercises as they worked together.

Karen recognized the effect of the teacher's inadequate knowledge of the students' skills on students' off-task behaviors at the end of the lesson. Her suggestion to assess students' readiness for the lesson is related to the focus of the next observation on assessment:

Near the end of the class time as the teacher walked around observing the students working in pairs, she realized that a few students did not remember how to multiply a mixed decimal (i.e., 4.375) by 100. Although it seemed as though a majority of the class knew how to compute the product, two students thought the product was 400.375. By calling the entire class together to discuss this, she interrupted the work of a majority of the students. This may have caused those students who knew how to calculate the product to engage in off-task behaviors [see Appendix C.2]. The teacher tried to involve the students who knew how to compute the product, but students were drifting off task. If the teacher had brought attention to this by including a Do Now example of some of the necessary computations, she might have been able to assess the students' readiness for the lesson at the beginning. This detour derailed the teacher's ability to bring the lesson to closure.

Karen was able to compare the discourse and level of student involvement in this lesson to what she observed in the previous assignment. She also realized that it is unfair to make generalizations based on one observation:

Similar to the previous observation, the discourse was controlled and dominated by the teacher. Unlike the previous lesson where only 46% of the students' voices were heard, every student had the chance to respond to a question or to a classmate at least once during this lesson. Also unlike the previous lesson, the teacher was inclusive, calling students to share their work at the chalkboard. This experience points out to me the importance of not making generalizations after observing just one lesson.

Grade 11 Lesson on the Law of Sines

Dorothy noticed that quiet students are not necessarily students who are on task. She also recognized the need to time the activities properly and, more important, to monitor the students closely to determine the proper timing. (See Appendix C.3 for the seating chart and the line graph.)

The teacher I observed has excellent control over the volume of her classes. Her students are virtually silent, and that seems to be the way she likes them. However, in doing this observation, I could see that a silent classroom does not mean that the students are all on task.

The class I observed had 20 students. At the start of the period, about 55% of the students were on task. However, the teacher left too much time for the students to do the Do Now. This caused many of the students to lose interest and come off task. This can be seen on the graph between 11:40 and 11:45 a.m., where the students were least attentive; only 3 students (i.e., 15%) were on task. When the teacher started to go over the Do Now at 11:50 (already 20 minutes after the period had started), most of the students (i.e., 95%) were on task.

Even when the students were off task they remained silent. During the first 20 minutes of class, the teacher was sitting at her desk, grading tests from another class. This should not have been done during class time. Had the teacher gotten out from behind her desk and walked around the classroom, she would have noticed that most of the students were finished with the Do Now and were sitting and daydreaming or working on homework from other classes.

Dorothy also noticed the relationship between the verbal interactions she noted in the previous observation and the task behaviors she noted in this observation. She recognized how the teacher's questioning style affected the learning environment, the level of task engagement, and ultimately what the students learned.

When I observed this class for Observation 6, I noticed that this teacher seemed to have very little interaction with her students. I have never seen her call on any particular student by name. When she asks questions to the class, she simply waits for some faceless voice to call out the answer. The entire classroom environment is very cold and impersonal. The fact that the students sit by in silent protest (as opposed to acting out by talking, etc.) adds to the already eerie setting. The students seem almost like robots; they carry out their task and then sit silently. I don't know what they are learning, but I can't imagine any concepts to be understood on a deeper level with so little student participation.

When it came to her conjecture regarding the teacher's knowledge of the students and of pedagogy, Dorothy seemed confused:

It is hard for me to judge this teacher's knowledge of pedagogy based on what I saw. I don't know whether she teaches this way because she doesn't know any better or because she just doesn't care. Maybe she believes that as a teacher she shouldn't have to take any work home with her and so she thinks it is OK to get her work done during class time. Or does she really believe that it is not her job to give students individual attention? I can't imagine that teaching in the way she does, she knows very much about her individual students.

Even though Dorothy was confused, she understood that there is a distinct connection between this teacher's beliefs and the low level of student participation in the class.

The next observation assignment concerns the assessment procedures used with the class. A discussion of methods of assessment is clearly a discussion of methods of monitoring and regulating.

Observation 8: Assessment (Monitoring and Regulating)

One of the main purposes of assessment is to help teachers better understand what students know and do not know and make meaningful instructional decisions based on that information. Within our model, this would primarily fall under the category of monitoring and regulating. Beginning teachers often think that assessment is synonymous with testing. This common misconception could not be farther from the truth. Assessment is an ongoing process that takes place within classrooms every day as students and teachers interact. The fact that it is usually undocumented information should not detract from our appreciating its importance. Ongoing student assessment is the teacher's main problem-solving technique—the problem being to help students learn mathematics. By monitoring student understanding and regulating the instruction based on the feedback obtained, teachers can maximize their chances of helping students learn. In short, assessment of student understanding must be an integral part of instruction.

Teaching has been recognized as a profession in which decisions are made every few seconds. This means that teachers must be flexible and able to change the path of their lesson based on their assessment of the students. Teachers frequently walk out of their classrooms feeling defeated because they were not able to "cover the material." Although it is important to adhere to a syllabus, we believe that teachers who cover the curriculum without regard to whether students are "with them" are making a big mistake. This kind of teaching is based on a belief that a teacher's number one role is to complete the curriculum and that student understanding is a distant second. We often tell student teachers, "If you could teach the same lesson with or without the students in the room, then something is radically wrong." The marks of an effective teacher are knowledge and flexibility to change the course of a lesson based on an assessment of student understanding. This on-the-spot decision making is very difficult for beginning teachers for two reasons. First, they are so concentrated on following their plan and what they are doing that they fail to recognize whether the students understand the work. Second, if they do recognize that the students are confused, they are at a loss for how to help them and are threatened by the thought of not following their preplanned script. Knowing how to change directions in a lesson takes expertise that usually takes years of experience to develop.

Assessment strategies are used not only to help teachers adjust their instruction but also as the basis for evaluation. That is, a part of every teacher's job is to assign some sort of a grade to represent the students' levels of understanding. How teachers formulate their grades is a reflection of what they value. For example, a teacher who thinks that it is important for students to be able to communicate orally and defend their mathematical ideas will probably count class participation as part of their grade.

A first step in learning how to engage in the monitoring and regulating that takes place during instruction is to observe it in other teachers' classrooms.

Observation Overview

The purpose of this assignment, which includes interviews with the teachers you observe, is to make you aware of the various forms of assessment. This assignment is designed to make you attend to assessment opportunities that occur during a class session, ways teachers can alter their instruction based on the feedback they receive from students, formal techniques teachers use to assess student understanding, and criteria they use to evaluate students.

Prior to the observation, read about "assessment strategies" in your methods text. The guidelines provided in Appendix B.8 will help you to focus on monitoring and regulating instruction and prepare the written report.

Observation Examples

What follows are excerpts from two observation reports. The first one is from George's report, prepared after he visited a Grade 4 lesson on the additive inverse, where the teacher was practicing principles of CGI (Carpenter et al., 1999). The second excerpt is from a report prepared by Danielle about a Grade 11 lesson on simplifying trigonometric expressions.

Grade 4 Lesson on the Additive Inverse

George noticed how the teacher's knowledge of her students helped her to target her questions, personalize instruction, and use feedback from students to develop her lesson:

> Throughout the lesson, the teacher continually monitored and assessed the students as she interacted with each of the 22 children in the multiethnic class. She knew her students so well that she personalized the word problems, assigning individual and pairs of children to discuss their thinking about the problems. As she listened and observed the children, the teacher made decisions related to the order of reviewing and discussing various problems that the children were called upon to discuss in front of the class. After one child, Princess, correctly explained the meaning of "$a + b - a = b$," the teacher asked

several children to explain in their own words what they heard Princess say and share examples to support their ideas. When the teacher was convinced that the children understood the additive inverse, she purposefully skipped over several planned examples to move on to a different "thinking problem": $a = b + 2$, where the children had to discuss and decide whether $a = b$, $a > b$, or $a < b$, providing examples.

By carefully observing and analyzing the teacher's behaviors, George was able to infer the teacher's goals for her students:

> The teacher's goals are to build on children's prior knowledge, to challenge children to become mathematical thinkers, and to offer children tools (e.g., manipulative materials, symbolic notation) for expressing their mathematical ideas.

After the lesson, George had the opportunity to interview the teacher. Although most of the teacher's formal methods of assessment are traditional, George questioned her use of class participation in the computation of grades without establishing a rubric:

> The teacher gives homework, quizzes, and exams as formal methods of assessing children's progress. To formulate grades, the teacher uses all forms of formal assessment and the quality of children's class participation. Using "the quality" of children's class participation for a grade is not clear. How is "quality" quantified? Shouldn't the teacher have a rubric posted so children know exactly how their class participation will be counted in the grade?

Grade 11 Lesson on Simplifying Trigonometric Expressions

Danielle recognized the connection between student questioning and ongoing assessment:

> I found very good ongoing assessment and a high rate of class partici-pation—something that is vital to good ongoing classroom assessment. I also found that the teacher did a pretty good job of questioning any answer a student gave—whether it was right or not—so that the students' confidence in their answer would have to be based only on how much mathematical sense it made to them and not on how the teacher was reacting to the answer. This way the teacher can assess better whether the students really know what they are doing or if they are just taking a shot in the dark and either sticking to it or changing their minds depending on the teacher's reaction.

Danielle also gave a good example of how a teacher regulated her instruction based on her assessment of student understanding:

> When one student wanted to take (tan x + sin $2x$)/tan x and just divide both tan x's to get sin $2x$, the teacher decided to take a couple of minutes to show why that doesn't work, especially because before, another student had taken (tan x × sin 2 x)/tan x and divided common factors of tan x and had not understood why he couldn't use the same process. Because no student was able to explain it better than to say "Because you just can't," she decided it was important to show them. She demonstrated it with the examples (8 + 4)/24 and (8 × 4)/24, which students could see more clearly. This was an example of using ongoing assessment to adjust a lesson plan according to the needs of the class. Not only that, but the fact that she first went to another student to answer a student's question, rather than at first answering it herself, shows that even one student's question is utilized for the assessment of other students.

Danielle demonstrated how this teacher's knowledge of content pedagogy allowed her to give the students an on-the-spot problem that would clarify the confusion.

Danielle pointed out that to be able to assess all of the students during class, the teacher should have called on all the students, which she did not do. Danielle gave two reasonable suggestions for involving all of the students, one of which supports the appropriate use of cooperative learning groups:

> There were at least two students whose mouths didn't open even once during the whole period, and probably four or five who were noticeably much less involved than the others. I think part of her wanting to keep the atmosphere nonthreatening goes a little too far—by just engaging students who may feel comfortable with being called on. The loss is that students who are uncomfortable being called on do not have the opportunity to demonstrate their knowledge through any avenue other than the tests. I think that if she thought of ways to bring these students gradually and gently into the conversation—ask them very simple things at first, for example—she may get the feeling that they are more willing to participate, and call on them more often, so that she can assess them in the classroom as well, rather than having to leave it completely up to her imagination whether or not they are following. Another way to maximize individual student involvement is to provide some cooperative group time. The teacher could have strolled around the room and listened in on students' conversations with each other. An adolescent would probably be more relaxed in a conversation with another adolescent than with an authority figure such as a teacher. By listening in on this kind of conversation, a teacher can gain insights and assessments that she couldn't get otherwise.

Danielle made some interesting conjectures regarding the goals, beliefs, and knowledge of this teacher:

> Judging from how the teacher insists that students use the correct mathematical language and how she questions them all the time, I can tell that she thinks it is important for them to communicate their thoughts and she really is interested in knowing what is in their minds. She was also very flexible about digressing from the lesson to make sure students understood a concept. The examples she gave really cleared up the concept and showed that she had good pedagogical knowledge.

Danielle was pleased to interview a teacher who used some nontraditional formal assessment and evaluation strategies:

> The teacher has a simple method for formulating grades. Students' class participation is one essential consideration. For every single student, she keeps an index card and at the end of each day, she jots down any students who had very good participation or poor behavior. When calculating grades, she looks at these index cards, along with tests, logs (the students in all of her classes keep daily logs), and portfolios. She does not weigh each item equally. For example, for the class I observed, she counted the portfolios and participation much more heavily than the two tests they had taken.

Danielle was impressed that the teacher made official documentation of students' daily participation on index cards. Such a technique not only enables the teacher to remember the incidences of participation more accurately but also demonstrates that the teacher genuinely values what students say during classroom instruction.

Although Danielle was impressed with this teacher's method of evaluation, she expressed some concerns:

> I felt this method of evaluation was very thorough. The only problem that I may see in it is that it's somewhat difficult and students generally prefer a more precise formula in order to figure out their grades. In addition, I don't think it is objective enough.

The issue of objectivity is a source of many discussions today as teachers consider alternative forms of assessment. It is good that Danielle is already sensitive to this issue.

Danielle recognized that this teacher's goals for student learning went far beyond being able to understand how to solve certain problems:

> Obviously this teacher placed a high value on having the students be able to explain mathematics both orally and in written form. From the way this teacher spoke to me in the interview and judging from the fact that in her

research class she counted her students' participation and portfolios more than their test grades tell me that she wants these students to appreciate mathematics and feel confident in their ability to express themselves.

It is encouraging to notice how Danielle has made the connection between the grading policy of the teacher and the goals the teacher has for the students.

From these examples it is clear that ongoing monitoring of students occurs in many ways through many sources. The teacher's ability to regulate instruction to meet the needs of the students is a critical aspect of teaching for student understanding. This being the case, it is important not only that teachers monitor the feedback they get from students but also that teachers' underlying assumptions of students' needs, interests, and abilities are accurate and unbiased.

The next observation assignment concerns the preexisting impressions and expectations teachers may have about different students or groups of students and how that is reflected in the discourse that occurs within their class and the tasks students are assigned.

Observation 9: Teacher Expectations and Stereotyping (Discourse, Tasks)

To be prepared for citizenship in our highly technological society, all students must learn mathematics—with particular emphasis on the word *all*. Students of all races, ethnicities, socioeconomic levels, physical conditions, religions, languages, and genders must have equal opportunities to learn mathematics. In other words, teachers must understand student differences in their approaches to learning and create learning experiences that are adapted to student diversity (Interstate New Teacher Assessment and Support Consortium, 1990). Most teachers would dispute the allegation that they allow stereotyping to interfere with their ability to offer equal opportunities to all their mathematics students. But teachers' deep-rooted beliefs about the abilities of different groups of students cannot help but be reflected in their discourse with students.

For example, teachers communicate their expectations of student performance by how they respond when students have trouble with some task. Teachers who believe students are capable of carrying out tasks scaffold their instruction, enabling students to succeed on their own. A teacher who believes students cannot carry out a given task tells them exactly what to do or performs the task for the students. When teachers do tasks for students, the students conclude that their teachers do not believe that they are capable of performing the tasks themselves. In time, students come to share the expectations of their teachers.

Another way that teachers communicate their expectations of student performance is through the length of wait time they use. As described in Observation 2, there are three kinds of wait time in the classroom. The first kind is the time between asking a question and calling on a student, which teachers should extend to give all students an opportunity to think about an answer in preparation for being called on. The second kind is the wait time between calling on a student and achieving some kind of resolution—receiving the answer, rephrasing the question, or moving on to another student for the answer. The third kind is the wait time between receiving a response from a student and following up on it. Research suggests that teachers tend to wait longer for students from whom they expect correct answers (Rowe, 1974, 1986; Tobin, 1983). They tend to wait longer for interpretative and opinion answers than for factual answers. They tend to wait longer for answers from boys in mathematics and science classes and longer for answers from girls in English classes. The significance of long wait time, then, is that it signals to students that you have confidence in their ability to answer questions, which in turn motivates students to try harder to answer it and thus to succeed.

A third way that teachers communicate their expectations of student performance is through the feedback they give to students regarding their academic performance. Although many teachers realize the instructive benefits of praising and correcting students on their written work, they are unaware and less conscious of the verbal feedback they give to students in the classroom. For example, gender studies have revealed that boys receive more feedback from teachers than girls do (American Association of University Women, 1992). Boys are both praised more for right answers and criticized more for wrong ones than girls are. One researcher even found sex-stereotyped variations on the type of feedback: boys are encouraged to try harder when they answer a question wrong but girls are praised for trying (Campbell, 1995; Oakes, 1990; Secada, 1992).

When students feel that their answers receive little response from their teacher, they have less reason to work hard. These are the students who learn less and are more likely to discontinue their mathematics studies as soon as they have the opportunity.

Observation Overview

The purpose of this observation, divided into two parts, is to sensitize you to subtle evidence of bias in the classroom and to heighten your awareness of how beliefs about students can directly shape the nature of the discourse within the classroom. The first part of this assignment requires that you attend to any evidence of stereotyping or teacher bias in the classroom. The second part requires that you attend to the classroom and school environment (e.g., bulletin boards, posters) for evidence of inclusiveness in mathematics (e.g., gender, ethnicity, handicapping conditions).

Prior to the observation, read about "stereotyping" in your methods text. The guidelines provided in Appendix B.9 will help you to focus on the teacher's expectations and stereotyping and to prepare the written report.

Observation Examples

What follows are excerpts from two observation reports. The first one is from Mitch's report, prepared after he visited a Grade 2 lesson on mental computation using number strings (Fosnot & Dolk, 2001b). The second excerpt, prepared by Nicky, is of a Grade 11 lesson on parabolas.

Grade 2 Lesson on Mental Computation

To analyze the teacher's interactions with her students, Mitch recorded the composition of the class, the task presented to the children, and the teacher's approach to calling on children. He noted an instructional strategy that he observed in another class, offering it as a suggestion to get more children involved in the discussion:

> The 20-minute lesson focused on developing the children's mental computation skills using number strings. The 25 ethnically diverse students sat around the perimeter of a rug in the meeting area of the classroom without any paper, pencils, or books. Of the 25 children, 15 were girls and 10 were boys; 3 were inclusion special education children; 11 were white, 9 were Asian, 2 were African American, and 3 were Hispanic. The teacher carefully selected number examples, scaffolding the ideas to help children recognize relationships among numbers (e.g., $19 + 4$; $19 + 14$; $29 + 4$). As she presented each example, writing it on a whiteboard, she asked the children to explain how they think of the numbers so they could compute the sum "in their heads." When the children wanted to share their thinking, they raised their thumbs and sat quietly, waiting for the teacher to call on them. For each of the 16 opportunities that the children had to speak (i.e., answering a question, commenting on a peer's response, or asking a question), the teacher waited at least 5 seconds before calling on a student. Only children who had their thumbs raised were called on, and the majority of those called on were girls (14 responses were from girls from each ethnic group, and 2 responses were from boys, 1 white and 1 African American), with 1 of the white girls being an inclusion student. I was surprised to see how much more aggressive and willing to participate the girls were than the boys. I think it's great that the girls are so eager to share their ideas, but I think that the teacher should have called on more boys (2 of whom are inclusion students), even if they did not raise their thumbs. I saw another teacher use popsicle sticks with children's names on them, with the name part hidden in a cup. She selected popsicle sticks randomly to call on students to get more children involved in the lesson and to add some "drama" to calling on children to respond. Sometimes she asked the child who responded to pick a popsicle stick to select the next child to speak. I like this idea very much, and I hope to use it when I have my own class.

The description that Mitch provided is testimony of the teacher's respect for the children and her attempt to develop their autonomy and independence in learning:

> The teacher always responded to the children by asking whether anyone thought of a different string. Whenever children explained their thinking, the teacher illustrated the string on the whiteboard, identifying the name of the child who shared the idea so that children could refer to each other's methods. The teacher was very patient and encouraging, never correcting, criticizing, or rejecting any students' answers. All responses were welcomed and were used to develop the lesson. The teacher asked the children to identify and explain why some strategies were more efficient than others. The teacher shared her ideas only after the children shared theirs. Although the teacher did not call on children who did not signal to her that they wanted to speak, I think that the teacher believes that all children can learn mathematics and she respects their individual learning styles.

Mitch observed in a school that was sensitive to issues of equity. He noticed evidence of equity in the textbooks and posters:

> The newer mathematics textbooks they used pictured as many, if not more, females engaged in mathematical activities than males. I found a fifth-grade mathematics bulletin board with two very interesting printed posters. One pictured a woven rug and had an inset with a Navajo woman weaving one of them; the text mentions the intricate geometric concepts and relationships inherent in the designs of these rugs. It highlights intuitive mental math and visualization skills exhibited in these handwoven crafts by the Navajo women. There was a second poster depicting a system of calculation used in India centuries ago.

Although one might object to the stereotype of women sewing rather than "doing math," the important thing is that Mitch was sensitive to the representation of mathematical ideas being credited to people other than white males.

Grade 11 Lesson on Parabolas

Nicky noticed evidence of gender bias in the way the teacher conducted the discourse:

> In this class, there were 20 girls and 13 boys. Whenever the teacher called on a girl to answer a question, he waited less than 5 seconds and then proceeded to explain the answer and the procedure for how to get the answer. In one instance, he called on a female student, and while she was answering the question, he proceeded to answer the question and drown out the girl's voice. I might add, from previous observations, I noticed this girl never speaks in

this class and now I understand why. On the other hand, when a male member of the class answered a question, he allowed the student to answer.

Nicky had strong feelings about the probable beliefs of this teacher regarding differential abilities of males and females: "I really think that this teacher doesn't have much confidence in the ability of his female students. He doesn't seem to want to waste time waiting for them to answer a question, and when they do try to answer a question, he cuts them off. I think he assumes they won't give the correct answer and if they do, they won't be able to explain it."

This observation assignment enabled Nicky, who was given the opportunity to teach a class of her own in the school, to become aware of her own biases: "This observation has made me aware of a few of my own gender biases. I have noticed that I tend to pay less attention to the female students because of the behavioral problems I have with the male students in the classroom. In this manner my female students suffer from not getting as much attention that they deserve."

Although the issue of discipline was not included in the original assignment, Nicky's findings precipitated an interesting class discussion regarding the effects of negative attention and how it might actually be encouraging the boys to misbehave.

Nicky also noted bias in the posters she observed in the school: "As for famous mathematicians, most of them pictured were of white men." She credited this problem with lack of knowledge on the part of the teachers: "I don't think that the reason the posters were all of white men was because the teachers were biased against females or other races. I think they are just not aware of the work done by females and people from other ethnic groups, and the posters of these people are not that available. This may point to historian's bias but I'm not sure."

The last observation assignment is a culminating activity that gives you the chance to integrate the ideas you have learned from the previous nine observations.

Observation 10: Culminating Observation

By the time you do this observation assignment, you will have already observed teachers' instructional practice from many vantage points. In the previous nine observation assignments, you noted different aspects of teachers' instructional practice and made conjectures that may have accounted for what you observed. You specifically critiqued the tasks, learning environment, and discourse, as well as the teacher's use of phases and monitoring and regulating of instruction. On the basis of this information, you then considered what the teachers' knowledge, beliefs, and goals were. At this point, you are ready to put all the pieces of the puzzle together and observe all the dimensions of teaching at one time.

Observation Overview

The purpose of this observation assignment is for you to observe and critique all aspects of instruction in one lesson and make conjectures regarding all aspects of the teacher's cognitions. The assignment consists of two parts: (a) an analysis of the dimensions of the lesson (see Table 2.1, chapter 2) and (b) an analysis of the teacher's cognitions during the three stages of the lesson (see Table 3.1, chapter 3). If possible, interview the teacher to gain insight into the teacher's postactive thoughts following the lesson. The guidelines provided in Appendix B.10 will help you to focus on the lesson dimensions and teacher's cognitions during the three stages of the lesson and prepare the written report.

Observation Examples

What follows are excerpts from two observation reports. The first one is from Shante's report, prepared after she visited a Grade 5 introductory lesson on decimals. The second excerpt, prepared by Maria, is of a Grade 10 lesson on nested triangles.

Grade 5 Lesson on Decimals

Overall, Shante was inspired by the lesson she observed. Regarding modes of representation, Shante noticed how the teacher shifted the children's thinking from whole numbers to parts of a whole by using Dienes's Base-10 blocks to represent decimals: "Large quantities of the large cube (i.e., one whole), the flat (i.e., one tenth), the long (i.e., one hundredth), and the small cube (i.e., one thousandth) were available to the five groups of 5 to 6 children in each group." She observed that the students were familiar with the tools from their work with whole number place value. Using ideas related to money, she wrote that the teacher elicited decimal notation to help children make connections between concrete and abstract representations of decimals.

What impressed Shante the most was the motivation of the lesson. The children were given about 5 minutes of free exploration time to study the blocks and to answer the question "How do these blocks 'speak' to you mathematically?" She indicated that this open-ended question allowed children of various ability levels to enter the lesson and join in the discussion when the teacher brought the class together. She reported, "The children were totally engaged and interested in comparing the different-sized blocks and discussing equivalencies with their peers."

With respect to the social and intellectual climate, Shante recognized the teacher's excellent rapport with the children and the children's respect for each other:

> In this diverse class, the teacher showed genuine respect for each child as she encouraged and elicited opinions. The children listened to and respected each other. Children have obviously played mathematics games in this class before. They cooperated extremely well, keeping on task, attending to each player's accumulation of pieces representing parts of the whole and the exchanges made. The children knew the classroom rules for using manipulative materials, sharing and working with each other, and completing the assignment.

Attentive to modes of instruction and pacing, Shante noticed the importance of making adjustments to the instructional plan based on students' reactions, and her suggestion for expediting exchanges could be viable:

> When the game started, the teacher told the children to accumulate one-thousandth cubes by rolling one die. After about 8 minutes, the children realized that the game could take "forever." The teacher agreed to allow them to use two dice. This still took a very long time. By the end of the 50-minute period, no one had made a whole. Perhaps the children could have used more than two dice, or perhaps they could have used two dice of different colors so that one color (e.g., white) could represent the thousandths and one color (e.g., red) could represent the hundredths. Depending on the children's ability, this might make the game more challenging and move it along more quickly.

Shante noted the teacher's strengths related to discourse. Specifically, it seems as though the teacher–student and student–student interactions as well as the teacher's questioning were exemplary:

> This was one of the most interactive classes I have ever visited! Throughout the entire period, the teacher was nonjudgmental and encouraging and elicited ideas from all of the children. She called on children who raised their hands as well as those who did not raise their hands, asking them, "What do you think?" "What do you notice?" The nature of the teacher's open-ended, thought-provoking questions required that the children provide detailed explanations, and the children responded to each other's comments, either agreeing or disagreeing and explaining why. The teacher listened to each child carefully, asking others to repeat what they heard in their own words. She determined who needed clarification and often asked other children to provide the clarification.

Shante's interview with the teacher confirmed her observations related to the teacher's cognitions. The teacher knows her students so well that she was able to arrange them in heterogeneous groups based on their social and academic skills: "Children worked extremely well together. The children were able to work independently without too much adult supervision."

The teacher acknowledged that "she believes that the children are responsible for their own learning and that they need to be active participants in all aspects of classroom life. This teacher is definitely a facilitator of student learning. Her teaching behaviors support what she says her emphasis is on, and that is student understanding. She designs and selects tasks based on her knowledge of her students' interests and abilities, and she knows how to put them in charge of their own learning."

Grade 10 Lesson on Nested Triangles

Maria was quite critical of the lesson she observed. It was apparent that she was sensitive to the weaknesses of the lesson that existed within every category.

For example, within the category of modes of representation, Maria explained that to clarify the distinction between nested triangles, the teacher should have used either different colored chalk or an overhead projector. Maria was disappointed that the only motivation used was extrinsic, that is, the threat of the state exam. It was a review lesson, so she took no issue with the sequencing or difficulty level.

As for the social and intellectual climate of the class, Maria was convinced that it was poor and gave good reasons for feeling so: "The students clearly do not like this teacher, do not feel he cares about them, and do not feel he respects their intelligence or thoughts. This is clear from some of the comments students said to me after class and from the way he treats them during class." Maria criticized the pacing because he never let students explain their ideas and whether they were right or wrong, he would just move on. Although she thought his administrative routines were good in that students settled in quickly, she had an idea to improve the procedure by writing the problems on a transparency, which would save time from having to write them on the board.

Maria had major criticisms of the discourse. Regarding teacher–student interaction, she wrote, "It was terrible! The teacher showed no respect for anything that any student said. He gave no positive feedback for either correct or incorrect answers, never asked how a student got an answer—showing that he really didn't care how their minds worked, but only what their mouths said." Notice how Maria is able to relate the teacher's instructional practice with the teacher's thoughts.

Regarding student–student interaction, Maria wrote, "There was basically none. No student was asked to comment on what another had said, no student was asked to explain something she or he understood to a student who didn't understand. The closest he got to that was something like, 'Did you hear what Jane just said? You multiply both sides by two.' This was a sorry attempt at having students share ideas with each other!"

Maria was also critical of the teacher's questioning: "The only types of questions this teacher asked were 'What do I do next to solve this problem?'" Maria had suggestions for better types of questions: "The class never considered questions such as, Why are we taking this next step? What would happen if we took this different next step instead? How do you know that is the next step to take? What is the question asking us? What should the answer look like—a number, a set of points, an equation?"

Despite the fact that Maria was so disappointed in the instructional practice of this teacher, she did recognize the possibility that the teacher knew the subject matter and probably knew his students:

> From what I could tell, the teacher had, in general, a pretty good knowledge about his students—which ones were following and which ones would most likely be able to follow. He knew that they cared about grades and their state exam scores (which isn't actually true of every class or every student) and knew which ones were the troublemakers, not doing their work and not trying. He definitely knew the actual mathematics, and he knew the state course of study—what the state exam will expect from the students.

Maria attributed what she believed was his inferior teaching style to his lack of knowledge of suitable pedagogy. She wrote, "I don't believe he understands how the students learn or what is best for their learning."

On the basis of what she observed, Maria was able to deduce this teacher's beliefs about his role and the students' roles in his classroom: "I think he sees his role as a teacher as solely to get them to do well on the state exams by showing them the material and forcing them to do work by means of holding grades over their heads. I think he sees the students as a passive audience who can sometimes contribute to his presentation (but only with right answers—he doesn't like wrong answers) and whose active learning takes place through homework."

Maria's conjecture regarding the teacher's beliefs about mathematics was not a result of her observation of how he represented mathematics to his students. Rather, she expressed her own belief about all mathematics teachers, which may or may not be accurate: "It was not clear from the class I observed that the teacher feels that mathematics is anything special or dynamic, but I must give him the benefit of the doubt and imagine that he does on some level. It is impossible for me to consider that someone would be a mathematics teacher and not have at least some positive beliefs about mathematics." Maria reasoned that this teacher was unable to transfer his appreciation for mathematics to his students because it was not part of his goals: "This teacher's only goal was to cause the students to do well on the state exam by means of learning some mathematics."

Maria recognized the distinction between monitoring as a means of finding out which students were on task and monitoring as a means to learn about what the students understood:

> The teacher definitely monitored the students to see whether they were following. He called on almost all of the students throughout the course of the period, many of whom had not had their hands up. However, he never asked how a student got an answer, so he really couldn't know whether the student who answered correctly was just guessing or what mistake the student who answered incorrectly had made. Therefore, his method of monitoring couldn't really give him an accurate assessment of the students' knowledge or thoughts.

Maria's idea that the teacher did not monitor for the purpose of assessing student understanding was reasonable because, as she pointed out, he did not seem to deviate from his planned lesson, despite indications from the students that maybe he should have.

Regarding the category of regulating, Maria wrote, "The teacher refused to adjust his proposed lesson to the needs of the students. When it was clear that a few of the students weren't positive about how to factor the quadratic, he said, 'You should know this' and just did it, not explaining how in detail or taking even a minute to explain (or better yet, have another student explain) what was happening."

Maria was disappointed, but not surprised, that this teacher did not have the time to talk to her about the lesson so that she could examine his postactive thoughts. However, from what she wrote, we can see that Maria has developed a keen observatory eye and is able to relate the underlying teacher cognitions that are probably at work. This is a giant step on the road to becoming a teacher who can engage in self-assessment and reflection at a deep level of understanding and insight.

6 Using the Model to Examine Your Own Instructional Practice and Cognitions

The fact that teachers' cognitions are the driving force behind their behaviors in the classroom makes it essential that whenever you analyze your own teaching, you incorporate assessments of your own thoughts and decision making as well as your instructional practices. In this book, the model we present provides the conceptual basis for approaches you, as a preservice teacher, can use to reflect on and assess your teaching in a structured way. As we suggested in previous chapters, the lesson plan you write and your instructional practice are only part of your work. The cognitions that you have before you write your lesson plan, the thoughts you have while teaching your lesson, and the thoughts you have after you have completed your lesson are also critical components of teaching. To facilitate analyses of cognitions and instructional practices before, during, and after lessons, we recommend participating in written and oral pre- and postlesson activities. Although you cannot be expected to write pre- and postlesson activities on a daily basis, writing your plans and thoughts when your supervisor or a peer observes you or for a videotaped lesson can be an excellent tool for professional growth. Moreover, if you get accustomed to thinking about your lesson in such a structured manner, it is likely that it will become a natural part of your reflective practice (even though it may not be in written form). It is this application of the model, explained and exemplified in the sections "Reflection and Self-Assessment with the Assistance of a Supervisor or a Cooperating Teacher," "Reflection and Self-Assessment with Peers," "Reflection and Self-Assessment Using a Videotape," and "Reflection and Self-Assessment Through Journal Writing and Online Communication," that is the focus of the remainder of this chapter.

Reflection and Self-Assessment With the Assistance of a Supervisor or a Cooperating Teacher

To prepare for a lesson that your supervisor or cooperating teacher will observe, write not only your lesson plan but also a description of your prelesson thoughts and concerns. Presenting these documents before starting the lesson gives your supervisor the background information she or he needs to get a good understanding of the lesson. After the lesson, meet with your supervisor to share your impressions and analysis of the lesson, the thoughts you had while teaching the lesson, and your own ideas about how you might do things differently if you were to teach the lesson again. After you have shared your thoughts, the supervisor can share her or his impressions of the lesson and what you have said. At this time, your supervisor can reinforce positive features of the lesson and give suggestions for further thought and improvement. After the conference, think about what you and your supervisor discussed, and at the next class meeting submit documents to your supervisor that include your postlesson thoughts and final assessments. Your supervisor can then use these materials to assess your ability to engage in the reflective and self-assessment skills so necessary for ongoing improvement in teaching. Each of these activities is structured in a way that is consistent with the conceptual model described earlier in this book. The details of these activities and excerpts from the work of our student teachers follow. Detailed guides for the written observation reports and the conference are in Appendix D.

Prelesson Thoughts: Reflecting on Your Preactive and Interactive Cognitions Before Teaching a Lesson

There are many reasons why it is important to write your prelesson thoughts and present them to your supervisor before teaching a lesson. First, it is a way to communicate with your supervisor and set the stage for your lesson. This is your opportunity to justify your plans for this lesson and a time to explain the dilemmas and frustrations you may be facing. You want to be sure that when the supervisor sits down to observe your lesson, she or he understands the context for instruction that has contributed to your decision making for that class. The second critical purpose of writing the thoughts you have before or during lesson planning is to make explicit to your supervisor, as well as to yourself, your over-arching cognitions. It is important that you write about the goals you have for your students and what you know about them. Becoming student focused helps you to advance more quickly from the initial stage of teaching, where content is the main focus, to the latter stages of teaching, where student understanding is the main focus.

We also suggest that you write about the knowledge you have of the mathematical content and the methods of pedagogy suitable for this lesson. This process encourages you to get a better understanding and appreciation of the content, see a bigger picture of the content, and focus on and consider alternative strategies for conducting the lesson. Including information about the resources you used to create the lesson encourages you to go beyond the textbook when making decisions about how to teach a lesson. Consulting a variety of sources (e.g., other texts, journals especially written for mathematics teachers, other teachers in the school, peers, books, the Internet) increases your knowledge and makes your lessons more interesting and effective.

Finally, although you might write a lesson plan with a detailed script to follow, remember that, as in every human endeavor, things do not always go as planned. As you become more experienced, you will be able to anticipate when problems might arise and what to do when they occur. This is the art of being able to engage in effective on-the-spot monitoring and regulating of classroom instruction.

To help prepare you for this challenge, try to anticipate the areas of difficulty you might face as you teach your lesson and create a plan for dealing with these difficulties in case they do arise. Expert teachers involved in Japanese lesson study anticipate student responses as they plan their lessons. For examples of such lesson plans, see Fernandez and Yoshida (2004).

Although beliefs are a key component of the overarching cognitions in the model, they are not directly addressed in your assignment for prelesson thoughts. There is an important and interesting reason for this. By the time you are ready for student teaching, you have a clear idea of the latest philosophies of mathematics instruction that are valued, and if asked about your beliefs regarding mathematics instruction, you know what your instructors want to hear and are probably very adept at saying it. In research conducted by Artzt and Armour-Thomas (1998), several student teachers gave wonderful lip service to their beliefs about student-centered instruction yet contradicted those ideas during their instructional practice. In fact, when interviewed as they viewed videotapes of their lessons, these students often contradicted their prelesson beliefs as they tried to justify their actions. Using the idea that "actions speak louder than words," the supervisor should save all discussion of your beliefs until after the lesson is concluded and you are called on to justify your actions. Deeply held beliefs are essentially indirectly revealed in all that you do as you teach your lessons.

The details of this prelesson activity and excerpts from the work of our student teachers follow.

Provide Personal Background Information

Although student teaching is usually cited as the most valuable experience in a teacher preparation program, it can be fraught with difficulties. For example, conflicts sometimes arise among the philosophies of the supervisor, the student teacher, and the cooperating teacher. Dilemmas sometimes exist between the desire to use interesting teaching strategies and the perception that they will take too long and impede the efforts to cover the content. Sometimes a cooperating teacher is reluctant to relinquish control of the class to an inexperienced student teacher. Student teachers placed in these kinds of difficult positions have to make serious decisions about the nature of their instructional practice. If any of these problems exist, it is important to inform your supervisor by including her or him in your prelesson thoughts. Jenny described her frustrations after student teaching for 8 weeks:

> Before I start writing about my prelesson thoughts, I think I need to write a little bit about the class, my cooperating teacher, and my experience with the class. I have been in front of the class only about five times so far, and only one of these has been to teach. My cooperating teacher is an extremely nice man but unwilling to give me any freedom in the classroom. He says that the ideas I share with him about teaching or certain materials are good, but he would prefer that I do things his way. That is why, in the lesson you are about

to observe, you will see that I am just going to explain the material to the kids in a very straightforward way.

Having read what Jenny said, the supervisor might have been more understanding than she would have been if she had observed such a teacher-centered lesson without this information. It was encouraging to note that Jenny was dissatisfied with the traditional teacher-centered approach she was asked to take. The question then was how to help Jenny formulate a student-centered approach that would be acceptable to the cooperating teacher.

In Catherine's prelesson thoughts, it is easy to sense her frustration with the dull problems she is about to use for the focus of her instruction:

> Before I delve into all the interesting problems I wanted to use in this lesson, let me start by saying that I never get to use any of them. My cooperating teacher wanted me to do a lesson on all the types of Pythagorean Theorem questions that are bound to show up on the state exam. Although I would have liked to teach this lesson with some examples from carpentry or bridge building or some other real-life example, I had to take all routine problems from the review book. They were very drab.

If the supervisor had not read these prelesson thoughts, she would have been unaware that Catherine had such good ideas for applying the Pythagorean theorem and was not using them because of the wishes of the cooperating teacher.

Write About Your Goals for Students

When you describe the goals you have for your students, take into consideration the development of both procedural skills and conceptual understanding. Even though research suggests that the overriding concern of most beginning teachers is content coverage, the important thing to realize is that content coverage has value only in relation to student understanding and skill development. You should also consider goals for your students that are supplementary but intertwined with performance goals. That is, it is important for students to understand the value of learning a specific aspect of mathematics. It is also essential that students feel capable of learning the material and communicating their understanding to others.

Anna explained her goals for students in the prelesson thoughts she wrote for a lesson on adding and subtracting radicals:

> One of my goals is that students will come to understand that adding and subtracting radicals is just an extension of their prior knowledge, and I am hoping that it will not be very difficult for them to do. Also, I want them to be able to check that the rules for this topic are correct by calculating the values of the expressions. By using the interesting real-life problem I found for this topic, I hope that I can help the students recognize and appreciate the use of

mathematics in the real world. They will also be required to use problem-solving techniques and think logically.

Anna's goals go far beyond mere procedural competency. She was concerned that students be able to link their new understanding to their past understanding. Furthermore, by having them check the rules, it is clear that Anna wanted the students to have confidence in what they are learning. Finally, she explicitly stated her concern that they see the value in what they are learning.

Write About What You Know About Your Students

The next section of your prelesson thoughts should contain a description of your students and what you know about their ability levels, personalities, and interests. In addition, you should describe the gender, language, and racial and ethnic backgrounds of your students. In the beginning of a semester, your accounts might be general in nature, but as the semester progresses, you should be able to be quite detailed in your descriptions. For example, it is not enough to say that students have difficulty learning different counting procedures. This is too vague a comment to provide a focus for the design of a lesson. Rather, you should outline the specific difficulties that the students are having. That is, it is more helpful to say that students have difficulty deciding when to use combinations and when to use permutations. Such comments will help you to design a lesson that focuses on and highlights clearly the difference between the two counting procedures.

Margaret identified a specific area of difficulty for her students:

> I feel that students need more time and practice with permutations, even though they've learned it in the past. Yesterday, while circulating, I realized that some students did not understand why $15!/14! = 15$. I saw that some students in class grasp probability ideas quickly, whereas others didn't know what we were doing. As time progresses, I learn more about each student. Now I think I know whom to pair up so that the ones who understand it can help the ones who don't.

Not only was Margaret specific in her evaluations of what her students understand but she also came to know their abilities and is now in a position to use that knowledge to their advantage in the classroom.

Nora chose to focus on the students' self-confidence and disposition toward mathematics when revealing her knowledge of students:

> To get them interested in quadrilaterals and make the concepts easier to understand, for homework I asked them to cut out strips of given lengths from cardboard I distributed. Some of the students commented, "I could not even pass algebra. How can I pass geometry?" It is really challenging to

motivate some of the students in this class because they are so disappointed with their abilities that they don't even try to understand.

It is clear that Nora was trying to adapt her teaching to the knowledge she has of her students' low self-esteem in mathematics.

An excerpt from Karen's prelesson thoughts shows that she considered the ability levels and language differences that exist in her elementary class:

> There is a wide range of ability levels in the class, so I will have to think of the brightest student as well as the slowest. I am concerned about some of the students who have language problems though. I am beginning to plan a lesson where they will have to describe various shapes. Although this will be difficult for them, I believe it may serve as a good practice.

Although Karen was not explicit about how she intended to meet the needs of the wide range of student ability in the class, it is good that she is aware that they exist and that her intention is to meet all of their needs.

Vanessa's prelesson thoughts show how her knowledge of students has been progressing over the course of the semester:

> I don't believe I have a firm grasp of my knowledge of students yet. My class seems average; I have some stronger students and some weaker. I also seem to have at least one student who absolutely panics when she sees a mathematics example. In past lessons I've been surprised by what the children did not understand. I'm getting more used to the fact that what may seem simple to me could be far from easy for my students.

Vanessa's last comment indicates that she arrived at one of the most important realizations a teacher can have. All too often, teachers are unable to put themselves in the place of the learner and recognize what may be problematic for them.

Finally, excerpts from Jasmine's first and fourth observations show how she learned to deal with a student, Roxanne, because she got to know her better. In her first observation, Jasmine described how she planned to use a small-group activity but had concerns about Roxanne:

> Because the students are not used to this type of activity, I worry that it can go totally wrong. I also have concerns about one student in particular. Her name is Roxanne, and other teachers have told me to watch out for her. She can totally change the course of a lesson. She tends to make wisecracks to me during class that are very disruptive. I'm not sure what her problem is.

By the fourth observation, Jasmine had taken the time to get to know Roxanne, whose behavior completely changed:

I have met many times with Roxanne after class and have spoken to her personally about why she makes the comments she does. Even though she couldn't give me any reason, I think she just needed that personal attention. I am embarrassed to say I had a preconceived opinion of Roxanne because of other people's opinion of her. I am very happy to say Roxanne has become one of my most treasured students in the class. Roxanne often does change the course of my lesson, but I wish I had a dollar for each thoughtful, wonderful question she asks during our lessons. When I introduced parabolas, Roxanne was the one to ask, "What happens if we turn it upside down?" I could not ask for a better way to introduce $y = -x^2$. I truthfully hope Roxanne learned as much from me as I learned from her this semester.

Jasmine learned the importance of taking the time to get to know her students so that she can better meet their needs and, in turn, they can better meet her needs.

Write About What You Know About the Content of the Lesson

The next section of your prelesson thoughts is a written account of what you know about the content. Each day's lesson does not occur in a vacuum. It is part of a mathematical story that unfolds throughout the course of the semester, so it is essential that you consider the whole picture when designing the lesson plan. In your prelesson thoughts, describe the mathematical content that came before and the content that will come after that particular day's lesson. Furthermore, describe the value of the content for students. Considering such issues about the content will help you to design a lesson that is sequenced appropriately and will attract the interest of the students.

Michael described his concerns about the complexity of the content when he was preparing to teach a second-grade lesson on place value:

I wonder why place value is in the second-grade curriculum. It is such a sophisticated concept, and the language related to exchanging "one 10" for "10 ones" seems to be cumbersome and confusing for young children, especially for those for whom English is not their native language. The children have played several versions of the "Exchange Game" in Base 3 and Base 10. For this lesson, my cooperating teacher wants me to develop the meaning of "place value" for Base 10. I have been struggling with this, trying to find the appropriate language to describe the powers of 10 as we move from the ones' place, to the tens' place, to the hundreds' place. It seems to me that if the children can read the numbers (e.g., "23" is "twenty-three") and they can decompose the numbers (e.g., "23" is "2 tens and 3 ones"), they should have a grasp of "place value," and more formal language and explanation can occur in the later grades.

Michael's analysis of the curriculum, his knowledge of the content, and his knowledge of young children will serve him well as he designs the activities for his second graders.

Yali described her knowledge of matrix multiplication, how it relates to what the students learned before and will learn in the future, and the importance of the topic:

> We have already studied matrix operations, such as addition, subtraction, scalar multiplication, and matrix multiplication. Also, we have evaluated the determinant of a 2×2 matrix. Today they will learn determinants of a 3×3 matrix by seeing that they must use what they know already (make the 3×3 into a 2×2). Later in the week, they will use the determinant in Cramer's Rule and solving equations. They will then be able to apply these concepts to linear programming, which has so many important applications in real life.

Yali's knowledge of matrices contributed to her ability to sequence the instruction in such a way that her students could build on their previous understanding of 2×2 matrices to learn about 3×3 matrices.

Michele demonstrated her overall knowledge of the content of counting procedures and their use in the study of probability:

> Students have reviewed simple probability, the counting principle, probabilities with two or more activities, as well as permutations. Students were also introduced to permutations with repetitions but did not study probabilities that involve permutations. During this lesson students will be introduced to a new concept—combinations. During the next several days, they will practice problems and find probabilities using either permutations or combinations, so they must learn to distinguish when to use which.

It is clear that Michele understood that students learn the counting procedures to solve problems in probability and that it is important for students to understand the distinctions between permutations and combinations. This broad picture is often what eludes students and makes topics confusing for them. Michele's depth of understanding is likely to facilitate her ability to help her students understand the concepts.

Write About What You Know About Pedagogical Approaches for the Lesson

When you write about your knowledge of different pedagogical approaches that might be suitable for your lesson, include descriptions of the roles that you and the students will play in the lesson. This will help you to decide which approach might work best. You should also consider which tools and motivational techniques will be most suitable for helping students to gain conceptual understanding. This task is designed to help you envision the engagement and interaction between you and the students during the lesson. It is also designed to help you consider different options for the representations that will work best in helping students to understand the concepts.

The following two excerpts from the prelesson thoughts of Julie and Eileen illustrate a focus on materials that would be most effective for their particular lessons. Julie wrote,

> Because my goal is to reintroduce area in Grade 5, I would like to build a lesson out of what they may already know about the topic. I would like to use something physical, where they can see that the area of a triangle is half of a rectangle with the same base and height. I would have liked to use geoboards; however, there are a few students whom I would not trust working with rubber bands. I may use large-box graph paper as a substitute for the geoboard, or use tangrams to explore area with problem solving.

Regardless of whether Julie made a good decision to forego using geoboards with her fifth graders, the important point is that she used her knowledge of students to affect her choice for instruction.

Eileen weighed the pros and cons of using different materials for a lesson on graphing parabolas:

> A graphing calculator can be used in this lesson so not as much time will be spent on graphing parabolas. On the other hand, students need practice in graphing, and perhaps it would be a little confusing to students to see that on a calculator the parabola does not look really as a smooth curve, and the units on the x-axis and y-axis on a calculator are usually not the same, so that the parabola drawn on graph paper and the one on the calculator may look a little different. Also, I am not super familiar with a graphing calculator, so I will choose to use colored markers, transparencies, and an overhead projector.

Eileen's inadequate knowledge of the graphing calculator influenced her choice of materials. However, she was able to come up with alternative approaches.

Latisha's prelesson thoughts reveal that her pedagogical concerns center on the mode of instruction she will use to discuss the fairness of a particular game of dice. Although Latisha was convinced that the game had to be enacted, she debated in her mind how to do it:

> I would have liked to have split the class into groups of three and have each group do the experiment so that we would have lots of trials and so that the students could work together and be more actively involved. However, I will not do it that way because my cooperating teacher said it would be difficult to get that many pairs of dice. So I will choose three students to do the experiment in the front of the room while the rest of the class watches.

It is clear that Latisha appreciated the value of getting all students actively involved in the lesson.

Finally, Katie's prelesson thoughts show that she was well aware of a variety of pedagogical strategies:

> In this lesson, I will use three types of instructional formats: small-group discussion, group presentation, and whole-class discussion. I am using these formats in the hopes that within the small groups, the students will get a chance to share ideas with their peers; within the group presentation, the students will get the opportunity to share their findings with the entire class; within the large class discussion, the students will get an opportunity to develop an understanding of algebraic expressions through hearing each other's questions and comments.

Katie indicated that she knows not only a variety of teaching strategies but also the specific advantages each has for student learning.

Write About the Sources You Consult for Designing the Lesson

In this section of your prelesson thoughts, describe the sources you used to get ideas for the lesson and the criteria you used to make your final selections. When designing a lesson, it is a good idea to use many different sources of information. Doing so encourages you to use different resources to increase your knowledge and expand your alternatives with respect to the design of the lesson. There is no reason to reinvent the wheel when designing a lesson.

Every school usually has a mathematics office with a small library. You might consult different textbooks for ideas. There is a wealth of interesting material published by the National Council of Teachers of Mathematics (NCTM). Furthermore, there are many materials created as a result of government and private funding. You can also find interesting ideas for lessons on the Internet. However, remember that there is no quality control on the Internet, and some of these materials have not been peer reviewed or edited. It is also important to consult with experienced teachers in your school who probably have a wealth of ideas just waiting to be shared. Keep in mind that the more sources you consult, the more ideas you will have to select from when planning your lesson.

Greg's prelesson thoughts clearly show that he has learned the value of consulting with other people as a source for good ideas: "The idea for this lesson (finding Waldo) came from Anna, a fellow student teacher, who in turn got it from her cooperating teacher, Etta. It worked well in their classes, so it seemed like it was worth a chance here."

In her prelesson thoughts, Angelina chose to describe the process she used in working with a variety of sources:

The materials I used for this lesson plan are: *Making Sense of Data: Addenda Series Grades K-8, Navigating Through Data Analysis and Probability in Grades 3–5, Used Numbers: The Shape of the Data,* and the textbook. I first reviewed the topic of graphing discrete data in the textbook to get a sense of how the textbook treated the topic. I then reviewed the addenda, navigation, and used numbers books to get ideas for involving the third graders in actual data collection. I realized that by using the ideas from *Making Sense of Data* for the lesson, I could assign examples from the textbook for homework.

Angelina's use of a variety of high-quality sources enabled her to move beyond the textbook, providing children with appropriate data collection activities.

Irina's prelesson thoughts demonstrate that she has learned to use different sources—other teachers and written sources—in combination: "I got this idea from the eighth-grade curriculum book that the district wrote. This is the first year they have implemented the new curriculum. I also researched ideas from the *Mathematics Teacher,* as well as conferring with my cooperating teacher and other teachers." Most schools have teachers who are eager to mentor novice teachers. It is unfortunate that many beginning teachers are too shy or embarrassed to take advantage of their expertise and generosity. It is good to see that Irina has availed herself of this wonderful resource.

Write About Difficulties You Anticipate and How You Intend to Prepare for Them

No matter how carefully you have planned your lesson, the likelihood is that things will not proceed exactly as planned. It is important that you develop the ability to sense when a change is needed and what the appropriate change should be. That is, you need to develop your ability to monitor the lesson and regulate your instruction accordingly. The trick to dealing with unexpected events is to anticipate what they will be and plan what to do should they occur. The more experience you get, the easier it will be for you to predict problems you might encounter and the appropriate adjustments to make. For example, you will come to know what concepts students tend to get hung up on and the examples you can give to clarify the confusion. You will learn good approximations for the length of time different pedagogical strategies will take. You will also learn how to predict certain students' behaviors and plan appropriate roles and activities for these students. Even though you are a novice teacher, it is not too early to begin to anticipate difficulties that may occur in your lesson and make appropriate plans.

In the excerpt from Sarah's prelesson thoughts, she demonstrated her awareness of the different attention spans and knowledge of her students and how that might affect her plans for her lesson on developing a formula for permutations with repetition:

> The problem I am anticipating is that it takes awhile to generate each sample space, and I think some of them lose interest, particularly those who fully understand and are bored. Also, a few of them may know the mystery formula, having learned it on their own. I hope they don't spill the beans. If someone does this, I'm going to insist that she or he justifies why the formula works. It is not enough just to substitute numbers in the formula.

Although Sarah did not express a plan for what to do if the students do lose interest, she did have a plan in case a student gives the formula away before the students develop it on their own.

Tara expressed two areas of concern in her prelesson thoughts:

> A main concern is avoiding arithmetic errors. I always second-guess myself. I rush to get the answer, and I make mistakes and look like an idiot. I've tried to familiarize myself with the examples, and I've written the answers down to avoid humiliation. My biggest concern is timing. The few times I've taught lessons, I've either run out of time or there's too much time. I can honestly say I have no idea how long it will take to finish each section. My cooperating teacher always says, "They're very bright, and you can move quickly." But sometimes I'm shocked at what it is they have a problem with.

Although Tara had a detailed plan for how to combat her problem with making arithmetic errors when in front of the class, she was still perplexed by the issue of timing. However, it is good to see that her concerns about timing involve her concerns that students understand the material.

Fran expressed concerns about behavioral problems when students work in groups: "Because I have had some behavioral problems in this class when [the students] work in groups, I am expecting some problems. However, this task is very specific, unlike other group work I have had them engaged in." It is reassuring to note that rather than giving up on using small-group work for these students, Fran instead planned a way to make it work better.

Finally, Ellie, who was teaching the family unit from the *Interactive Mathematics Program* (Fendel & Resek, 1997), showed an awareness of the difficulty students may have with a particular lesson:

> I believe that the most challenging part of this lesson will be getting started on the families. Some students may become bogged down by the usage of *at most, at least,* and so on. As such, I plan on walking around while they are working in their groups and helping elicit a better understanding of these terms. In addition, I will call the class to attention and have some of the students explain their understanding of these terms and how they use this understanding to construct their families.

It is reassuring to note that Ellie intended to monitor the understanding of her students. Although she did not state how she would resolve confusion about the words, she prepared herself for the time the trouble might arise.

Summary

By giving descriptions of your prelesson thoughts, you not only are encouraged to think about the overarching cognitions that drive your lesson but also give your supervisor, who subsequently observes the lesson, insight into the decision making and reasoning behind your lesson. Knowing why you do what you do when you are teaching makes it easier for your supervisor to understand and assess the instruction she or he observes. Directions for writing your prelesson thoughts are in Appendix D.2.

Creating a Lesson Plan Consistent With Your Cognitions

The prelesson thoughts that you write should serve as the foundation for the creation of your lesson plan. Starting with the objectives for student performance and understanding set forth by the NCTM (1989, 2000), you can set goals that go far beyond mere performance objectives. You want students to value mathematics, have confidence in their ability to do mathematics, and engage in such mathematical processes as problem solving, reasoning and proof, communication, and connections and representations.

You can derive the structure of your lesson from your knowledge of the students, content, and pedagogical strategies. The sequencing of the tasks must come from your knowledge of the logical sequencing of the content and students' prior understandings. The motivation for the lesson may be developed through the creation of a void in the students' knowledge, in which case you need a clear awareness of students' level of understanding. Motivation may also be created by linking the concept to something in real life that is of interest to your students. Such a motivational strategy can be effective only if you are well informed about the interests and backgrounds of each student. Different content areas lend themselves to different motivational strategies. Therefore, a thorough understanding of the nature of the content is needed to design appropriate motivational approaches. Finally, you can derive effective instructional strategies from your knowledge of the content, students, and pedagogy. For example, the discovery approach lends itself only to content that is within reach of student ability and can be derived from students' previous knowledge. You must have a good grasp of the content and the ability levels of your students to use this approach effectively. Furthermore, you must be aware of how different instructional strategies can facilitate or impede student discovery. For example, in many cases, a small-group approach, in which each student in the group works on a similar activity to derive a pattern and generalization, is the most effective way of facilitating discovery learning. You need to be well versed in small-group strategies to enable such an approach.

The phases of the lesson also grow out of a teacher's underlying cognitions. That is, the *initiation* of a lesson requires that you establish your students' readiness for learning the new content. This necessitates that you have a good understanding of the content and the prerequisite knowledge that is needed to learn the new content. The *development* of a lesson requires the building of new understandings. In the creation of the plan, you must employ all that you know about different pedagogical approaches, the structure of the mathematical concepts, and the distinct abilities and interests of the students to design an effective development. The *closure* phase of the lesson is the time when the new concepts are integrated with the students' previous understandings and, when possible, extensions of the concepts are made. Creating culminating activities that promote the integration and extension of concepts demands a depth of understanding of the concept that goes beyond the mere requirements of the curriculum.

With the exception of Kim's lesson plan (presented later), which we included to support her prelesson thoughts, this chapter does not contain samples of lesson plans because this aspect of your instruction should be well covered in the methods textbook that you are using in conjunction with this book. However, Appendix E.2 includes a broad outline for writing a lesson plan.

Reflecting on Your Instructional Practice During the Lesson: Monitoring and Regulating

Effective monitoring and regulating is a part of teaching that is often described as the art of teaching. It consists of the thousands of moment-to-moment decisions that teachers make during the course of their lessons based on the feedback they receive as they enact the lessons. Often these decisions take the lessons down paths that the teachers did not plan. Being able to diverge from the original lesson plan to meet the needs of students is the mark of quality teaching. Beginning teachers are often distressed when they do not accomplish all their plans for their lessons. They need to view this in a more positive light, understanding that teaching is much like problem solving. That is, you may set out with a specific plan, but if things are not proceeding the way you wish, you must have the flexibility to make some alterations. Also, as in problem solving, it is essential to monitor the progress of the lesson. This entails engaging students in a way that allows them to tell you, through their remarks and behaviors, whether they are indeed learning. You must then have the willingness and ability to change the course of your lesson if necessary.

Your postlesson conference is a good time for you to reflect on and assess the monitoring and regulating you engaged in during the course of your lesson.

Reflecting on Your Instructional Practice After the Lesson: Evaluating and Revising

After you complete your lesson, set aside time to meet with your supervisor to reflect on and assess your instructional practice and your thoughts related to that practice. Keep in mind that it is important that you express your ideas before anybody else gives you input regarding their reactions to your lesson. This is the first step in your becoming an independent learner of teaching. Through most of your career, you alone will be in the class with your students, and you will have to reflect on and assess your instruction on your own. Your ability to engage in such self-analysis will determine your professional growth as a teacher. Therefore, it is important for you to develop the habit of being the first critic of your own teaching. We have found that student teachers often have a difficult time analyzing their lessons. They tend to make such general comments as "I think it went OK" or "That was a disaster." Some students just draw a blank and cannot even remember what happened. This is why we provide a detailed structure that, through appropriate questions, allows you to analyze every aspect of your instructional practice and your cognitions. This structure is explained in the following sections.

Express Your Thoughts About the Lesson to the Supervisor

With the help of the written guide given in Appendix D.1, assess your own lesson while the supervisor and cooperating teacher sit quietly and listen to what you are saying. First, examine how your prelesson thoughts, your lesson plan, and your lesson enactment are related. For example, recall your original goals for the lesson, how you addressed them in the lesson plan, and to what extent you believe you accomplished your goals. You should compare what you planned to do in the lesson to what you actually did. Explain how you decided to deviate or not to deviate from your original plans. That is, you should explain your monitoring and regulating behaviors as you taught the lesson. For example, you might describe what feedback you received from the students and how it informed your practice.

Following this discussion, in case all aspects of the lesson were not addressed, further assess your lesson with a focus on the elements: tasks, learning environment, and discourse. Think about, describe, and evaluate the nature of these elements as they unfolded in your classroom. Consider reasons that might have contributed to the nature of your lesson. Finally, consider suggestions you might have for improving your lesson if you were to teach it again.

The Supervisor Shares Her or His Thoughts About the Lesson and the Thoughts You Have Expressed

After you complete your own postlesson reflection and assessment, your supervisor and cooperating teacher should share their thoughts regarding the lesson. The supervisor can provide positive reinforcement when appropriate and request clarification of issues by using the model as a basis for helping you to think about and appreciate what new knowledge you have gained or beliefs you may have changed as a result of teaching the lesson. Your supervisor might ask questions such as the following: What have you learned as a result of teaching this lesson? What have you learned about the content, the students, or the best ways of teaching the lesson? What beliefs did you have about the content, the students, or the best ways of teaching the lesson that changed in some way?

It is important for you and the supervisor to remember that the focus of this conference is not to judge how good or bad the lesson was. Teaching is a learning process, and we hope you are in it for the long haul. Therefore, the primary goal of the conference is for you to learn more about yourself and your teaching so that you will continue to improve. In our program, we base student teachers' grades not on our judgment of the quality of the lessons they teach but rather on what we believe they have learned from the process of learning how to teach. We are most interested in how student teachers reflect on and assess their lessons after having conferences with their supervisors. That is the purpose of the written postlesson, postconference activity.

Write Your Postlesson, Postconference Reflections, and Assessment

After the conference with your supervisor, put your thoughts about the lesson in writing. Written documentation of your thoughts and assessment serves at least two purposes. First, it gives you the opportunity to reflect on and assess the lesson once again and integrate and synthesize your ideas and those of your supervisor regarding the lesson. Second, it gives the supervisor the opportunity to assess what you have learned from your experience and how you have internalized the ideas that you discussed. With this assessment, she or he can help you improve. Appendix D.3 provides a guide to writing your postlesson thoughts and assessment.

To help you assess the nature and quality of the dimensions of your lesson, first complete the Self-Assessment of Instructional Practice form that appears in Appendix D.4. This form asks you to rate and describe each dimension of your instructional practice. For example, according to Table 2.1, which lists the lesson dimensions and dimension indicators, the indicator for a quality motivational strategy for the tasks dimension: "Uses tasks that capture students' curiosity and inspires them to speculate on and to pursue their conjectures. Takes into account the diversity of student interests and experiences. The substance of the motivation is aligned with the goals and purposes of instruction." On the basis of that description, you can rate the motivational strategy used in your lesson. In addition to rating the dimension, the form requires you to make a short comment. For example, a student who gave herself a high rating for motivation made the following comment: "The 'Matho' game was motivational because it caught the students' attention."

The guide in Appendix D.3 asks you to revisit some of the questions you addressed during your conference, reflecting on the degree to which you accomplished your original goals for the lesson. You describe how your knowledge or beliefs were changed in any way as a result of the teaching experience and the conference. You also describe the thoughts you had and the basis of your decisions while teaching the lesson. An important question you are asked to consider is how well you think you evaluated your own lesson prior to hearing the ideas of your supervisor or cooperating teacher. Finally, you highlight the strong points and areas of the lesson that need improvement and the cognitions that might have been the contributing factors to these aspects of your lesson. Include suggestions of ways to improve the lesson, and submit a revised lesson plan if your suggestions are extensive.

To show how some of our student teachers have integrated their understanding of the relationship between their cognitions and their instructional practices, we give in the following sections sample responses to the questions that appear in Appendix D.3.

Goals. In Marissa's response to the question regarding goal accomplishment, she distinguished between students' understanding of the concepts and their ability to carry out the procedure. Her perception was that the students did not arrive at a conceptual understanding of the content:

> I did not accomplish the goal that I had to have the students understand the use of the property of zero and factoring to solve quadratic equations. I know this because at the end of my lesson I asked the class, "Why did the quadratic equations have to be equal to zero before we could solve them?" They had no idea. One boy read the rule about $ab = 0$, but he didn't know how it was connected to the factoring and the equation.

However, she recognized that it was surprising that the students, despite their lack of conceptual understanding, were able to solve the problems: "I did accomplish the goal that was to have the students learn the procedure for solving a quadratic equation. I know this because at the end of the lesson, I went around to see how they were doing with the last three questions, and they were solving the equations."

Marissa wisely used student feedback as the source for her assessment of whether her goals were accomplished.

Knowledge. In her postlesson comments, Janine indicated that she learned much about ways of improving dimensions of her instructional practice. She indicated her increased knowledge of how to conduct discourse when she said, "I learned that when students are very quiet, say less and let them say more." Her change in knowledge about what constitutes motivation is evident in her comment, "I learned that an 'attention catcher' is not necessarily motivation. Motivation is the question that comes from the attention catcher. The motivational question should be stressed." Janine also indicated her increased knowledge about how to teach concepts:

> I learned that before I present a general concept to the class, I should give several specific cases first as well as some nonexamples. In this lesson, I presented only one case of parallel lines. I should have given three or four examples of parallel lines and at least one case where the lines were not parallel. This way the students could have discovered the pattern of the slopes when two lines are parallel.

Beliefs.   Leah's comments reveal a change in her beliefs about her role as a teacher: "The students were very responsive and asked many interesting and important questions. It is unfortunate that I felt obligated to answer every question. I should try to throw the questions back to the class. I tend to listen to what the student is asking, but then I answer the question myself instead of involving the class." It appears that Leah was beginning to reconsider her belief that her role is to be the "answer person" for the students.

Following her lesson, Lauren found she had new beliefs about students' knowledge:

> I also believed that my students remembered what they had learned before about solving linear systems of equations. Unfortunately, many students forgot what a system of equations is. From this experience, I learned that we should never assume that students remember past lessons. We should poke their memories by spiraling homework that pertains to the upcoming lesson.

Lauren not only changed her beliefs about how much students retain from past lessons but also had a plan for how to cope with the problem.

After her lesson, Sonya questioned her beliefs about students:

> I previously believed that students (particularly seniors) understood that when I begin looking at and talking to the whole class and a problem is being solved on the board, they are to listen. Apparently, you have to spell that out, as after the Do Now was put up and there was a discussion going on, a group of boys on the side were not with us because I didn't specifically tell them to be!

Monitoring and Regulating.   Beryl mentioned two very different instances of monitoring and regulating during the course of her lesson. In the first instance, she monitored student involvement and made a decision she felt worked out well:

> One thought that I had during the lesson was, "Wow, the students are really tired and out of it." I knew that I had to do something about this. I decided to ask students to go up to the board to solve problems while the rest worked at their desks. As they worked, I walked around and asked the tired students, "Are you OK?" After asking this, these students woke up and participated.

In the second instance, she monitored the work that was on the board and made a decision she felt worked out terribly:

> While going over the homework, I noticed that one of the assigned problems was not on the board. At first I thought that the best way to handle this situation was to forget about the problem. However, I saw that many students had problems with this question. Thus, I decided to ask a student to go to the board and do the problem. This decision, however, was not wise. While the student was writing her answer on the board, the other students sat idle. I will never do this again.

The important point about Beryl's comments is that she revealed her sensitivity to what was going on in her class and her willingness to make on-the-spot adjustments.

Nora also revealed her insight into on-the-spot decision making during her class. She mentioned two interesting situations. In the first instance, she described how monitoring and regulating served to clarify a concept: "I am getting better at monitoring the understanding of the students, such as when Melanie drew a perpendicular in the triangles and everyone became confused. I saw the confusion and was able to clear it up by tracing the two triangles with colored chalk." In the second instance, Nora described how she monitored a situation, but her lack of regulating contributed to the failure of the lesson:

> Although I knew the class was not proceeding as expected, I was aware the task was taking too long, but I did not make the cognitive connection to change the task from one of discovery to one of modeling. Because of that, we ran out of time and I don't think the students learned very much. ... I believe this will come with time, as every time I sit down to write a lesson plan I am able to anticipate more and more places where trouble may arise and how to compensate for it. This should have been something I anticipated, and now after experiencing it, it will be something I will be more prepared for in the future.

Nora recognized that becoming an effective on-the-spot decision maker is critical to good teaching and that experience is gradually helping her to become better at it.

Evaluating and Suggesting. Carla's postlesson comments reveal that after teaching the Grade 6 lesson, she had only a general impression of the quality of the lesson and was not able to identify the specifics:

> I believe my overall impression of the lesson was correct at the postlesson conference, that being it was a disaster. Yet at the time I was not aware of all the reasons why. I see now that the problem was never posed correctly, that the mode of representation was not followed through as planned, that the lesson plan had major gaps in it, that I did a poor job of monitoring and regulating, and that I could never plan to summarize a lesson with goals that were never really set.

Carla taught this lesson at the beginning of the semester. It is interesting to note how she improved in her ability to critique her lessons over the course of the semester. The following is what she had to say about the postlesson analysis she gave for a lesson she taught at the end of the semester:

> Now that I can think straight after my lesson is over, I notice that I always tend to vent the worst things at the postlesson conference. Again, because

the mode of representation was not the most appropriate one, I believed the goals of the lesson were not accomplished. I no longer believe this to be the case. The children did do the required examples, even though we did not get to the further explorations. ... I believe I tend to deemphasize some of my most important attributes, such as my rapport with the children. The classroom is a friendly environment where the students feel free to express themselves.

It is interesting to note that by the end of the semester, Carla became so self-critical that she tended not to acknowledge the positive aspects of her lessons.

Because the point of this book is to help you see the relationship of cognitions and instructional practice, the questions in this section that ask you to assess the strengths and weaknesses of your lesson do not include examples, because they focus mainly on the nature of the instructional practice and are quite standard in teacher education programs. These questions require you to identify the strong points of the lesson, the parts of the lesson that need improvement, and the ways to improve the lesson. The self-assessment form for summarizing these aspects of your instructional practice is in Appendix D.5.

Supervisor Evaluates Your Reflections and Assessments

In addition to your self-assessment, your supervisor evaluates your ability to reflect on and assess your instructional practice. At this point, your supervisor has observed you teaching a lesson, has had a conference with you, and is in possession of some critical documents: your prelesson thoughts, your lesson plan, your ratings and summary statements of your assessment of your instructional practice, and your written postlesson thoughts and assessment. Your supervisor has already shared her or his thoughts about your instructional practice and is now in a position to focus on your ability to be a reflective, insightful, self-critical mathematics teacher. Not only will your supervisor make comments on the written documents you have submitted but she or he will also evaluate your cognitions, using the form found in Appendix D.6. Beginning with preactive indicators, your supervisor evaluates the quality of the goals you have for your students and your knowledge of your pupils, the mathematical content, and the pedagogical strategies appropriate for teaching the lesson. Using the categories set forth in the model, your supervisor evaluates your lesson plan. An important aspect of the evaluation is your ability to reflect on and assess your lesson when you just finish it, before you have received any input from others. The hope is that by the end of the semester, your self-analytic comments following the lesson will be so detailed, extensive, and on-target that the supervisor will have little to add. Finally, the supervisor evaluates your ability to understand and assimilate the ideas shared at the conference and your ability to give insightful suggestions for improving your lesson. Your ability to excel in all these areas indicates that you will continue to improve on your own throughout your career as a mathematics teacher.

So far in this chapter, we have outlined how the different elements of the model are put into play when a supervisor observes a student teacher. However, we have examined each element in isolation. In the following section, we will show how Kim put all the elements together in her lesson, which her supervisor observed.

An Example of Using All Elements of the Model Together in a Supervised Lesson

Kim taught a first lesson on plotting a sine curve on a coordinate grid. Her prelesson thoughts, lesson plan, postlesson thoughts, and revised lesson plan reveal that Kim learned a great deal from the experience.

Prelesson Thoughts

Kim's prelesson thoughts indicate that she values both procedural and conceptual understanding of graphing the sine curve:

> My goals for this lesson are that students be able to graph a sine curve and understand its connection with the unit circle. I will start with the unit circle drawn on the board and ask the students to fill in the coordinates at 0, 90, 180, 270, and 360 degrees. Then I want to have them make the connection between degrees and radian measures. They know how to convert from one to another, but I do not think they have really made the connection yet. From the unit circle, I will have them plot the points on a graph emphasizing the connection between the graph and unit circle. This will take a new concept (the sine curve) and cognitively connect it to familiar knowledge (unit circle). I could just graph the curve using the graphing calculator, but I think having them plot the points first will help them understand where it is coming from.
>
> I also want students to think about the change of behavior the curve will have if we increase amplitude and frequency coefficients. They do not know this yet. I could have them graph the curves on the graphing calculator and come up with a conclusion, but instead I want them to conjecture as to what effect these coefficients will have on the curve. Then we can confirm our hypothesis with the use of the calculator.

The way she planned to structure the lesson by linking students' prior knowledge about the unit circle to the graphing of the function indicates both her knowledge of the content and the importance of sequencing as an effective pedagogical strategy. Her decision to use the calculator as a means for reaffirming hypotheses shows her thoughtful approach to motivation as a critical pedagogical issue.

Kim revealed her knowledge about the level of difficulty of the different concepts in her lesson when she explained a problem that she foresaw: "I do not anticipate much difficulty with the amplitude. I do, however, anticipate some confusion with the curves involving frequency changes, as this is a harder concept for them to grasp." Unfortunately, Kim did not plan a solution in case the problem came up—and it did. She also anticipated that she might be overambitious in her plan for the lesson: "The lesson is set up for one period, although if we have trouble developing the sine curve, we may not get as far as anticipated. I expect this may happen because other teachers have taken one full lesson to develop the sine curve and then another to introduce amplitude and frequency." As it turned out, Kim was quite rigid about covering so much content. This eventually led to the downfall of her lesson.

Finally, in her prelesson thoughts, Kim described where she got her ideas for the lesson: "The source for today's lesson was taken from a resident teacher, other than my cooperating teacher, and has been modified to accommodate the needs of this class. I find the teachers in this school are a wealth of information and are usually happy to share it." It is good to see that Kim understood the value of consulting experienced teachers for ideas.

Lesson Plan

Because there are many appropriate formats for lesson plans, some of which are most likely discussed in your methods textbook, we do not prescribe a set format. Details related to actual lesson planning are beyond the scope of this book. However, depending on the expectations of your cooperating teacher or the mathematics department in the school where you do your student teaching, there may be a format required for designing a lesson plan. The lesson plan developed by Kim follows a standard format. Suggestions related to the clear formulation of the aim and objectives aligned with her prelesson thoughts, the need for details related to the other curves to be explored, the need to formulate clear key pivotal questions, the need for specificity related to the practice examples, and the limitations of the enactment of the plan were discussed at the postlesson conference and influenced Kim's decision to prepare a revised lesson plan (see Table 6.1).

Postlesson Thoughts

Contrary to the student-centered focus of the prelesson thoughts, the discourse that took place during the lesson was predominantly teacher centered and impeded the effectiveness of this lesson. Kim rushed through the development, doing most of the explaining herself and accepting student answers without explanations. Despite the students' confusion with the graphing of the sine curve, Kim rushed through the examination of amplitude and frequency and was perplexed by the students' lack of interest. In her postlesson conference, Kim was aware that she tried to do too much in one class period, but she was not aware of how her style of discourse prevented her from monitoring the understanding of the students and adapting her lesson to fit their needs. Kim's written postlesson thoughts indicate that she learned a great deal about the importance of monitoring and regulating during a lesson.

Table 6.1 Kim's Original and Revised Lesson Plans

Original Lesson Plan	Revised Lesson Plan
Topic: Sine curve	**Topic:** Sine curve
Aim: How do frequency and amplitude affect the sine curve?	**Aim:** What are the characteristics of the graph of $y = \sin x$?
Objectives: Students will understand how to plot the sine curve. Students will understand the relationship between the sine curve and the unit circle. Students will see how the amplitude and frequency affect the sine curve.	**Objectives:** By the end of the lesson, the students should be able to do the following: 1. Graph the sine curve, $y = \sin x$; 2. Describe the relationship between the sine curve and the unit circle; 3. Compare the graphs of selected functions created by hand and by using the graphing calculator (e.g., $y = \sin x$; $y = 2 \sin x$; $y = \sin 2x$); and 4. Define "amplitude," "frequency," and "period" of specific sine curves.
	Materials: Overhead projector, transparencies, markers, TI graphing calculator view screen, handout sheet, and graphing calculator for each student.
	Do Now: Have students fill in the unit circle with coordinates, degrees, and radian measures.
Motivation: Create a Void Ask students to plot points and graph $y = \sin x$. Using a handout sheet (with the clear overhead copy), students will learn how to plot the sine curve using coordinates and radian measures obtained from the unit circle. Working off the unit circle, have students determine and plot the sine coordinate for theta = 0, 90, 180, 270, 360 degrees.	**Motivation: Create a Void** Ask students, "What do you think the graph of $y = \sin x$ looks like?" "How do you think we can find out?" Using a handout sheet (with the clear overhead copy), students will learn how to plot the sine curve using coordinates and radian measures obtained from the unit circle. Working off the unit circle, have students determine and plot the sine coordinate for theta = 0, 90, 180, 270, 360 degrees.

(continued)

Table 6.1 (*continued*)

Original Lesson Plan	Revised Lesson Plan
Exploration: Q: What do you think the curve of 2sin$x$ will look like? Q: What might change? Q: How, increase, decrease …? Does it affect the period of the function? Call on students to graph it on the overhead. Graph with the graphing calculator on the overhead while students work on calculators. Q: Does our graph 2sin$x$ agree with the graph on the calculator? Continue exploration with other sine curves. Have students describe verbally the change in behavior of the curves.	***Exploration:*** Q: What do you think the curve of $y = 2$ sin x will look like? Q: What might change (e.g., frequency, amplitude, period)? Call on students to graph it on the overhead. Graph with the graphing calculator on the overhead while students work on calculators. Q: Does our hand-constructed graph of $y = 2$ sin$x$ agree with the graph on the calculator? Continue exploration with other sine curves (e.g., $y = \sin 2x$; $y = 2\sin 2x$). Have students describe verbally the change in behavior of the curves.
Further Exploration: Q: How do you think the graph of sin2x will vary from sin x? Q: What will it look like? Have a student draw it on the overhead. Q: Does this change the period of the function? Why or why not? Continue exploration by graphing other curves. Compare results on the graphing calculator. Describe verbally the change in the behavior of the curves.	***Further Exploration:*** Q: How do you think the graph of $y = \sin 2x$ will vary from the graph of $y = \sin x$? Q: What will it look like? Have a student draw it on the overhead. Q: How does this change the period of the function? Continue exploration by graphing other curves (e.g., $y = 1/2 \sin x$; $y = \sin 1/2\ x$). Compare results on the graphing calculator. Describe in writing the change in the behavior of the curves.
Practice: Write the equation of the curve on the handout. Have students think, and then let one write equation on the overhead. Ask students if this is correct and why or why not.	***Practice:*** Write the equations of the curves on the handout. Have students share their equations. Call on students to write their equations on a transparency to display on the overhead projector. Ask students whether they agree or disagree with the equations displayed and why or why not.
Summary: Ask students to write about what they learned about the amplitude and frequency of trigonometric function.	***Summary:*** 1. What are the characteristics of the graph of $y = \sin x$? 2. How are radian and degree measures related? 3. What is the amplitude of the sine curve? 4. What is the frequency of the sine curve? 5. What is the period of the sine curve?

Goals. Kim realized that she did not meet the goals she had established for this lesson:

> At the conference, I said "yes" and "no" when asked whether I accomplished my goals. At the time of the conference, I believed I had accomplished some of the goals of the lesson, but on reflection, I do not believe this to be so. For if I had accomplished the students' understanding of the sine curve and how to plot it, then they would have been able to apply this knowledge to plot $y = 2\sin x$, and they could not. I believe, as you stated in the conference, that this is due to incomplete development of the lesson.

Believing now that she did not accomplish her goals, Kim suggested a good idea for improvement:

> To improve this, I would use a Do Now, having students fill in the unit circle with coordinates, degree, and radian measures. I would have one student do it on an overhead transparency so she or he could display it for the class to see and compare. After I was sure the students had this in their notes, we could proceed to create a table of values using the unit circle. I think I would stress more the relationship between the radian measure being the x value on the curve and the y coordinate being the y value of the curve. A chart on the board would have helped to clarify this.

Kim went on to describe another unfulfilled goal and an appropriate suggestion for improvement: "Another goal was to have them explore how the amplitude and frequency affected the sine curve, but before trying to accomplish this, I should have done a more complete job of defining these terms. I could have accomplished this better had I had the students write the definitions on the board and in their notes after they discussed them." These ideas are reflected in Kim's revised lesson plan (see Table 6.1).

Knowledge and Beliefs. In her discussion regarding knowledge and beliefs, Kim showed that she learned that students can become enthusiastic about a subject only if they understand the subject:

> I have learned from this experience that we can't rush into things just because we want to teach them. If the students are not ready to receive this information, no matter how hard I try, they will lose interest because they are unsure of what is going on. I saw this firsthand because I felt disappointed when the students weren't more enthusiastic about the changes in the sine waves when we changed the coefficients. I now realize that this was not because they weren't interested but because they did not understand what was happening.

Again, Kim included a good suggestion for improvement: "I feel this would have been tremendously improved had I spent more time plotting points and developing a few of the other curves with them. Then, as we changed the coefficients, they would have realized why the change was occurring and therefore how it affected the curve."

Kim realized the importance of listening to experienced people who may have more knowledge than she and showed that her beliefs regarding the essential nature of monitoring and regulating are beginning to develop:

> Although I had anticipated that this class may not be ready for this lesson, I went ahead and did it anyway. My cooperating teacher had apprehensions about this lesson, and I should have worked more closely with him on adapting the lesson plan to fit the needs of these students. I should have been more prepared to deviate from this lesson and give more development to the sine curve itself.

Monitoring and Regulating.   Kim went into more detail on how she should have improved the interactive aspects of her lesson:

> Again, I believe I was so determined to pull off this lesson that I did a very poor job of monitoring and therefore regulating. I saw the loss of motivation, but I did not connect it to a loss of understanding at the time. If I had done a better job of monitoring, perhaps I would have ended up spending the entire lesson on just developing different curves on the page. But instead I was asking the class to make conjectures on curves they did not yet understand. Live and learn!

Evaluating and Suggesting.   Not only was Kim disappointed in her lesson but she was also disappointed in her inability to assess her lesson accurately at the postlesson conference:

> Although a lot of my postlesson conference evaluations were accurate, such as my questions getting better, remaining more neutral, the climate being good, as I stated earlier, I do not believe my assessment of goal achievement was accurate. I also stated my mode of representation was good, but I now see that my board work was poor, leaving much uncertainty and confusion among the students.
>
> I was disappointed in the outcome of this lesson. I was expecting it to be so much better. I believe my biggest problem was wanting to forge ahead with a lesson they were obviously not ready to approach in the mode of representation I had planned. The biggest lesson I learned from this experience, besides clarifying definitions and such, was learning to be ready and willing to adapt. That was the biggest downfall in this lesson. I was unwilling and unprepared to take a step back and fill in the development that they were lacking. I expected too much and did too little.

Kim learned one of the most important lessons about teaching: You must use student feedback as a means for making decisions about whether and how to change the course of a lesson. A common mistake among mathematics teachers is acting like a runaway train in an effort to cover the content, disregarding the fact that the students in the class are no longer on the train. By using the model as a means of structuring her reflection on and assessment of the lesson, the supervisor was able to help Kim analyze her lesson in a complete and thoughtful manner.

Reflection and Self-Assessment With Peers

In addition to being observed by your supervisor and cooperating teacher, there is much to be gained by engaging in observations with your peers. Because your peers are experiencing problems similar to yours, having them observe you is a powerful technique for reflecting on your own practice. This is why we suggest that you engage in at least one peer observation during your student-teaching semester. Select a fellow student teacher who will observe you and whom you will observe. Use the same forms and procedures that your supervisor uses to observe you. That is, before the lesson, give your observing peer a copy of your prelesson thoughts and your lesson plan. After the lesson, engage in the same type of conference with your peer that you do with your supervisor. Following the conference, write your postlesson thoughts and share them with your observing peer. Submit all the forms from this peer observation experience to your supervisor. In addition, you should both write reports that document your reactions to the peer observation.

The following peer observation report written by Gerard reveals what he learned from observing his friend Susannah teach. The first thing Gerard noticed when observing Susannah was that watching her was somewhat like watching himself:

> I have to admit, when I first heard that we would have to do a peer observation, I thought it was a good idea, but little did I know just how great an experience it would be. As I watched Susannah work, I saw someone who was just as fresh in teaching as I was, trying all the same teaching methods that I try in my classroom, also. This was the advantage of observing my peer versus observing a seasoned teacher; I was basically watching myself. It was amazing just how alike we all teach, trying to incorporate discovery learning, cooperative learning, board work, and so on, and I was able to see how it looks from the outside. I was able to see which techniques worked, which did not, and ways to improve on them. For example, I noticed that Susannah used colored chalk in her lesson, and this really inspired the class. One of the girls who went to the board (another thing Susannah did well) wrote her answer in multiple colors, changing from red to blue halfway through the answer. Though it was time-consuming, I noticed that every

student in the class was paying attention as the student went over her answer. The next day I went out and bought colored chalk. I also noticed that by having students to the board often, it created a good learning environment in the class. I feel this way because the students seemed very willing to ask any questions that they had and were not hesitant to express their views on how to do the problems.

It is encouraging to note that Gerard used student involvement as a means of assessing the effectiveness of the strategies that Susannah was using.

Prior to this observation experience, Gerard was passing judgment on all student answers. To empower the students, he needed to remain neutral to student responses and let the class debate the issues. Only after Gerard observed Susannah doing the same thing, and the effects it had on her students, was he able to make the change in his own instruction. The following is what he said about it in his observation of Susannah:

> I also observed the negative effects of not remaining neutral to student answers. Susannah seemed quick to praise students' answers, and though the praise was good, I noticed that on one of the questions when Susannah said "good answer," one of the other students looked at her friend and said "I have no idea." The student then asked his question, but in a class where students may be more shy, Susannah's not remaining neutral to an answer may keep students from asking questions they have.

Gerard noted the big difference he found between watching Susannah and watching the many seasoned teachers he had observed in the past:

> Susannah did a superb job teaching her class. To me, she has been able to master many of the techniques that we have been taught in our methods class, and the class responded well to her because of it. I hadn't noticed just how few teachers bring students to the board at any point during their lessons, because as I watched Susannah I felt like this was the first time I had seen many of these teaching techniques being used on such a large scale. And I have to say, I like what I saw. The students seemed so happy to be in her class. They were thrilled when they were called to the board. When they had questions, the first person they looked to for the answer was their classmates.

Again, it is refreshing to see that Gerard used student behavior as the barometer for evaluating Susannah's practice.

Gerard indicated the powerful effect this peer observation had on him in the following statement, which, incidentally, was supported by our subsequent observations of him: "Overall, I noticed that the following day I was using many of the techniques that Susannah used, and the techniques that I kept as my own now that I had more confidence in them because I had seen them in action."

In his comments, Gerard documented the many advantages that can be derived from peer observations. Somehow you are able to see yourself in your peer. This is the most objective view you may ever get of yourself, and it can be used to great advantage. According to Gerard, it enabled him to see the effects of the discourse on student learning.

We hope that you will carry the value of peer observations with you so that when you enter the teaching profession, you will continue to engage in such practices with your colleagues. A great deal happens during a lesson, and your thoughts and decisions are colored by your perception of what happens. It is always worthwhile to invite someone into your classroom to observe your lesson from a different vantage point and provide a fresh perspective of the events that transpire. A teacher who can observe your teaching from the back of the classroom is likely to see things you may not have noticed and can provide added feedback for the interactive decisions you make during the course of a lesson. Likewise, when you observe your colleagues' teaching, you can take a more objective perspective of the effects of certain instructional practices on student learning.

Reflection and Self-Assessment Using a Videotape

Videotaping is a powerful tool that can help you develop as a teacher. Although the process of being videotaped can be threatening and viewing the tape can often be uncomfortable, the advantages are well worth it. We have found that videotaping is one of the only ways that teachers can assess the interactive nature of their instruction. That is, you can closely examine the degree to which you are monitoring what is going on in your classroom and how well you regulate your instruction accordingly. It is also one of the only ways that you can carefully assess the discourse that occurs in your class. It is for this reason that we encourage you to videotape as many of your lessons as possible over the course of the semester. It is a good idea to make one of your first videos when your supervisor is observing you. This way you can compare what your supervisor sees with what you perceive while you are teaching and what you observe when you watch the videotape. Often student teachers claim that they did not really believe what their supervisors said until they saw it with their own eyes. From her videotape, Annie noticed a behavior she had been resistant to change:

> I learned a lot from watching my video. I saw many things that my supervisor said that I needed to improve. I did not give the students the "floor" as I should have. For example, I saw that while one of my students was at the board, I stood in the front with him. I even went so far as to redo one of his problems. I realize that I should have allowed the student to correct his work or should have allowed him to call on someone for help.

Jackie's video helped her change her beliefs about her role in the classroom:

When I first started student teaching, I felt it imperative to be the answer woman. I took quite an authoritarian position, not because I didn't think the students were capable of answering but because I honestly thought it was my place to answer each student's question. I was not aware of the negative connotations or even that there were better ways to handle this until it was pointed out to me on my first observation and I was able to see it on the video. It was then that I decided to make this a point of self-growth.

At the end of the semester, you should make another videotape. This video serves at least two purposes. First, it allows you to document any changes you notice from your first videotape. Second, it forms the basis for independent reflection and self-assessment. That is, after at least four structured observations by your supervisor and one peer observation during the course of the semester, you should be able to assume the role of being your own supervisor. Toward that end, as part of your final self-assessment project, prepare a lesson in which you supervise yourself. Videotaping this lesson not only will help you remember what occurred during the lesson but will give you an improved perspective, more similar to that of an observer. In preparation for this lesson, complete the same forms you use when you are going to be observed by your supervisor. That is, write your prelesson thoughts and your lesson plan. After you teach your lesson and observe it on videotape, write your postlesson thoughts and complete the appropriate forms that document your analysis of the lesson. Continuing in the role as your own supervisor, you should then complete the forms that document your own assessment of your cognitions. As your own supervisor, what do you think about your goals for the lesson? What do you think about the level of knowledge you have indicated and exhibited about your students, the content, and the pedagogy? How well do you think you monitored and regulated your instruction? How well do you think you were able to evaluate your lesson and make suggestions for improvement?

After completing this self-assessment project, you should have a final conference with your supervisor. Share segments of the videotape and your written work that explain why the lesson looks as it does. That is, show what you perceive are both good points and weak points of the lesson, and address the cognitions that you feel are responsible for these teaching episodes. You should stop the tape at points when you made specific decisions and explain what your thoughts were at that time. Finally, address any new knowledge you have gained or beliefs that you have changed as a result of engaging in this self-assessment process. You can also use the videotape to document any cases where evidence of change (from an earlier videotape) is clearly indicated. The directions for this final self-assessment project appear in Appendix D.7.

Student teachers notice many things on the videotape that they never realized before. For example, Carol noticed that her listening skills were lacking:

> Another thing I did bothered me; I don't know if you can tell on the videotape, because the camera wasn't focused on me, but while the students were explaining their work at the overhead, I didn't really listen. I was walking around the room making sure everyone else was attentive, but I really didn't pay attention myself. I wasn't concerned that a mistake would go by unnoticed, I was more upset with myself that I lost track of what I was supposed to be doing. I was off task!

Lisa had been struggling with discourse since the beginning of the semester. She got into the habit of passing judgment on all student responses. She was pleased with the change she noticed on her final videotape: "As I watched my last video, I was happy to see all the long fragments where I said nothing. The students talked by themselves. They were the ones who were deciding if something was right or wrong."

Joyce also noticed an improvement from her earlier videotape:

> The tapes reveal that my questioning techniques have improved. In the beginning, I did not wait long enough for hands before calling on a student. Thus, I did not give all students a chance to ponder the questions I asked. The first video illustrates this. Furthermore, I did not leave enough time in between each question. Fortunately, however, the second video shows how I have drastically improved in both of these areas.

Pascale recognized the progress she had made by comparing her two video-taped lessons:

> The segment I selected from my first video is the one that shows me repeating what the student says. At the beginning of the semester, I did this a lot. In the second video, you'll see me asking students either to repeat what they said or asking them to speak up. At the beginning of the year I really didn't think it was such a big thing when I repeated what the students said. But over time, I realized that if I keep repeating the student, the other students are going to tune out when any student is speaking. And because I want the students to listen to each other and respond to each other, it was important to make sure I stopped repeating their answers. The more I got students to answer each other's questions or sort out confusion, the more dynamic the class became. Students wanted the opportunity to explain things to their peers.

Jessica gave a convincing written testimony to the value of the videotape for improving discourse:

> All semester I knew what I was having problems with, but nothing brought it home as well as this videotape. There's just something so much more under-standable about the mistakes you're making and how to improve them when

you actually get to see them. I know now how teacher centered I really am and that just planning to call students to the board more often doesn't fix this. It's the questions you ask and the explaining you encourage your students to do that are important. Now I see that I give the students absolutely no responsibility—I do everything for them. I also know from the video how boring and ineffective this is. My biggest problem all semester has been not knowing how to change, but I think this stemmed from not knowing how bad my discourse actually was. I now understand how much more involved I have to get every student in every lesson. The reason every student is not involved in my lessons is that I never call on anybody. This is something else that must change. If I concentrate more on calling on every student, I will have to talk less and force myself to get them to explain more. This will get them actively involved in their learning, which is best for everyone!

When discussing her plans for the future, Jessica added, "When I do get a job, I will have to tape my lessons frequently to monitor my discourse."

As these student teachers have discovered, videotaping is the best way you can view the interactive nature of your instruction. It allows you to examine the discourse carefully as well as identify the moments in which you monitor and regulate your instruction. For this reason, if you wish to contribute to your own professional growth, continue to videotape your teaching throughout your career. It is even more helpful if you can watch the videotape with a colleague. Teaching need not be an isolated endeavor. The more communication you have with your colleagues regarding professional matters, the more rapidly you will improve.

Reflection and Self-Assessment Through Journal Writing and Online Communication

Most teachers will agree that a large percentage of their thoughts about teaching come to them throughout every day, outside the classroom. Using the premise that teaching can be considered a work in progress, teachers can record their thoughts and feelings about what occurs in relation to their instructional practice. This process allows you to revisit the experiences and analyze them from an organized perspective. Teaching offers moments of great satisfaction and great disappointment. Writing is a vehicle through which you can express your emotions and when necessary resolve problematic situations. It is also a way for you to communicate with your supervisor and peers and get feedback about your concerns on a daily basis. The model provides a structure that you can reflect on and use to make better sense of the many teaching experiences you have. Although our student teachers have used the journal to discuss all aspects of their cognitions and instructional practice, we have found that their most common focus is on the monitoring and regulating they do during instruction. The journal seems to provide the opportunity they need to rethink the decisions they made during the course of instruction. Many student teachers use the journal to express concerns they have about their goals, knowledge, and beliefs.

We have recently taken advantage of the Internet to provide open lines of communication among student teachers and supervisors. We established a private Web-based bulletin board where student teachers post their inquiries and announcements. Student teachers visit the site daily and are given the option to raise issues and concerns related to challenging experiences or to share their successes. As supervisors, we promote peer interactions by allowing the online conversations to occur without immediately intervening. Depending on the severity of the comments and inquiries, we may respond after one or two student teachers react, or we may wait several days before sharing our thoughts so that other student teachers can participate in the exchange.

The following excerpts from student teachers' journals and online exchanges exemplify how they have used the model to help them reflect on critical moments of their classroom practices. Supervisors and peers can raise questions and provide helpful feedback by reviewing student teachers' journals. The examples in this section focus on the student teachers' overarching cognitions (i.e., goals, knowledge, and beliefs) and the interactive stage of their teaching (i.e., monitoring and regulating).

In her journal, Alison discussed two different types of goals she had for her students. The first goal was of a general nature. She expressed a possible conflict between the goals of her administration and her own goals. Observing a fellow teacher served as a catalyst for her thoughts on this matter:

> Today I observed one of the most organized teachers at the school. This teacher functions as a well-programmed robot. Yet, with all her great organization skills, she is a classroom dictator. There is no room for any creativity or discourse in this class, all pure mechanics. I keep on questioning myself, What makes for good teaching? Why are those who are teacher centered and dominant generally celebrated by the school administration? Is it because their students do so well on the state exam? I hate state exams! I was told by some teachers that teaching for passing them must be the goal. How about teaching for understanding or showing the beauty of mathematics?

Alison faced the dilemma that most teachers face. Unfortunately, it is very difficult to meet the demands of a standardized exam and at the same time engage students in exciting problem-solving activities. The model has helped Alison understand that her dilemma concerns decisions about the goals she has for her students, which hinges on her beliefs about what is most important for them as learners in her class.

Alison wrote about her goals for a particular lesson: "I can't say it went perfectly; however, I achieved most of my goals for this lesson. They spoke mathematics! I was able to conference with all students, I did not lose control of the class, and they solved a lot of challenging problems. I believe this lesson gave a chance to many of the students to believe in their abilities because there was a lot of tutoring in groups." From a supervisor's perspective, reading this journal entry confirms the idea that Alison's goals for her students extended well beyond merely covering the content and maintaining control. That is, she wants them to communicate mathematically, she wants them to become problem solvers, and she wants them to become confident in their abilities.

Judy, another student teacher, wrote about her lack of knowledge, which impeded her ability to regulate her instruction: "There are times when I'd like to go back and change something, rephrase a question or complete a concept, and because I am not very comfortable teaching yet, I don't know how to handle the situation." The fact that Judy was able to verbalize her problem with monitoring and regulating demonstrates that she is indeed monitoring her instruction and is aware of the need to regulate her instruction. The supervisor uses Judy's journal entry as an opportunity to praise her for this awareness. Her admitted lack of knowledge about how to handle the situation indicates that she is motivated to learn more about what to do. Issues such as this are brought up for classroom discussion during the weekly student-teaching seminar.

In addition to student teachers thinking about their own beliefs on teaching mathematics, they quickly become aware that they must consider their students' beliefs as well. In the following excerpt from her journal, Yelena showed her awareness of the conflict between her beliefs and her students' beliefs and how it worked to the detriment of her lesson: "Class today was a little bumpy. I tried to have the students discover the area of a trapezoid by dividing it up into two triangles. What a flop! After the lesson, my cooperating teacher suggested that the kids just wanted to know the formula—that's all they cared about. She said that she heard one of the students say, 'We don't care where it comes from—just give us the formula.' Oh well, live and learn." This short journal entry was grounds for much conversation with the supervisor and Yelena, especially because her comment "live and learn" leaves one confused about how she stands on the issue. Her desire to engage the students in the derivation of the formula demonstrates that Yelena believes it is important for students to understand where a formula comes from, which was contrary to the students, who believed the only important thing to learn was the formula. The question for Yelena is "Why do you think students believed that only knowing the formula is sufficient?" This conversation, of course, leads to the issue of assessment. Most students want to learn what they are expected to reproduce on their examinations. Therefore, if a teacher truly believes that understanding formulas is important, then she or he should include test questions that assess their students' understanding of the derivation of the formulas.

Yelena's journal entry served as a good opportunity to discuss the connection between beliefs and assessment techniques in instructional practice.

Monitoring and regulating instruction by questioning students was a concern raised online by Georgia:

> My cooperating teacher knows exactly what to ask her students and when to ask them certain questions. I feel like I ask too many questions. I always ask

the students why they did a step when solving equations. I ask the students about every little step I take. Is there such a thing as "too many questions"? Today I asked a student why he divided by 3 first in the equation $3x = -45$, and he replied, "I don't know, because that's how I did the other problem." From this I concluded that these students don't have a clue WHY we do certain steps. I ask many questions because I want to see whether my students understand what I am trying to teach them or what they have already "learned."

Reacting to Georgia's entry, Eric also monitors his students' learning by asking questions and encouraging his students to ask questions. Unlike Georgia, he is not concerned about asking too many questions:

I also ask a lot of questions, but I do not think I ask too many. I try to determine my students' readiness to move on in the lesson by asking many questions. I always try to elicit from the students why they did what they did on a given problem. I also try to encourage students to ask questions, both of me and of fellow students.

After 2 days and nine reactions to Georgia's concern, the supervisor supported their comments and shared her reaction:

It is so interesting to read all of your comments about how posing questions can help you to monitor and regulate your instruction. As Toula indicated, including key pivotal questions in your lesson plan can help you to identify the important questions needed to elicit the big ideas of your lesson. It is more challenging to formulate questions on the spot, after carefully listening to what your students are saying and not saying and the questions they are asking. I think Georgia's concern about asking too many questions could be overbearing. Eric's approach to encouraging his students to ask questions can help to promote student–student interactions. All of you will need to help the students become comfortable with your teaching style and adjust to any expectations that may be different from those of your cooperating teacher. All of this takes time and perseverance.

Such online exchanges are extremely fruitful and keep the student teachers and supervisors in touch with each other. Often the online discussions spill over into the weekly seminar meeting at the college campus, allowing for further applications of the model.

In her journal entry, Arlene indicated how her awareness of her students' confusion and her desire to bring clarity to all of her students led her to change her lesson in ways that created more confusion:

Today was somewhat disturbing. For the first time, I experienced a disaster lesson. The object of the lesson was to derive the distance formula. I decided to let students discover the distance formula while looking at a specific case. The students had no trouble doing this. However, when the general case was introduced, I lost most of the students. Many of them showed that they didn't understand. This made me feel very uncomfortable. I didn't know what to do.

I knew that I couldn't proceed with the lesson until everyone understood. I went back to the specific case and then tried to make the connection with the general case. More students started to understand. However, I was not satisfied. I wanted the entire class to understand. So I went back to the specific case again. I noticed some students were getting bored and started to misbehave. Luckily the bell rang, and my moment of horror was over. My cooperating teacher said that the best way to handle this situation is to proceed with the lesson. Eventually the ones who do not understand will pick up the concepts later after they do practice problems.

Arlene described a situation that most teachers of mathematics encounter on a daily basis. Rarely do all of the students understand things at the same time. Arlene is to be praised for her awareness and concern that some of the students were confused and for her efforts to resolve the confusion. Although her cooperating teacher's idea just to proceed might be good advice in some cases, the issue deserves further analysis. That is, there are many other courses Arlene could have taken at the moment of confusion, as well as methods she could have used to prevent the confusion in the first place. At this point, the supervisor can help Arlene think of other tasks or teaching strategies that would have been helpful. For example, when she sensed misunderstanding, she could have had the students break up into pairs and try to explain it to one another. Also, Arlene might have been able to prevent the confusion altogether by adjusting the task she created for her students. To help Arlene reflect on this matter, her supervisor might ask her how many specific cases she gave her students before asking them to make a generalization. If she gave them only one case, then surely that would be grounds for confusion. To recognize a pattern leading to a generalization, students need a minimum of three specific cases. Arlene's journal entry served as a good opportunity for the supervisor to help Arlene recognize other options for regulating her instruction at the moment or regulating her plans for teaching that lesson another time.

People who enter teaching are often surprised by the amount of work that is required. As you well know, it entails far more than just walking into a classroom and telling students how to do mathematics. Teachers spend endless hours preparing lesson plans, homework assignments, quizzes, exams, projects, and other interesting activities. The same process you use to reflect on and assess your instructional practice should be used in relation to the written materials you create for your students. One means of documenting your work as a teacher is to assemble a portfolio. That is the focus of the next chapter.

7 Using a Portfolio to Document How You Engage in Self-Assessment and Reflection

A portfolio is a useful tool for both professional and personal development. You can use it for professional purposes: It is not unusual to be asked for a portfolio when you apply for a teaching position, and it is required for National Board Certification. Or you may want to create a portfolio for personal use, as a means of documenting your professional growth and collecting your best pieces of work for future reference. Whatever your goal, you can use the guidelines given in this chapter for creating a portfolio. A description of each of the elements for the portfolio (i.e., lesson plan, homework assignment, project, unit plan, quiz, unit exam, and peer observation report) and suggested rubrics for grading the elements and the portfolio can be found in Appendix E.

Using the model as a conceptual basis for linking your instructional practice to your underlying cognitions, you can create a portfolio that documents your growth as a teacher. The portfolio we recommend goes far beyond a mere collection of lesson plans, homework assignments, projects, and assessment instruments. These documents have more meaning when they are accompanied by your written thoughts on what went into their creation and your reflections following their implementation. (Note that these written reflections are required for National Board Certification.) For each piece that you include in your portfolio, you should include a written rationale that explicitly states what you know about the students, content, and methods of pedagogy and defines your goals for your students. Furthermore, every lesson plan, written assignment, and assessment you include should be accompanied by a written reflection on how your students reacted.

To help you better understand the types of pieces that you can include in a portfolio, this chapter presents examples from actual student teachers' portfolios. These examples are more important for the thoughts that accompany them than for the quality of the specific lesson plan, homework assignment, or assessment instrument. That is, the process of ongoing professional growth lies in your ability to know why you do what you do and to then evaluate whether it works effectively and how you might be able to improve its effectiveness. Teaching has often been described as a continual learning process. It is the act of learning that should be the highlight of the portfolio.

Kelly included a good description of the value and purpose of a portfolio in her portfolio overview:

> For me, this portfolio has been one long work in progress. Each day, each lesson, every class, test, and student interaction has been an extension of the last. There was always a piece of yesterday's mistake being corrected or improved on in today's lesson, and the same will hold true for every tomorrow to come. There are no perfect lessons or best ways to approach a topic. I will always be striving for the better way to accomplish student understanding, because for me this is the most important goal.

This chapter presents examples of a lesson plan, a homework assignment, a long-term project, and a quiz. Each example includes quotations from the student teacher's written thoughts before and after the activity. The chapter concludes with a critique of a section of a textbook that a student teacher included in her portfolio. These particular pieces were chosen because they exemplify how the model can be used as a basis for analyzing the materials used and activities created for students. Note that portfolios should consist of many other pieces that document your work as a teacher. Some of our student teachers have included mathematical autobiographies, résumés, observation reports of other teachers, observation reports of themselves, unit plans, unit exams, alternative assessment instruments, videotapes of lessons, samples of student work, and samples of letters from students—and much more.

Lesson Plan

Writing lesson plans is a major part of every teacher's work. The format of a plan can range from thoughts in a teacher's mind to a detailed written script for what a teacher will do and say and specific activities for students. However, regardless of the format of the plan, it contains messages about the teacher's goals, knowledge, and beliefs. These cognitions are evident in Bryan's prelesson thoughts:

> The goal of this lesson was to have the students using manipulatives to "discover" the relationships of angles formed by transversal lines. I wanted to teach transversal lines using discovery learning because otherwise they would find learning the properties boring. So I found a way to allow them the chance to figure out the properties for themselves and explain them to each other. I know the students love when they become the teachers and explain the properties. I tried to address most of the anticipated difficulties in the lesson itself. I have to make sure that I have enough time at the end of class to derive the properties from what the students had discovered.

Bryan values a student-centered approach to teaching and is aware of the interests and desires of his students. His lesson plan follows.

Topic: Angles formed by parallel lines cut by a transversal

Aim: What relationships exist among the angles formed by parallel lines cut by a transversal?

Instructional format: Individual exploration leading to a whole-class discussion

Motivational activity: Have a ruler and two pieces of pattie paper on students' desks at the start of class. Challenge the students to see whether they can discover a set of fundamental relationships between the angles formed by parallel lines cut by a transversal using only the given materials.

Instructions: Using transparencies, perform each step to demonstrate.

1. Have a student define parallel lines.
2. Have all students draw a set of parallel lines separated by the width of the ruler on their pattie paper. Make sure they label their lines AB and CD.
3. Instruct students to use the ruler to draw a nonperpendicular diagonal line that crosses through both parallel lines. Label this new line EF.
4. Have the students label the angles formed from 1 through 8 and indicate on a diagram on the chalkboard.
5. Have the students trace what has been written on the first piece of paper onto the second.

Discovery: Students will work in pairs.

1. Ask students if just by looking at the pieces of paper they can make a conjecture regarding whether any angles have equal measures. Ask them how they can confirm their hypothesis (leads to use of pattie paper).
2. Demonstrate how to line up different angles using the separate pieces of pattie paper. (*Note*: This item was inserted following the lesson, after Bryan discussed his lesson with his supervisor and cooperating teacher.)
3. Inform students that there are at least eight sets of these relationships. Challenge them to see who can find the most.
4. Indicate that there is another relationship between some of the angles that is not that of equality. Challenge them to find it.

Final summary and conclusion:

1. Randomly select one student from each group to write on the board the relationships that their group discovered.
2. Engage students in a discussion of these relationships and arrive at a statement using the terms *alternate interior angles, corresponding angles, alternate exterior angles,* and *interior angles* on the same side of the transversal.

Bryan's postlesson thoughts indicate that this lesson proceeded quite well and, in Bryan's estimation, needed only slight adjustment. His comments show that he was able to address the concepts planned for the lesson and at the same time capture the interest and understanding of the students. Very often teachers find that their greatest challenge is to cover the content and achieve student understanding all in one lesson.

> This plan did proceed as I had expected. The students were able to derive every property in a very short amount of time. Once they discovered that the pattie paper could be flipped around it was easy for them to find the angles with equal measure. To my surprise, three of the students in the class were able to come up with the supplementary angles. When I observed this lesson being taught in another class using a teacher-centered method of just telling students the properties, I found the students were quite bored and uninterested. I was glad to see that my class responded with a high level of enthusiasm. The only problem I had was that in the original plan, I had not prepared them to understand how to use the pattie paper to determine which angles have equal measure. That is why I inserted a demonstration in my revised lesson plan [see Discovery Item 2]. I will use this method of teaching this lesson again in the future, for it not only uses discovery learning but also suggests to the students that these properties work every time (because each student had different angles formed and yet they all came to the same conclusions).

Bryan's assessment of his lesson is based on his analysis of the interest and involvement of his students.

Homework Assignment

Most teachers agree that homework is a critical part of the teaching–learning process. Learning mathematics necessitates active involvement on the students' part. Giving students problems to do on their own in the privacy of their homes affords them the opportunity to practice what they have learned, to discover what it is they do not understand, and possibly to extend their learning through new applications. In addition to thoughtfully assigning problems from the text, teachers should try to assign interesting problems by consulting other sources and using their own creativity. The following homework assignment was created by Jeannette to alert students to common mistakes they make. Jeannette described the assignment as follows:

> The homework assignment referred to here consisted of 15 algebraic problems that represented a fictional quiz taken by a fictional student. The homework assignment required the students to make corrections to the fictional student's work. The following directions were given:

Mrs. Tuttle gave the following problems as a quiz to her algebra class. Below are the solutions given by her student, Pat Mathlover. She needs your help correcting this quiz. Each solution has at least one error in it. Determine where Pat made mistakes, and give the correct solution to each problem. Then write an explanation for why you corrected the problems as you did. For every 3 problems you properly correct and explain, Mrs. Tuttle will give you an extra point on your upcoming exam (for a possible total of 5 extra points).

One of the examples on the test was as follows:

Problem: Simplify $x^2 + 2x - 3 / (x^2 + 3x)$ to lowest terms.

Pat's work:

$$\frac{(x+3)(x+1)}{x(x+3)} = \frac{(x+3)(x+1)}{x(x+3)} = \frac{x+1}{x} = \frac{x+1}{x} = 1$$

Corrections:

Explanations:

This is Jeannette's rationale for creating this homework assignment:

The assignment includes 15 problems representative of the topics covered for algebraic fractions. The students are to mark the answers provided by a fictional student. The incorrect solutions include some obvious and not-so-obvious mistakes that my students tend to make. I hope that the students, by recognizing the errors in this manner, will better digest them. For each problem, a corrected solution is required, along with a detailed written explanation (using appropriate mathematical reasoning). Requiring the students to communicate the mathematics should, I hope, reinforce their knowledge of it. Because it is really a homework assignment, the point values given are not extremely large, but nonetheless the motivation is there and it will help the students study.

Jeannette's comments reveal much about her goals, knowledge, and beliefs. First, by creating the problems, she demonstrates that she is aware of the common errors and areas of misunderstandings of her students. She appears to believe that having students see the errors made by others will help them understand the concepts better. It is clear that her goal is to have students communicate mathematically by requiring them to provide written explanations, because she believes that this is a means for improving their learning. Finally she reveals her goal of creating an assignment that will be motivational for the students, based on her belief that motivation is an aid for getting students to study.

In her postassignment reflections, Jeannette revealed her disappointment:

> I thought this assignment was a great idea, as did some of the teachers I showed it to where I student teach. However, my students found it extremely difficult. Perhaps this is because I made the errors match the typical mistakes they tend to make. Many of them wrote only brief explanations of the corrections, if any at all. I think my students still have this fear of writing about mathematics, or rather have confusion about it. They seem to be able to write only about the procedural aspects of mathematics. I am trying to get them to go deeper than this.
>
> Out of a possible total of 5 extra credit points, the average granted was a mere 1. Many students did not even complete the review sheet (which is unacceptable because it was a homework assignment). A few students got 4 or 5 points, but most of the students just tried to do the minimal amount of work. The feedback and comments I received were that it was very hard, although some admitted that it was a good idea. I had expected much better results and for it to be met with greater enthusiasm. I think the problem is that these students are not so accustomed to change or variety. I know they like it though; it just takes some getting used to.

By reflecting on her students' performance and reactions to this assignment, Jeannette learned more about her students and how she is beginning to form new beliefs. She recognized that her students fear writing and change and that they focus only on procedures. However, she recognized that the students like the idea of something different. Therefore, rather than reverting to the usual types of assignments, Jeannette was determined to keep pushing the students to engage in activities that she feels will improve their learning.

Long-Term Project

Another type of homework assignment is a long-term project. Projects can be a wonderful motivator for students, especially those who are disinterested in mathematics. Projects can give students the chance to learn about mathematics and engage in mathematical problem solving. We encourage our student teachers to design at least one interesting project for their students. In line with the model, they must explain the thoughts that went into their design of the project, and then they must use the students' work as a means for assessing and reflecting on the quality of the project design.

The following project, created by Stella, is highlighted here not because the assignment was so innovative or successful but because of the quality of her cognitions with regard to the assignment.

The project Stella assigned to her precalculus students was to count for 20% of the final grade. She gave them a choice of three topics: exponential growth, sports statistics, and masters of math. For each topic, she included a thorough description. To summarize, the exponential growth project required the students to estimate how the world's population would grow in 50 years. The sports statistics project required the students to select two professional players or teams and compare the historical performance statistics over the years. The masters of math project required the students to choose a mathematician and write about her or his life, contribution to mathematics, and discoveries. Whichever topic they picked, students were given the following instructions: "You should use as many mathematical tools as possible, such as charts, graphs, tables, and so on. You have to use information from books or from the Internet. You must list your sources in the last page of your paper." They were told that their grade would be based on "content, creativity, use of mathematical tools, and oral presentation."

In her written rationale for this project, Stella stated, "When I was constructing the project assignment for my class, I tried to find a topic that is related to precalculus. I also wanted a topic that would attract my students' interest, so the project would be a fun assignment for them, especially because my students had never been asked to do a mathematics project." Stella focused on her students, and her goals are both cognitive and affective. She wanted them to learn something related to precalculus, and she wanted them to enjoy it.

Stella next described her rationale for each of the three choices: "All the topics that I researched were great topics for projects, but they were suitable for either lower-level students or calculus students. Exponential growth was the only topic that I could think of that was related to what we had learned in class. I thought this topic could be slightly difficult. However, I put it as part of the choices because there might be some students who would like to do research on it." Stella's comments reveal her concern for choosing a task that is at the appropriate level of difficulty for her students.

Stella also described her rationale for choosing the sports topic: "I was confident that a project on sports would draw many of my students' interest because some of them belong to a sport team in the school." This comment shows that Stella has knowledge of both her students' interests and their involvements.

Finally, this is Stella's reason for choosing the topic about mathematicians: "For the other topics, students have to use a great deal of statistics. Thus, I wanted something different for the third topic. Some of my students are good in English, and they do not see mathematics as a fascinating subject." Stella's goal to hook students into appreciating mathematics is clearly evident in this remark.

Stella's respect for her students and knowledge of her students' needs are evident in the process she used to help students begin their work on the project:

> I made sure that this assignment was ready to be given out before the winter break, so students would have enough time to work on it. I prepared a sheet that they had to fill out with their chosen topic, sources, questions, and time of free period. Writing a topic and sources would pressure them to start working on this assignment right away. The questions that students may write would help me see what needs to be clarified about this project. I wanted to

know when my students' free periods are in case I found it necessary to meet with them individually later on.

By giving the students adequate time to do the project and by scheduling meetings at the students' convenience, Stella established a respectful social and intellectual climate with her class. Moreover, by giving the students opportunities to ask questions about the assignment, Stella demonstrated her desire to monitor and regulate the students' work on this project.

Much to Stella's surprise, most of the students did the project: "Surprisingly a huge number of students handed in the project. Only three students did not hand in their projects. One of these students told me that he had to finish it when I asked him about it. However, a few days passed and he did not hand it in. A day before the project was due many students came to me and asked me for an extra day, so I gave it to the whole class." By extending the deadline, Stella again demonstrated her flexible position and kind attitude toward her students.

Stella's kindness perhaps was overextended in her grading, which she described as follows: "Since I wanted this to be a good experience for the students, I did not want to be too strict grading the papers. Thus, most students got A's, a few got B's, and only one student got C+ because he just printed a table from the Internet as his paper. Certainly, those students who did not do the project received F's." Although Stella's grading policy can certainly be debated, the point taken here is that Stella was consistent with her original goal for students that they appreciate mathematics.

The work Stella did on her postproject assessment reveals a few issues Stella needs to think about. Contrary to the detail of her preproject comments, her postproject comments are rather general and never discuss in detail the quality of work the students produced. As she becomes more experienced, she might revisit her decision to count this one project as such a high percentage of the grade if she is going to be so generous with her marks. She also might revisit her criteria and figure out a more detailed rubric to use when grading the work.

Quiz

Quizzes and exams are integral parts of the teaching–learning process. When teachers create assessment instruments, they must have clearly defined rationales for what they require students to do. Kaye created the following quiz question:

1. State the distance and midpoint formulas.
2. Jack just learned the distance and midpoint formulas. He was assigned the following problem: ABCD is a parallelogram. Its vertices have the following coordinates: A(–6,8), B(2,10), C(6,4), D(–2,2). M, N, L, and O are the midpoints of sides AD, AB, DC, and BC, respectively. What kind of quadrilateral is MNLO?

3. Jack's sister Ann is in seventh grade and loves geometry. She looked at the graph and suggested that MNLO is a parallelogram. Prove or disprove Ann's assumption. Show all your work.

In her rationale, Kaye stated,

> As I constructed this instrument, I had several objectives in mind. I wanted to check, first, whether the students know the formulas of distance and midpoint and if they can apply them and, second, their reading comprehension, that is, if they can read the problem and understand what is given and what they have to do to find the information or prove it. Third, I wanted to improve the students' critical thinking skills, that is, let them choose a correct assumption and carry out an argument. Using such proofs gives students a good opportunity to review the definitions of a parallelogram, a rhombus, a rectangle, and a square and to see the relationships among them.

Beyond wanting her students merely to solve the problem, Kaye understood the necessity for them to develop their mathematical reading comprehension skills and understanding. Kaye demonstrated her own knowledge of the question and the underlying skills that are needed to solve the problem.

In her postquiz reflections, Kaye stated,

> The quiz was graded on a 10-point scale. Knowledge of each formula was worth 1 point. Another 8 points were distributed between identifying the problem, being able to choose the correct assumption, and carrying out a proof.
>
> Since I evaluated the reading comprehension in the beginning of the semester, I was able to see that many of the students made significant progress. The grades ranged from 5 to 10. The average was 7.8. Students' problem-solving abilities increased. Many of them were able to apply Pólya's steps for problem solving: identify the problem, derive a plan, carry out the plan, go back and justify the solution.

Kaye's postquiz reflections show that she placed a higher value on process than on product. The rubric she used for grading the quiz and the way she described how the students performed on the quiz reveal that she is committed to helping the students with both their reading comprehension and their problem-solving abilities.

Critique of a Section of a Textbook

Considering the fact that textbooks are the main sources that teachers use when constructing their lessons, it is important that teachers assess them carefully. The reflective processes they use on the activities they create for their students should be extended to the materials they use with students that others have created, specifically textbook writers. Marion not only found weaknesses in the section of the text she was using but also designed a worksheet for her students that would compensate for these weaknesses. Here is her description of the text's section on inverse functions:

> When it comes to sequencing and promoting student discovery, the text is really awful. There is no room for student discovery, and it is very hard to read. The material is just presented, rather than leading the student to it before stating it clearly. There are only 3 examples and their solutions in the section, and 2 of them are of the same type, while the exercises require the student to solve at least 5 different types of problems, which the book does not model for them.

Marion clearly understands that the way tasks are sequenced has pedagogical implications. Her comments also reveal that she believes it is important for students to discover new concepts on their own. What was most impressive was that Marion took the time and effort and had the knowledge of how to improve the textbook. She wrote, "I have constructed and attached a group worksheet that promotes student discovery by having them do simple review type exercises and then examine the results in order to derive the properties of inverse functions." Marion's approach was to have one person in a group doing one set of problems and another person in the group doing another set of related problems. After they finished, she asked them to compare their results to come up with a conclusion. For example, in one case, she had two people create different graphs of a function and its inverse and asked them, "Examine both graphs, and the relationship between the graphs of each function and its inverse. From these examples, can you notice a special property about the graphs of pairs of inverse functions? What do you notice? Why do you think this happens?" The guided discovery worksheet that Marion created integrates her knowledge of sequencing and pedagogy with a goal for student-centered instruction.

Marion showed her sensitivity to the modes of representation the textbook promotes when she said, "The text does not promote the use of technology at all. This is unfortunate because a graphing calculator is really helpful to demonstrate the fact that inverse functions are reflections of each other in the line $y = x$. Even something as simple as tracing paper or the overhead projector can enhance a lesson in discovery of the graphs of functions and their inverses." Her reference to the use of a graphing calculator, tracing paper, and transparencies for an overhead projector show that Marion has a good understanding of which representations would facilitate students' discovery of the properties of inverses. Again, she demonstrated how she has integrated her knowledge of the content, her knowledge of modes of representation, and her knowledge of pedagogical content knowledge with the goal of empowering students to become independent learners.

Finally, Marion revealed her sensitivity to the types of questions that were asked in the textbook, noticing that it rarely provides occasion for students to explain any of their ideas:

> The text promotes student writing minimally, but hardly models examples for them. Rather than having an example of an "explain" question and a good answer, these types of questions are rare and appear only at the very end of the exercises, as "challenge exercises." In my group worksheet, there are some examples of opportunities for student writing as part of describing what properties they've discovered about inverse functions.

Indeed, Marion's worksheet includes several opportunities for students to explain their results.

So far this book has presented practical methods for observing and analyzing lessons, both yours and others', and techniques for documenting your learning and your experiences. This approach entails a great deal of reflection, introspection, and hard work. You certainly have the right to question whether this approach really works. The next chapter provides the evidence. It describes case studies in which we have documented the impact of this approach on the teacher preparation of some of our student teachers.

Part III

Evidence—The Model in Action

8 Case Studies of the Model in Action
Five Cases

The fundamental premise of this book is that teachers' classroom practices and their underlying cognitions must be predominantly student centered for students to learn mathematics with understanding. In the preceding chapters, we described the development and use of our model as a way to understand and appreciate the complexity of student-centered teaching. This chapter consists of five case studies that show various issues and concerns that arise when student teachers engage in the process of reflection and self-assessment about their cognitions and instructional practices. For the student teachers, Maria, Iris, Mindy, Elizabeth, and Kyungso, we describe their experiences and their professional growth by organizing their comments under the following headings: Identifying the Problem, Owning the Problem and Searching for Resolution, and Growth in Self-Understanding. Furthermore, we include a commentary section to share our own analysis of the student teachers' experiences and to suggest probable trajectories for their progress in becoming student-centered professionals. As you read the comments of these student teachers, watch for the unspoken contradictions in what they say and what they do, feel their emotional struggles as they try to make their practice consistent with their cognitions, and share in their breakthrough moments when they confront and seek resolution of acknowledged problems. In shadowing their experiences, you get a glimpse of the complexity of the dynamic interplay between goals, knowledge, and beliefs and classroom practice and an appreciation of what it takes to understand one's own teaching.

The Case of Maria: How Knowledge and Beliefs Affect Discourse

Maria's use of the model helped her change her questioning style from overusing chorus responses to calling on individual students and thereby increasing the level of student involvement in her classes. The reflective writing required by the model helped Maria to identify explicitly the contradictions between the advice of her cooperating teacher and that of her college supervisor. The writing forced her to confront the conflicts between what she felt comfortable doing and what she was learning about questioning techniques in her college course. Furthermore, the model helped her acknowledge that her conflict was between her knowledge and her beliefs. When she considered the fact that chorus responses filtered out wrong answers and allowed her to hear only correct answers, she recognized that her beliefs about the value of chorus responses had to be reconsidered.

Maria can be described as a self-made woman. She received most of her high school education in Puerto Rico, and despite her later-recognized gift for mathematics, she graduated with few credits in the subject. She came to the United States with three children, no husband, no job, and little money but with a strong desire to learn and to attend college. After getting A+'s in several mathematics courses, her desire to teach mathematics emerged. "I knew that with my mathematics background, I wanted to teach kids. I am a young Puerto Rican mother who has been there, done that, and I'm good at mathematics. I hope I can reach some of these New York City kids in ways other teachers cannot." It was clear from the start that Maria's focus was connecting to her students. At the beginning of the semester, Maria wrote in her journal that she "was very nervous and scared of how the class would take to me." It is interesting to see how her concerns about her relationship with her students influenced the nature and quality of her discourse with them, which may have negatively affected their learning.

Identifying the Problem

In the first visit from the supervisor, Maria conducted what might be called a "chalk-and-talk" lesson. In keeping with that, the only questioning technique she used was to ask a question and then accept the answer that the whole class called out—the chorus response.

Owning the Problem and Searching for Resolution

In her written postlesson thoughts and after conferencing with her supervisor, Maria understood why the chorus response was not the best approach: "I was told that the chorus responses had to go. I was so happy to be getting so many good responses that I wasn't even concerned over this. But I realize that some students are being left out. This will be another goal of mine; to get the kids to not call out!" Although she specified this as her goal, she did not explain how she was going to accomplish it. That is, she gave no specific plans for how to prevent the students from calling out their answers. In response to Maria's postlesson thoughts, the supervisor requested that Maria think about a definite strategy for inhibiting students from calling out. It is not surprising that in her second observation 2 weeks later, the chorus response was still evident. In her prelesson thoughts, Maria again made no mention of her plans for changing her questioning techniques. At the postlesson conference, Maria was aware that the students were still calling out, but as she later explained in her postlesson thoughts,

> I was not aware of how many questions I answered myself or the way I led the class into giving me the answers I wanted. I was not aware of how many students were being left out of the lesson because of the chorus responses. ... At first I didn't believe, really, that chorus responses were always wrong.

My cooperating teacher does it, and I thought, I'm glad someone is responding. I now feel this is wrong, and I'm not just saying this. I know that as a result of chorus responses some students are lying back and not participating because there is no need to.

Maria's postlesson thoughts for her second observation included a method for how she would eliminate the chorus responses:

Before asking a question, I will tell the students to raise their hands. I will raise my hand, and I will respond to those students who have raised their hands. I also will try to wait after I ask a question so that the class has time to think about it, and hopefully I'll see more hands and new hands. Also, on some days I am going to concentrate on calling on certain areas of the class so that as I alternate areas, all students will be involved.

Maria's specific ideas for ways to change her questioning style convinced the supervisor that the next observation would reveal a change. And sure enough, there was.

Although Maria did not mention anything about changing her discourse in the prelesson thoughts of her third observation, her supervisor noted a big change in her instructional practice. In fact, she did all that she said she planned to do in the postlesson thoughts of her previous lesson. That is, before asking a question, she reminded the students to raise their hands before answering. As a reminder to students, after asking a question, she would raise her own hand. In her postlesson thoughts, she revealed what was impeding her efforts to change and what finally convinced her of the need to put an end to the chorus response. Apparently, her cooperating teacher was supporting her use of the chorus response.

The cooperating teacher stated to me how we are just content with the fact that the class is responding and not to worry about it. As a new teacher, that hit the nail on the head for me. I was so happy the class was answering my questions that I didn't want to stop. Besides, my cooperating teacher teaches this way all the time. So, I decided, why change something that was going so well?

Maria then shared with another student teacher how in her observations she kept being told to eliminate the chorus response and how she was reluctant to do it. The student teacher's response made a big impression on Maria, who related the story as follows: "Then one day I was speaking to another student teacher. I told her what had happened at my conference after the observation and about my decision that I was happy that at least the kids were responding to me. She then asked, 'So you hear only the right answers?' This really made me think. Did she have a point? Was I listening only to the answers that I wanted to hear?"

Growth in Self-Understanding

In evaluating her learning experiences, Maria commented on the impact the supervisor made when confronting her true beliefs about encouraging chorus responses from her students:

> At the conference, the supervisor saw right through my BS about having to change my chorus responses. She knew I really wasn't going to try to change this because I really didn't believe yet that I had to. She opened my eyes some more. I saw how chorus responses only cheated the students from actually learning. I have since tried to change the chorus response in my classes. But one major hurdle that I still have is that I observe only my cooperating teacher and am with her all the while I am at school. See, she has chorus response in her class all the time, and I get used to hearing it to the point that I don't notice it unless I remember to.

Commentary

Through the use of the model, the supervisor was able to help Maria work through the contradictions between her knowledge and her beliefs about best pedagogical approaches. Furthermore, by putting these issues in writing, Maria was able to alert the supervisor to the contradictory messages she was getting from her cooperating teacher and the supervisor. Through Maria's writing, the supervisor was able to help her focus on the most important question: When the children were responding in chorus, how was it contributing to their learning? Only if she truly believed that most students were not getting the chance to think and that the wrong answers were going unnoticed would she be able to accomplish the difficult task of changing a routine that was set for her by the cooperating teacher.

Because Maria experienced such extensive focus on this problem and exhibited clear awareness, we can reasonably expect that when she is no longer under the guidance of her cooperating teacher, she will blossom into the student-centered teacher she wants to be.

The Case of Iris: Difficulty in Monitoring and Regulating Instruction

Iris's use of the model helped her change from being unresponsive to student input to conducting lessons that were dependent on student input. The writing activities required by the model served as a vehicle through which she could acknowledge her own insecurities about deviating from her lesson plan. The structured postlesson conferences and postlesson written reports enabled her to articulate a compelling rationale for using student input as a means for understanding the thinking of her students, which served as her motivation to overcome her difficulties with what she called "thinking on your feet."

Iris had worked in finance for several years before deciding to be a teacher. She was overwhelmed by fear when she first began student teaching. Here is what she wrote in her journal toward the end of the semester:

> I think I felt that way because the shock was considerable. My expectations of doing well from day one were high. I had wonderful training, knowledge of mathematics, and love of children and learning, with good human relation skills. There should have been no reason why I wouldn't walk in and be a good teacher from the beginning. I did not account for the nerves, the stage fright, the questioning, and the idea of thinking on your feet. I mistakenly thought these and many more aspects of teaching would be second nature to me.

As it turned out, Iris's neglect of this very important concept in teaching—thinking on your feet—contributed in no small way to her early difficulties in the classroom.

Identifying the Problem

Observation of the first lesson by the supervisor revealed that Iris tended to ignore students' incorrect answers. During the postlesson conference, the supervisor discussed with her the importance of monitoring student understanding and regulating her instruction during the course of the lesson—thinking on your feet. In the second observation, there was still no change in Iris's classroom behavior. She continued to ignore student input. During the postlesson conference, the supervisor again made a point of stressing the need to monitor student understanding by carefully listening to students' ideas and regulating the instruction accordingly.

Owning the Problem and Searching for Resolution

This time the postlesson conference made an impact on Iris. She admitted the following in her postlesson thoughts: "I also need to value students' ideas more and to follow their ideas and not mine. An example of this was when Annie asked to show what she found on line symmetry, I showed them what I found instead. When students came up with their own ideas, I was reluctant to go with them—partly because of my insecurities and partly because I am afraid to go off the beaten track of my lesson plans."

During the third observation, Iris began encouraging students to express their ideas, whether they were correct or not. In fact she designed a lesson on the intersections of loci that was totally dependent on student input. She told students that they were to embark on a treasure hunt in the classroom. Students were required to work in small groups, draw diagrams on the chalkboard, and come up with different ideas for where the treasure was hidden. Contrary to her other lessons, in this lesson plan she indicated how the main ideas would come from the students. In the development section, she wrote, "Have a student come to the chalkboard to draw the diagram of the room. … Break students into groups and then have one student from the group come up and explain how to do the problem. ... Have a student summarize how to find the intersection of loci." In her written postlesson reflections, she indicated her commitment to understanding the thinking of her students: "I should have had the student come to the board to explain her work; first, because the other students would be able to hear the student more clearly. Then second, because the student is the better person to explain how she came to the conclusion than I am at guessing how the student was thinking. It also encourages the student to become more of an active member of the class."

Growth in Self-Understanding

By the end of the semester, Iris noticed how much she had improved her interactive classroom behaviors. In her last postlesson written comments, she noted how she monitored the understanding of one student to gauge how to proceed with the lesson. She said, "Rosemarie said she didn't understand. Rosemarie has strong mathematics skills and is also a very conscientious student. So when she didn't understand part of the problem, I knew that other students might have had the same problem. Furthermore, her question pertained to a concept, not a procedure. At this time, I introduced a new and simpler problem aimed at clarifying the concept."

In her final evaluation of herself, Iris indicated that she still needed to focus on the interactive aspects of her teaching. She explained, "I am aware of the continued need for growth and development. The value of students' ideas and thoughts, by listening to them and refining their ideas instead of imposing mine, are all elements of my style I need to develop."

Commentary

As Iris noted in her final reflection, "thinking on your feet," or as we would say, the interactive aspect of teaching, "is a critical aspect of good instruction." During a lesson, teachers must continually assess the understanding of their students to regulate their instruction in ways that will meet their needs. The fact that Iris became aware of and was able to apply these cognitive strategies in the classroom with consistency indicates that she is well on her way to becoming a student-centered professional.

The Case of Mindy: How Beliefs Affect Motivational Tasks

As a result of using the model, Mindy changed her motivational activities from being mere attention getters to being questions that would be of interest to her low-ability students and sustain their desire to learn throughout the lesson. After several unsuccessful attempts to convince her that the tasks she created were not sufficiently motivating for her students, Mindy revealed a clue to her reluctance to change her practice in her postlesson reflections. It appeared that she believed that her choice of tasks provided the kind of motivation that was appropriate for what she felt was a "low-level class." Using the model, Mindy was able to get to the root of her problem: her incomplete knowledge of the meaning of motivation and her beliefs regarding low-ability students.

Mindy entered student teaching after teaching at a religious school for 3 years. She felt that teaching mathematics would be an easy transition to make. At the end of the semester, she expressed this in her journal: "At the very beginning of the student-teaching semester, I thought teaching mathematics would be a breeze. All you had to do was write a lesson, carry it out, and give and grade tests. I felt since I had been teaching for three years, that carrying out the lesson would be simple. I was confident that I felt comfortable in front of the class." Mindy's rather simplistic notions about teaching belied more serious issues concerning her beliefs about students and the effect these beliefs had on their motivation to learn.

Identifying the Problem

In her first observed lesson, Mindy created the following problem for students:

> I went to the doctor last week, and he said I need to be on a diet and am allowed to have only 130 calories for breakfast. This morning I had an English muffin with butter. I know that they totaled 130 calories, but I don't know how many calories are in each of them. For some reason the labels don't tell me the amount, but I need to figure it out! The muffin has $300/x$ calories and the butter has $180/2x$ calories. All I know is that together they total 130 calories, but how many calories does the muffin have and how many calories does the butter have?

Although the problem started off sounding realistic, the algebraic expressions were not based on anything meaningful, and the students were given no reason to want to solve this problem. During the first postlesson conference, the supervisor discussed with Mindy the role of motivation in student learning with understanding and how her choice of the problem was unlikely to sustain student attention and interest.

It was clear from her written postlesson comments that Mindy's ideas about motivation changed only minimally: "I believe that the muffin story was appropriate for this low-level class. It was an attention getter—which is something they need (especially at 7:30 a.m.). For a regular class or an honors class, this story would be inappropriate, as it does not have mathematical validity. Instead, a real-life-related problem, perhaps using conversions, would be more appropriate." Mindy's comments indicate that she has made a distinction between motivation for low-ability students and for high-ability students. In her opinion, meaningless attention getters are sufficient for low-level students.

Mindy's attention-getting approach for low-ability students persisted in her next lesson. In her prelesson thoughts, she wrote, "This class is a low-level class, so the raisin activity should be a good motivational activity for them. They will enjoy it and have fun!" Her deficient understanding of motivation was reflected in the lesson, which had the students counting raisins in a box to learn how to use the stem-and-leaf plot. Although the materials in this lesson did capture students' interest, their true motivational potential was not realized. In the raisin lesson, instead of having students recognize the need to organize data and the value of the stem-and-leaf plot as an easy means of organizing the data, Maria had the students read off the numbers in numerical order and then she plotted them.

Once again, the supervisor discussed with Mindy the weak motivation of the lesson and how she may need to reexamine her beliefs about why she thinks motivation is different for low-ability students. This time an impression appeared to have been made.

Owning the Problem and Searching for Resolution

In her postlesson comments, Mindy surmised that a weak motivation might have contributed only to partial fulfillment of her goals:

> My goals for this lesson were for the students to understand the need for a stem-and-leaf plot and be able to make one and read one. Not all of my goals were accomplished. We never discussed any advantages to the stem-and-leaf plot. Why did we need to learn this? I should have created a need to organize the data. While all the numbers were up on the board in no particular order, I should have asked, "What is the mode?" This would have created some need for organization of the data.

At this point, the supervisor felt more confident that Mindy was gaining a better understanding that motivation goes far beyond mere attention getting.

Growth in Self-Understanding

By the last lesson that Mindy was observed teaching, she demonstrated an improved understanding of motivation. Her lesson involved an extension of the positive integers to the negative integers. In this lesson, although she still used hands-on materials—a long rope that acted as a number line—she focused more attention on creating a motivational question. The problem she presented to students was, "The weather in Alaska in January was –20 degrees Fahrenheit. The next day it was –25 degrees Fahrenheit. Did the temperature get warmer or cooler?"

In her postlesson conference, Mindy was able, on her own, to point out the value of her motivational question. She said that it worked fairly well because at the beginning of the class, the students debated which day was warmer, and by the end of the class, when they returned to the question, they felt satisfied that they had resolved the issue. The supervisor reinforced her satisfaction with the motivation, and Mindy revisited the issue again in her written postlesson thoughts: "The lesson started out with the motivational activity. I had a good motivational question, and it was good that I got back to it. I was very happy that this lesson had a good motivational activity. I have had trouble with the actual motivation in the past, but this lesson shows my improvement."

In her self-evaluation, Mindy again noted the change in her understanding of the role of motivation in student learning:

> Throughout the semester, I have been working hard to correct my weaknesses. The hardest one to correct was my lack of motivation. I am finally getting better at it! I understand the need for all lessons to be motivating. I understand what motivation is. I even understand how to incorporate motivation into a lesson. In my video observation, I had the 5 questions on the board that the students did not know how to solve. This was a void in their knowledge, and therefore the students were motivated to use the chips to solve these problems.

Commentary

Mindy's understanding of the relationship between student knowledge and motivation improved significantly. By the end of the semester, she recognized that toys and silly stories are inadequate methods of motivation for any students, regardless of their ability levels. Providing that she has no other hidden beliefs about low-ability students, she will continue to deepen her understandings of the complexities of motivation for student learning.

The Case of Elizabeth: How Goals Affect the Learning Environment

Elizabeth's use of the model helped her to slow down her fast-paced method of instruction, giving her students a chance to think and giving herself a chance to understand their thinking. In the first postlesson conference, Elizabeth's supervisor asked her to assess whether she accomplished the goals for student understanding that she had outlined in her prelesson thoughts. Recognizing that because she rushed the lesson, she limited student input and was unable to assess student understanding, and she began to realize that her instructional practice needed changing. Through her postlesson thoughts, Elizabeth was able to articulate the necessity of reconsidering her goals for content coverage as a means of creating a learning environment that would support her goals for student understanding.

As a teaching assistant in college, Elizabeth would simply go over homework problems that the students had difficulty doing. Elizabeth explained how she used to rush through explanations to students so that she could cover as many problems as possible in the allotted time. This experience might have contributed to the early difficulties she encountered during student teaching.

Identifying the Problem

In observing Elizabeth's first lesson, the supervisor noticed its very fast pace. Elizabeth pushed things along by constantly saying, "Right? It's logical," and then moving on. During the postlesson conference, the supervisor asked Elizabeth to reevaluate her use of time and consider the benefits of allowing students to investigate incorrect answers.

Owning the Problem and Searching for Resolution

The discussion during the postlesson conference had a big impact on Elizabeth's thinking, as she revealed in her written postlesson thoughts: "One weak point of the lesson was that it was too rushed. I always feel like I am on a timed schedule. Now I see that I can rush all I want, but if the students don't understand, it was wasted time anyway. When I sat back later and thought about it, I realized that they were not ready for the proof at the end. I guess I was trying to fit in too much, and this caused a problem." Based on these comments, the supervisor felt quite certain that the pacing in Elizabeth's next lesson would be noticeably slower. And so it was.

Growth in Self-Understanding

In her next lesson, Elizabeth slowed down the pace of her lesson by allowing time to get adequate feedback from the students and meet their learning needs. Her recognition of the importance of the relationship between use of time and student learning was also evidenced in her prelesson thoughts:

> My goal for the lesson was for the students to understand the ratios that exist in the right triangles and how useful they can be in solving problems. I was hoping to try to introduce it in a way that they wouldn't forget. I know that the students love to be involved and up and around, so I was hoping that by having them role-play being the angles of the triangle that they would get involved and have some fun. I figured that I would try to introduce it slowly, as I need to be gradual with the preparatory classes when I teach them new things. I see a possible difficulty with getting the sides confused, which is why I want to spend a lot of time making sure they understand the differences. I am using this day solely to introduce the ratios and am fairly sure that I will be able to fit in most of my lesson. If I have to sacrifice some of the examples so that they are clear on the ratios, then I will, as their understanding of the ratios is crucial to their success in trig.

In her subsequent lessons, Elizabeth sustained her slower-paced instruction. In her postlesson comments, she again made specific reference to her pacing and was pleased that she gave sufficient time for students to answer questions.

Moreover, she noticed the connection between pacing and monitoring student understanding: "I could see by the looks on their faces if they understood or not, so I had to modify the length of time we spent up there until I was able to see all students were comprehending. I spent a little longer up there than I wanted to. However, it was necessary in order to make sure all students got it."

In her final self-evaluation at the end of the semester, Elizabeth commented on her improvement once more:

> I know that at the beginning of the semester, I really moved at a quick pace; however, I still wanted the students to learn, and wanted to help them. I soon realized after being observed and from [my supervisor's and cooperating teacher's] comments that I can go as fast as I want, but if they are not learning, then I am wasting my time altogether. I also would want a response to a question right away at the beginning of the semester; however, now I tend to ask a question to a student and then just sit on a desk, or something else that will keep me from jumping down their throats. I also have used the "1–Mississippi, 2–Mississippi" method. These are the ways that I keep myself from having too short of a wait time.

Commentary

Elizabeth learned one of the most important lessons about teaching for understanding and made the change to slower-paced student-centered teaching.

The Case of Kyungso: How Beliefs Affect Classroom Practice

Kyungso's use of the model helped him change from a transmission approach to one that promoted more student involvement. The model gave Kyungso many chances to confront explicitly his deeply held beliefs regarding the right way to teach. Having learned mathematics in China, Kyungso was convinced that teaching is synonymous with telling and that learning is synonymous with listening. It was difficult for him to come to terms with the inherent contradiction between his stated goals for his students and his instructional practice. However, through the constant reflection and self-assessment required by the model, Kyungso explicitly identified early signs of change in his interactions with students he was tutoring.

Kyungso had been a computer programmer and made a career change into teaching. His beliefs about teaching mathematics were consistent with a transmission view of learning, as is evidenced in his journal writing at the end of the student-teaching semester:

> At the beginning of the student-teaching semester, my perception of teaching mathematics was rather naïve. I thought that all you needed to do was to think of an interesting problem to get the students motivated in the beginning. Then, just present the lesson pretty much as the textbook has it written. I was

imagining that the students were attentive and asking questions. I love to deal with children, and I love to be the one to provide the correct answers. I had the image of me just teaching and talking for the entire period, like a preacher, with the students absorbing all the knowledge that I impart to them.

Kyungso's deeply held beliefs about the right way to teach made it very difficult for him to explore practices that were more likely to promote student learning of mathematics with understanding.

Identifying the Problem

Kyungso's lesson involved the computation of probability for compound events. In his prelesson comments, he spoke in general terms that suggested superficial knowledge of both the content and his students:

> The goal in this lesson is to help the students to understand the concepts of compound events, independent events, and the counting principle and finally to understand how to use the aforementioned knowledge to compute the probability of compound events. The students had reviewed some of the basics of probability during the previous lesson. In that lesson, the students reviewed the definition of outcome, sample space, and event. They also reviewed the basic rules of probability.
>
> Based on the experience of the previous class, there is, in general, a fair level of interest among the students for the subject matter. Maybe because they were exposed to this matter in their last course, the students seem to be able to pick up on the material without too much difficulty.

Although Kyungso mentioned in his prelesson thoughts that he wanted his students to understand the material, he did not specify what they were finding difficult and how he would help them gain understanding. He suggested that students did not find the material particularly difficult. Because probability is usually a very difficult unit for students, Kyungso's comment indicates that he may not have been monitoring his students' understanding very well, if at all. Furthermore, although Kyungso mentioned several topics, he never discussed any of the details of these topics.

Kyungso's lesson plan consisted of an interesting and potentially motivational problem that required the students to take a multiple-choice quiz consisting of three questions: When is Neil Armstrong's birthday? How long is the Nile River? What is the diameter of Jupiter? The questions had three, four, and two choices, respectively, and the choices were close in value. He outlined a tight script for his lesson:

> I was going to give them the quiz and then prod them to recognize the compound events by asking them if they had noticed any difference between what they did yesterday (rolling a die and spinning the spinner) and what

they are doing now. I was expecting the students to come up with the correct answer—compound events. I would then write the aim. Following the aim, I then planned to ask the class what was needed to find the probability of getting all three questions correct on the quiz. I was expecting the class to reply that we needed to know the sample space. This would have provided the opening to investigate the sample space of this activity. The sample space investigation was to be a tree diagram to provide the necessary clarity. This was to be followed by asking the students for an easier way of getting the sample space—the counting principle. After establishing the counting principle, the plan was then to compute the probability of getting all three quiz questions correct by knowing the number of elements of the compound event or the number of ways that the compound event can take place. As a finale to the lesson, I was going to cover the counting principle with probabilities by asking the students if there is an easier way to compute the probability of the above compound event.

These prelesson thoughts reveal potentially significant problems with this lesson. Kyungso's focus was mostly on what he was going to do, with specific expectations for what the students were going to say. It was not surprising that the lesson did not proceed as Kyungso had envisioned.

The first problem he encountered was with the discourse. After the students took the quiz, one boy yelled out the correct answer to the probability question Kyungso had not yet asked (What is the probability that you will get all of the multiple-choice questions correct?). Kyungso told the student that he was correct, and then he was at a loss for what to do. For the remainder of the lesson he lectured, giving the definition of a compound event and writing out a tree diagram of the sample space for the students. The students were passively taking notes, and the potential motivation of the interesting task was all but lost.

In Kyungso's postlesson conference, the supervisor raised a number of questions for discussion. Kyungso was asked to review his original goals for the lesson and see whether they were met. When he stated that he covered all of the material he planned, he was asked whether he helped the students understand the concepts, as he had stated in his original goals. He said he had tried but wasn't sure whether the students understood. He was asked why he didn't know, and he said, "The class was quiet. It was just my voice." He was then asked about his beliefs regarding the best ways to help students understand. Did he think it was by explaining everything to them as he had done? Through this questioning, Kyungso began to recognize that to help students understand and be able to know whether they understood, he needed to include more informative discourse in the class. He admitted that he would have to "ask more probing questions," that he would have to "hear students explain their answers," and that students would need to "respond to other students' questions." Kyungso was then asked to reconsider his knowledge regarding students. He was asked whether he still thought the students did not have much difficulty with the topic, as he had stated in his prelesson thoughts.

He stated again that the class was very quiet. He was asked to consider the reason for their silence. Did the fact that one student knew the answer to the unasked question at the beginning of the class mean that each of the students in the class knew the answer as well? Even if they knew the answer, did it mean that they understood why that was the answer? Perhaps it was a lucky guess. How would the teacher know if it was a lucky guess?

Kyungso was also asked to examine the nature of the task in which he engaged the students. He thought the quiz was very motivational, but the motivation ended when the student gave the probability. He was asked how he might have maintained the motivation. How could he have sustained the task so that he could develop the other concepts, such as sample space? Kyungso realized that the quietness of the class was a result of the awkward learning environment. He was asked how he might have actively engaged the students. After much questioning, Kyungso suggested that he might have recorded each of the students' answers on the test. This would have helped in developing the idea of sample space and at the same time have engaged each of the students.

Owning the Problem and Searching for Resolution

Needless to say, Kyungso was very disappointed with his lesson, but as his postlesson reflections indicated, he seemed to come to terms with many of the problematic issues of his recently enacted lesson:

> One of the major problems with my lesson was my inability to capitalize on the make-believe quiz to motivate the class to learn the subject matter. My approach was too dry and too inflexible. The class was not motivated. Some students were heard asking what was going on. I was too anxious to get the words *compound event* out of the students' mouths so I could write the aim. Why not stir up enthusiasm by asking the class what is the probability that anyone in the class has answered all three questions correctly? Challenge the class to determine how many students answered all three questions correctly. This should lead naturally into the examination of sample space of the activity. When I did ask that question on sample space, one student answered correctly (not understanding why, however) and I applauded him for the correct answer and then went on to obtain the sample space by doing the tree diagram. I did all the explanation and all the talking. Big mistake! I should have used this opportunity to assess the students as to their understanding of sample space. Instead of applauding the student's answer, I should have asked why and how he arrived at the answer. As a matter of fact, I should have addressed this question to other students to see what they were thinking. I should have asked the students for their answers on the quiz to highlight what sample space is. Ask the students how could we determine the entire sample space. This would have been a better opportunity to ask the students to observe the difference, if any, between the type of sample space in this activity (having three outcomes) and

those that involve rolling a die or spinning a spinner as they had learned in the previous lesson—as a way of introducing the concept of compound event.

In subsequent postlesson conferences, Kyungso's supervisor asked him to reexamine the impact of his teacher-centered approach on students' learning. Because he had very positive experiences in China with learning through listening, it was very difficult for him to give up his transmission approach to teaching. However, after taking a second look at various elements of his lesson—tasks, learning environment, and discourse in light of his stated goals for students—Kyungso realized that his students were not paying attention, much less learning, while he engaged in "chalk and talk." Also, through reflection and self-assessment, Kyungso came to realize that he was not monitoring student understanding sufficiently or regulating his instructional practice to fit the needs of his students.

Growth in Self-Understanding

In Kyungso's final self-evaluation at the end of the semester, it appeared that he had become aware of the negative impact of his teacher-dominated approach to teaching on student learning:

I must get rid of my old habit of tightly following the script of my lesson plan. It is a habit that I still follow in the classroom setting although I am much more aware of it now than before. In a classroom setting, I have got to learn to use the lesson plan only as a guide. I see that I am not assessing the understanding of the students continually. It is interesting that, being aware of my bad habits, I tried to observe my tutoring technique for the past few days. What I have noticed is that I do not make many of the big mistakes as I have done in the classroom setting. During tutoring, I asked a lot of questions to assess the learning level of the students, and I tended to allow the students to learn by prodding them with questions instead of just teaching by talking away.

Commentary

It is encouraging that Kyungso is aware of the negative impact of his beliefs about teaching mathematics on student learning with understanding. Recognition of one's problem is an important first step in the process of self-generated change. With habitual use of reflective and self-assessment strategies with respect to both his cognitions and practice, Kyungso will eventually demonstrate with consistency the kinds of classroom behaviors commensurate with student-centered professionalism.

Conclusion

Learning to teach is a complex process. After reading this book, you must realize that for improvement to occur, you will have to give a lot of thought to both what you do and why you do it. However, there are so many facets of teaching that you won't know where to start or what to do unless you think about your work in a structured manner. The model we present in this book serves as a conceptual basis for the structure you can use to self-assess and reflect on your classroom teaching.

We admit that using this approach is labor intensive for both you and your college supervisor. But only a multidimensional, complex program of study can hope to prepare you adequately for a lifetime career in teaching. In our teacher education program, we have found the model to be a powerful tool for enabling teachers' growth. Perhaps the best evidence of the usefulness of the model comes from the statements made by our student teachers.

At the end of the student-teaching semester, Carol wrote, "Most of the work done as a student teacher was essential for self-awareness. I think by being focused in on pre-lesson and postlesson thoughts, I became able to focus on them subconsciously."

Larisa said, "The fact that we had to write pre- and postlesson thoughts helped me to time and to plan my lessons better. I was also able to identify my goals for the lesson and the particular unit of work and also to see how my ideas and beliefs had changed during the semester."

Elise acknowledged that putting into practice what she learned is very difficult: "I think that focusing on the model for teaching gave me some valuable insight into my teaching. The only problem was that I found it difficult to make the changes I realized were necessary after reflecting on my teaching. Maybe this should come immediately, or maybe it takes years."

Eileen had this to say about the benefits of the model:

> I would like to say that the model for teaching played an important role in my teaching development. I have learned what looks good on paper doesn't always work in a classroom. I have been able to reflect on the reasons why. Sometimes it was just a minor change. Other times there was a fundamental problem, routed deeply in a belief system. I have also been able to evaluate myself. I have seen very sound and wonderful lesson plans gone wrong due solely to my inexperience as a teacher to be able to anticipate, monitor, and regulate. I realize this will come with time and have seen small improvements throughout the semester.

Teaching well is hard. Even if you have a good deal of natural talent, there is a huge amount to learn, and learning takes time. Teachers have "developmental trajectories" in which their skills evolve, moving from talented beginnings to the point where they are truly accomplished professionals (but they *never* stop learning!). The most effective teachers—the ones whose professional growth is the fastest—are those who continually reflect on their teaching, striving to improve it. This book has provided you with the tools you can use for reflecting on your own instructional practice. We cannot say that it will be easy—but it will get easier as you engage in it and make reflection a habitual part of your teaching. Such reflection will ultimately be the key to your teaching expertise.

Appendix A

Research Results of Exploratory Study

Appendix A.1: Summary of Patterns of Lesson Dimensions

Lesson Dimension	Dimension Indicator	Student-Centered Group	Mixed 1 Group	Mixed 2 Group	Teacher-Centered Group
Tasks	Modes of representation	Multiple accurate representations that facilitate content clarity and enable students to connect prior knowledge and skills to the new mathematical situation	S S S	B S	Ineffective and/or inappropriate modes of representation that impede students' efforts to build on their past mathematical understandings
	Motivational strategies	Relevant, interesting tasks integrated throughout lesson	B B B	B B	Tasks unrelated to student interests and/or not aligned with the goals of instruction
	Difficulty level/ sequencing	Tasks challenging yet within reach of students' abilities and sequenced so students can progress in their cumulative understanding	S S S	B B	Tasks often too easy or too difficult for students and illogically sequenced
Learning environment	Social/intellectual climate	Relaxed yet businesslike atmosphere; lesson centered on student in put	S S B	S S	Tense, awkward atmosphere; superficial requests for and use of student input

	Modes of instruction/ pacing	Instructional strategies that support student involvement and allow time for thoughtful student input and exploration of ideas	B B B	B T	Instructional procedures that discourage student participation and paced either too fast to involve students or too slow to maintain interest
	Administrative routines	Effective procedures for organizing and managing the class; students actively involved in the lesson	S S S	S S	Administrative routines are disorderly; students tend to be uninvolved in the work
Discourse	Teacher–student interactions	Teacher shows accepting attitude toward students' ideas and responds in a variety of ways to encourage students to think and reason; students explain and justify their responses	B B T	B T	Teacher judges student responses and resolves questions without student input; students tend to give short responses lacking explanation or justification
	Student–student interactions	Students listen to and respond to each other's ideas and questions	T T T	B B	No interaction between and among students
	Questioning	Variety of levels and types of questions; appropriate wait times	B B T	B T	Low-level, leading questions; inappropriate wait times

Source: Coding method: S = lesson dimensions resembled those of teachers in student-centered group; T = lesson dimensions resembled those of teachers in teacher-centered group; B = lesson dimensions resembled those of teachers in both groups. From "A Cognitive Model for Examining Teachers' Instructional Practice in Mathematics: A Guide for Facilitating Teacher Reflection," by A. F. Artzt and E. Armour-Thomas, 1999, *Educational Studies in Mathematics*, 40(3), p. 231. Copyright © 1999 by Kluwer Academic Publishers. Adapted with kind permission from Kluwer Academic Publishers.

Appendix A.2: Summary of Patterns of Cognitions

Cognition	Component	Student-Centered Group	Mixed 1 Group	Mixed 2 Group	Teacher-Centered Group
Overarching	Knowledge of pupils	Had specific knowledge of students' prior knowledge, abilities, and attitudes	S T S	S T	General and superficial knowledge of students
	Knowledge of content	Viewed content in relation to entire unit and past and future study	S S S	T T	Content viewed in isolation of past and future study
	Knowledge of pedagogy	Anticipated specific areas of difficulty and planned suitable teaching strategies	S S S	T T	Primary focus on time-saving management strategies to cover the content
	Beliefs: Student's role	To think, discover, communicate, and take responsibility for learning	T B T	S S	To stay on task
	Beliefs: Teacher's role	To ask questions that challenge students to think for themselves and interact with one another	T B T	S S	To model how to do problems
	Goals	Focused primarily on conceptual understanding, procedural skills, and appreciation of content	B S B	S T	Primary focus on content coverage and students' procedural skills
Preactive	Lesson planning: Objectives	Focused on problem-solving processes, conceptual meanings, and underlying procedures and results	T T T	B B	Focused on procedures and results

	Lesson planning: Structure	Sequenced problems logically from easy to more difficult; built ideas on students' past knowledge	S S S	B B	Sequenced problems illogically; made large leaps in concepts and gave confusing examples
	Lesson planning:	Integrated initiation, phases development, and closure appropriately	S S S	B B	Content within phases inappropriate in relation to other phases
Interactive	Monitoring	Called on students to increase participation, evaluated understanding, and adjusted instruction	T B T	S S	Called on students to keep them on task
	Regulation	Excluded examples to save time and added examples to increase student understanding	T B T	T B	Made no changes from original plans
Postactive	Evaluation	Evaluated goal accomplishment in terms of student understanding and content coverage	T T T	S S	Evaluated goal accomplishment in terms of content coverage
	Suggestions	Gave ideas for better monitoring of students and clearer and more interesting instructional techniques	T T B	S S	Gave ideas for better time management

Source: Coding method: S = lesson dimensions resembled those of teachers in student-centered group; T = lesson dimensions resembled those of teachers in teacher-centered group; B = lesson dimensions resembled those of teachers in both groups. From "A Cognitive Model for Examining Teachers' Instructional Practice in Mathematics: A Guide for Facilitating Teacher Reflection," by A. F. Artzt and E. Armour-Thomas, 1999, *Educational Studies in Mathematics,* 40(3), p. 232. Copyright © 1999 by Kluwer Academic Publishers. Adapted with kind permission from Kluwer Academic Publishers.

Appendix B

Observation Guidelines

Appendix B.1: Observation 1— Nature of the Content (Tasks)

Before observing the lesson and writing the report, refer to the "nature of mathematics" in your methods text and to the overview and examples related to Observation 1 provided in chapter 5 of this book. Use the following guidelines to prepare the written report.

1. Observe the mathematical content of the lesson from two perspectives:
   a. Examine the accuracy of the content. In your report, record and correct any mathematical errors, misconceptions, or misrepresentations you observed.
   b. The National Council of Teachers of Mathematics (NCTM) Standards (1989) states that one goal for students is that they learn to value mathematics. When teachers believe in and understand the value of mathematics, they can teach in a way that reveals some of the following aspects of the nature of mathematics:

   - Mathematics helps us to understand our environment.
   - Mathematics is the language of science.
   - Mathematics is the study of patterns.
   - Mathematics is a system of abstract ideas.

   i. Describe each time that the teacher explicitly pointed out the value of the mathematics that the students were learning. (For example, the teacher said, "This problem shows how algebra can help us to understand the world around us.")
   ii. Discuss other opportunities the teacher could have used to get the students to appreciate and understand the value of the mathematics they were studying.

2. Based on this observation, make conjectures regarding the teacher's knowledge of mathematics, her or his beliefs about the nature of mathematics, and her or his goals for what the students should learn about mathematics.

Appendix B.2: Observation 2— Questioning (Discourse)

The two parts of this observation require observing two different mathematics classes. The first part focuses on the types of questions the teacher poses to the students. The second part focuses on the interactions between the teacher and the students.

Before observing the lesson and writing the report, refer to "questioning" in your methods text and to the overview and examples related to Observation 2 provided in chapter 5 of this book. Use the following guidelines to prepare the written report.

Part 1

Focus: Teacher's Questions

Two of the goals for students outlined in the NCTM Standards (1989) are that students learn to communicate and reason mathematically. Through effective questioning, teachers can foster such communication and reasoning.

1. Using the Questioning Skills Chart below, keep a tally of the types of questions the teacher asks throughout the lesson. Record divergent questions that resemble those provided in the list at the end of Part 1.
2. In addition to categorizing the type of questions the teacher asks, keep another tally of whether the questions encourage chorus responses, volunteered responses, or teacher-selected responses.
3. Using a watch that has a second hand, keep track of the time between when the teacher asks a question and when he or she receives an answer (i.e., *wait time*). Because the amount of time that the teacher waits after receiving a response from a student can be very critical as well (Breyfogle & Herbel-Eisenmann, 2004), record the *after-answer wait time* also. Calculate the mean for each type of wait time.
4. Based on the data you have recorded, write an overall description of the teacher's questioning style and how it affected the verbal communication that took place in the classroom. Specifically, describe how it affected the verbal participation of each student.
5. Give suggestions for how you feel the questioning could have been improved to maximize student understanding of the lesson.
6. Using the information you have gathered regarding the teacher's questioning of students, make conjectures regarding

a. the teacher's knowledge of the content and knowledge of the students in this class;

b. the teacher's beliefs about students, how they learn mathematics, and their ability to learn the mathematics being taught in this class; and

c. the teacher's goals for the students in this particular lesson.

Questioning Skills Chart

Directions. In the column titled "Cognitive Level," record examples of each type of question you hear during the lesson. In the column titled "Form of Question," keep a tally of each time you hear an example that fits the form.

Cognitive Level	Form of Question
Memory: Factual questions	Overlaid or multiple question *Example:* Which two triangles are congruent and also share a common angle?
	Elliptical question *Example:* How about these two angles?
Convergent: Narrow questions	Yes–no guessing question.
	Ambiguous question *Example:* How does the law of sines differ from the law of cosines?
Divergent: Broad, open-ended questions as suggested in the NCTM Professional Standards (1991)	Whiplash question *Example:* The slope of this line is what?
	Leading question *Example:* Wouldn't you say that triangle ABC is equilateral?
	Teacher centered *Example:* Give me the solution set of the equation.

Responses

Type	Number	Percentage of Total
Chorus		
Volunteered		
Teacher-selected		
Total		

Wait time. For each question posed by the teacher, use a watch that has a second hand and in the table below, record the wait time following the question and the wait time following the response. Calculate and record the mean wait time for both columns.

Question Number	Wait Time in Seconds Following the Question	After-Answer Wait Time in Seconds
1		
2		
3		
4		
5		
…		

Mean wait time: _____   _____

Some Sample Questions (Adapted from NCTM, 1991, pp. 3–4)

1. Helping students work together to make sense of mathematics
   "What do others think about what Janine said?"
   "Why do you agree or disagree?"
   "What is another way to explain the answer?"
   "Ask the rest of the class that question."
   "Explain in your own words what they are saying."
   "How can you convince the rest of us that that makes sense?"
2. Helping students to rely more on themselves to determine whether something is mathematically correct
   "Why do you think that?"
   "Why is that true?"
   "How did you reach that conclusion?"
   "Explain why you think your answer makes sense."
   "How can you make a model to show that?"
3. Helping students learn to reason mathematically
   "How can you show that your method will always work?"

"Do you think that is true for all cases? Why or why not?"
"What might be a counterexample?"
"How could you prove that?"
"What assumptions are you making?"

4. Helping students learn to conjecture, invent, and solve problems
"What would happen if ...? What if not?"
"What pattern do you see?"
"What are some possibilities here?"
"Predict the next one. What would you predict for the last one?"
"How did you think about the problem?"
"What decision do you think he should make?"
"What is alike and what is different about your method of solution and hers?"

5. Helping students to connect mathematics, its ideas, and its applications
"How does this relate to ...?"
"What ideas that we have learned before were useful in solving this problem?"
"Have we ever solved a problem like this one before?"
"What uses of mathematics did you find in the newspaper last night?"
"What is an example of ...?"

Part 2

Classroom discourse can be observed through many different lenses. In the second class you observe, view the discourse by tallying the turns that the teacher and the students take in conversing during the lesson. (See "Typical Classroom Discourse" for the definitions of the different types of turns.) Use the chart below to record the number of turns taken by the teacher and the students.

Turns	Teacher	Student
Initiations		
Request for answer		
Request for explanation		
Responses		
State answer		
Restatements		
Explanations		
Reconceptualizations		
Expansions		
Rephrasing		
Evaluations		

After you have made the tallies, create a bar graph that is a frequency distribution of teacher and student conversational contributions.

1. Write an analysis of the bar graph. What does it tell you about the discourse in the classroom and how does it compare to what is being recommended by the NCTM Standards documents (1989, 1991, 2000)?
2. What conjectures do you have about the teacher's beliefs about the role of the teacher and the student in the discourse that takes place in the class?
3. What suggestions do you have for changing the pattern of discourse to increase student learning?

Typical Classroom Discourse

Initiations

Request for answer. Speaker (i.e., teacher or student) asks another speaker (i.e., teacher or student) to provide specific declarative information without further elaboration. This category, for example, includes yes–no questions and questions about a specific computational result.

Request for explanation. Speaker asks another speaker to elaborate on an answer previously given.

Responses

State answer. Speaker provides information necessary for satisfying a request for an answer (i.e., specific information).

Restatements. Speaker (i.e., teacher or student) repeats verbatim what another speaker said.

Explanations. Justifications or rationales support an answer. Explanations can be statements or a demonstration of a concept using a visual model or a description of procedures, such as an algorithm.

Reconceptualizations

Expansions. Speaker repeats what another speaker said but completes the statement by adding other necessary information.

Rephrasing. Speaker modifies previous utterance, but the meaning of the original statement is preserved.

Evaluations. Speaker makes an explicit statement about the computational accuracy, conceptual correctness, completeness, or relevance of a prior statement.

Figure B2.1 Typical classroom discourse.

Appendix B.3: Observation 3—Motivation and Teaching Strategies (Tasks, Learning Environment, Discourse)

Before observing the lesson and writing the report, refer to "motivation and teaching strategies" in your methods text and to the overview and examples related to Observation 3 provided in chapter 5 of this book. Use the following guidelines to prepare the written report.

1. Describe how the teacher tried to motivate the students to want to learn.
   a. What motivational techniques did the teacher use? What was the motivational question or questions?
   b. What teaching strategies did the teacher use to make the motivational question interesting for the students?
   c. What teaching strategies did the teacher use to maintain student motivation throughout the class period?
   d. What student behavior gave you the impression that the students were indeed motivated to learn?
2. How could the motivation for this lesson have been improved?
   a. What changes, if any, would you make to the motivational technique used by the teacher? What changes, if any, would you make to the motivational question or questions? If there were no motivational questions, what question or questions would you ask?
   b. What changes, if any, would you make to the teaching strategies that were used to improve the motivation? Why do you believe this would help?
   c. What changes, if any, would you make to the teaching strategies that were used to sustain the motivation? Why do you believe this would help?
   d. What types of student behaviors would you look for to be sure that the students were motivated to learn?
3. What are your conjectures about the teacher's beliefs about motivation?
   a. How do you think this teacher would define *motivation*? Do you agree with this definition? Why or why not?
   b. What do you think this teacher believes her or his role is in motivating the students to learn? Why?
   c. What do you think this teacher believes the student's role is in being motivated to learn? Why?

4. What are your conjectures about the teacher's knowledge of her or his students?
   a. What did the motivational and teaching strategies reflect about the teacher's knowledge of the students' abilities?
   b. What did the motivational and teaching strategies reflect about the teacher's knowledge of the students' interests?
   c. How would you assess this teacher's knowledge of the students?

Appendix B.4: Observation 4— Homework (Tasks, Learning Environment, Discourse, Phases, Monitoring, Regulating)

This observation also includes an interview with the teacher to provide insight related to the teacher's philosophy about homework. Before observing the lesson and writing the report, refer to "homework" in your methods text and to the overview and examples related to Observation 4 provided in chapter 5 of this book. Use the following guidelines to prepare the written report.

1. Describe the content of the homework.
   a. Discuss the apparent purpose of this particular homework assignment (i.e., review of previous day's work, motivation for new lesson, etc.).
   b. Was spiraling evident? Describe.
   c. Describe and evaluate the quality and quantity of the problems.
2. Describe the procedure used for going over the homework from the previous day.
   a. During what time period of the class was it reviewed?
   b. How long did it take?
   c. Comment on the efficiency and effectiveness of the homework review.
   d. Suggest ideas for improving the procedure used for reviewing the homework.
3. Describe the procedure used for checking the students' homework.
   a. Was individual work checked?
   b. How many students had their homework examined? When?
   c. What criteria (e.g., accuracy, completeness, neatness) were used for checking the work?
   d. Comment on the efficiency and effectiveness of the homework checking.
   e. Suggest ideas for improving the procedure used for checking the homework.
4. Make conjectures regarding this teacher's underlying cognitions about homework.
   a. What do you think are the teacher's beliefs about the purpose of homework?

   b. How did the homework assignment and method of going over and checking the homework reflect the teacher's knowledge of her or his students?
   Of the content? Of methods? Of pedagogy?
5. Interview the teacher to find out more details about the homework procedures
   that may not have been observable to you. Use the following questions as a
   guide. Write your reactions to the responses of the teacher.
   a. How frequently do you assign homework?
   b. How do you create the assignment? What types of questions are
   assigned? How long are the assignments?
   c. What methods do you like to use to go over the homework? Do you go
   over all of the problems?
   d. Do you check the work that students do on their homework? If so, how?
   Is it graded? If so, what criteria do you use?
   e. Do you ever assign problem-solving projects, research projects, or term
   papers to the students? If so, please describe them.

Appendix B.5: Observation 5—Use of Class Time (Phases, Tasks, Learning Environment, Discourse)

Before observing the lesson and writing the report, refer to "the use of class time" in your methods text and to the overview and examples related to Observation 5 provided in chapter 5 of this book. Use the following guidelines to prepare the written report.

During the Observation

1. Use a watch (preferably with a second hand) to record the classroom activities. Here is a sample of two entries:

   9:00–9:05: Students enter class and open books (5 minutes)

   9:05–9:12: Teacher explains homework from previous night (7 minutes)

   a. Note where the teacher is in the room during each period of time and what she or he is doing.

   b. Note what the majority of the students are doing during each time period.

   c. Note the instructional strategies used by the teacher, such as cooperative learning, students explaining their work at the board, teacher lecturing, and so on.

   d. Note the phase of the lesson: initiation, development, closure.

Postobservation Report

2. Write the lesson plan that you believe best fits the lesson that you have observed. Identify what you believe were the teacher's main objectives of the lesson.

3. Describe how the teacher's use of time and the instructional strategies employed impeded or facilitated the accomplishment of the main objectives of the lesson. Give suggestions for how the use of instructional strategies and use of time could have been changed to accomplish better the goals of the lesson.

4. Describe the effect, if any, on the students of the teacher's movement or lack of movement about the room.

5. Were all three lesson phases present in this lesson? Discuss whether their presence or absence had any discernable effect on this lesson. Give any suggestions you may have for improvement.
6. Describe how the tasks, learning environment, and discourse affected the use of class time in this lesson.
7. On the basis of your observations of how this teacher made use of the class time, make conjectures regarding the teacher's knowledge, beliefs, and goals.

Appendix B.6: Observation 6—Verbal Behavior of Students (Discourse)

Before observing the lesson and writing the report, refer to "discourse" in your methods text and to the overview and examples related to Observation 6 provided in chapter 5 of this book. (Keep in mind that for Observation 7, you should try to revisit the same class with the same teacher conducting a different lesson so that some comparisons can be made.) Use the following guidelines to prepare the written report.

1. Create a seating chart on a piece of blank paper. To the best of your ability, record such characteristics as gender, socioeconomic background, ethnic or cultural differences, or any characteristics that might differentiate one individual from another.
2. Use the Legend for Verbal Flow Observations (see Figure B6.1) to guide you in using the appropriate notation to record the verbal flow of the students. An example of a completed Verbal Interaction Chart can be found in Appendix C.1.
3. In your analysis of the verbal flow you have observed, include responses to the following questions and any other observations you feel are worthwhile.
   a. How many students used their voice during class? Who did and who did not? What was the percentage of students who spoke?
   b. Was there an observable difference between talkers and nontalkers by gender, race, seating pattern, or achievement?
   c. Was there an observable difference between those who were directed to respond, those who always gave correct responses, and those who gave irrelevant responses? (Use same descriptors given previously.)
   d. Did an individual or a small group dominate? Explain.
   e. How did responses, statements, questions, and so on differ?
   f. Was there an observable difference in characteristics between those who talked about the mathematics and those who talked about nonsubject matter?
4. Discuss the tasks, learning environment, and questioning style of the teacher and how you think they affected the verbal behavior you documented.
5. Make a conjecture regarding the following:
   a. the teacher's knowledge of the students in this class;
   b. the teacher's beliefs about specific students or groups of students, how they learn mathematics, and their ability to learn the mathematics being taught in this class; and
   c. the teacher's goals for the students in this particular lesson.

Legend for verbal flow observations

Symbol	*Meaning of Symbol*
1.	Student volunteered a relevant or correct response.
2.	Student volunteered an irrelevant or incorrect response.
3.	Student volunteered a question about content.
4.	Student responded to a teacher question appropriately.
5.	Student responded to a teacher question inappropriately.
6.	Students talked to each other about the subject matter.
7.	Student talked to his or her peer about the subject matter.
8.	Student talked to his or her peer about the subject matter 4 times.
9.	Students talked to each other about non-subject matters.
10.	Students talked to his or her peer about non-subject matter.
11.	Students talked to his or her peer about non-subject matter 3 times.
12.	Students conferred with the teacher.

Figure B6.1   Legend for verbal flow observations.

Appendix B.7: Observation 7— Task Orientation of Students (Tasks, Learning Environment, Discourse)

Try to revisit the same class with the same teacher (conducting a different lesson) that you visited for Observation 6, so that some comparisons can be made. Before observing the lesson and writing the report, refer to sections that address how to develop tasks and activities as well as sections that address classroom management in your methods text and to the overview and examples related to Observation 7 provided in chapter 5 of this book. Use the following guidelines to prepare the written report.

1. Construct a chart resembling the seating pattern of the class, indicating the gender, race, ethnicity, or any identifying characteristics of each individual. If there are no changes in the students' seating arrangement in the class you observed for Observation 6, you may use the same seating chart.
2. Systematically examine the behavior of each student to note whether the students are on task or off task.
3. Write the letter denoting the observed behavior, "O" for on task and "F" for off task, in the box on the seating chart representing that student. Repeat this procedure for each student.
4. Repeat Steps 2 and 3 throughout the period, after which time you will have several numbered and lettered observations noted in each box representing the various students.
5. Before you can adequately analyze task data, it is necessary to do some summarizing. First tally the total number of each observed behavior recorded at each time interval. Then construct a table with the times of observation along the top row. In the next row under each time, record the number of students observed to be on task. In the bottom row under each time, enter the number of students off task. For example,

	10:40	*10:45*	*10:50*	*10:55*
On task	17	20	25	21
Off task	13	10	5	9

6. Using the data from the table, construct a line graph of the on-task behavior. (Use the number of students on the *y*-axis and the time on the *x*-axis.)
7. Using the information in your table, answer the following questions:
   a. How many students were in this class?
   b. How many students started work at the beginning of the lesson? What is the percentage?
   c. How long did it take before everyone was at least prepared to work?
   d. At their most attentive time, how many students were working as the teacher wanted them to? What is the percentage?
   e. At their least attentive time, how many students were working as the teacher wanted them to? What is the percentage?
8. Analyze the data in terms of the following:
   a. the variety of behaviors exhibited;
   b. the relationship between the behaviors and the different phases of the lesson;
   c. the relationship between the behaviors and the tasks, learning environment, and discourse; and
   d. any other interesting relationships you notice.
9. On the basis of your responses to Item 8, suggest ways the teacher might have improved the percentage of on-task behaviors.
10. On the basis of what you observed regarding the task orientation of the students, make conjectures regarding the teacher's knowledge of pedagogy and knowledge of students. What do you think are the teacher's beliefs regarding her or his role in keeping students on task during the lesson?
11. If you had the opportunity to visit the same class that you visited for Observation 6, describe any relationships you noticed between the data you gathered from Observation 6 of this class and the data you gathered from this observation. You may state these relationships regarding individual student's behaviors or the behaviors of the class as a whole.

Appendix B.8: Observation 8—Assessment (Monitoring and Regulating)

This assignment has two parts. For the first part you will focus on one teacher's use of questioning to assess students' understandings. For the second part, if possible, you will interview the teachers you observe to inquire about their assessment philosophy and strategies.

Prior to observing the lesson and writing the report, refer to the section that discusses assessment strategies in your methods text and to the overview and examples related to Observation 8 provided in chapter 5 of this book. Use the following guidelines to prepare the written report.

Part 1

Examine the questioning and responses of both teachers and students. That is, when a teacher asks a question, what is she or he trying to assess? When a student responds to the question, what assessment of student understanding can the teacher make? How does the teacher use the feedback obtained from student responses? When a student asks a question, what evaluative judgment can the teacher make? How does the teacher use that feedback to improve instruction?

1. Record any episodes of discourse that reveal how a teacher assesses during instruction, and show how the teacher used this assessment to alter the instruction. Try to include at least five examples.
2. On the basis of the assessment, record any missed opportunities for making changes to the lesson you notice the teacher might have made. How would you have changed the lesson at that point? Justify.
3. On the basis of what you notice about the assessments that can be made of student understanding in this lesson and the presence or lack of regulation of the instruction, make conjectures regarding the teacher's knowledge and beliefs about pedagogy. Does the teacher believe it is important to monitor student understanding? If so, does the teacher know what to monitor or when to monitor? Does the teacher know how to change the course of the lesson to adapt to student needs?
4. On the basis of the quality of the ongoing assessment you observe, make conjectures about this teacher's goals. For example, is the teacher's goal just to cover the content or do the goals incorporate student understanding? Comment.

Part 2

1. Interview each of the teachers whom you observe to find out the following information:
   a. What formal methods do they use to assess student understanding (e.g., written exams, quizzes, projects, oral exams, homework, etc.)?
   b. What methods do they use to formulate grades for their students?
2. Report the results of your interviews and write your own reactions to what they said.
3. Based on the information you have gained from the interview, make conjectures about what each teacher believes is of value for students to know, to believe, and to be able to do. That is, what do you think are this teacher's goals for her or his students?

Appendix B.9: Observation 9— Teacher Expectations and Stereotyping (Discourse, Tasks)

This assignment, composed of two parts, is designed to sensitize you to subtle evidences of bias that might exist in the classroom and to heighten your awareness of how beliefs about students can directly affect the nature of the discourse within the classroom. The first part focuses on the teacher's expectations and any evidence of stereotyping or bias revealed in teacher–student interactions or in instructional decisions. The second part focuses on any evidence of stereotyping or biases in the classroom or school environment. You will need a stopwatch or a watch with a second hand for this observation.

Before observing the lesson and writing the report, refer to the sections that discuss teacher expectations and stereotyping in your methods text and to the overview and examples related to Observation 9 provided in chapter 5 of this book. Use the following guidelines to prepare the written report.

Part 1

1. Use a stopwatch to record the discourse that takes place between the teacher and each student in the class by doing the following:
   a. Make a seating chart of the class, indicating any observable characteristics of each student (e.g., gender, race or ethnicity, handicapping condition, language).
   b. Use the abbreviations indicated in the following table to describe the nature of the response the teacher gives to each student.

Teacher Behavior	Symbol
Telling how or doing for	
Solves the problem for the student	T–
Carries out a task or procedure for the student	T–
Gives a student a hint for solving the problem	T+
Provides scaffolding for the student to do the work on her or his own	T+
Wait time	
Waits less than 5 seconds	W–
Waits 5 seconds or more	W+

Teacher Behavior	Symbol
Giving students feedback	
Accepts a student's answer	F+
Praises a student's answer	F+
Corrects a student's answer	F–
Criticizes a student's answer	F–
Rejects a student's answer	F–

    c. Identify patterns of discourse that may have occurred with any specific groups of students.

    d. Make some conjectures regarding this teacher's beliefs about the abilities of certain groups of students. Justify your ideas.

Coding Method

Interaction 1: Telling How or Doing For
– = Solve a problem for a student
– = Carry out a task or procedure for a student
+ = Provide scaffolding to support solving a problem
+ = Encourage students to share ideas for carrying out a task or procedure

Interaction 2: Wait Time
– = Wait time of less than 5 seconds
+ = Wait time of 5 seconds or more

Interaction 3: Giving Students Feedback
+ = Accept a student's answer
+ = Praise a student's answer
– = Correct a student's answer
– = Criticize a student's answer
– = Reject a student's answer

    2. Analyze the problems that are assigned to students. Are there signs of stereotyping? For example, are certain problems geared more toward the interest of boys rather than girls? How are people of different genders, races, or ethnicities pictured in the textbook being used in class?

Part 2

Analyze posters, bulletin boards, and other materials visible in the mathematics classrooms or hallways of the school. How many women and how many men are pictured? How many people of different races or ethnicities are pictured? Are any people with handicapping conditions pictured? How are they described? What are these people doing? Do any of the images or words reveal stereotypes? What do these representations suggest about the beliefs of society in general regarding the abilities of certain groups of people?

Appendix B.10: Observation 10— Culminating Activity

In the previous nine observation assignments, you were asked to note different aspects of teachers' instructional practice and to make conjectures for the underlying teacher cognitions that may have accounted for what you observed. You were specifically asked to critique the tasks, learning environment, and discourse, as well as the teacher's use of phases and monitoring and regulating of instruction. Based on this information, you were asked to consider what the teachers' knowledge, beliefs, and goals were. In this observation, you put together all that you have learned by observing and critiquing all aspects of instruction in one lesson and making conjectures regarding all aspects of the teacher's cognition.

This assignment consists of two parts: (a) a focus on the dimensions of the lesson and dimension indicators (see Table 2.1, chapter 2) and (b) a focus on components of teacher cognitions during the three stages of teaching (see Table 3.1, chapter 3). The report for this assignment should be done in the form of a list, with discussion given for each of the following nine subcategories.

Assessing Instructional Practice

Use the three broad categories you have focused on all semester (i.e., tasks, learning environment, discourse) to assess the instructional practice of the teacher. In addition to focusing on all of the variables outlined in your previous observations, use the nine subcategories identified in the following outline to organize your report.

Tasks

1. *Modes of representation.* Give a description of the symbols, materials, and so on that the teacher used, and evaluate their effectiveness in facilitating content clarity and enabling students to connect their prior knowledge and skills to the new mathematical situation.
2. *Motivational strategies.* Describe the strategies used to capture students' curiosity and assess whether they inspired students to speculate and pursue conjectures about the mathematical concepts. Discuss whether the diversity of student interests was taken into account and whether the substance of the motivation was aligned with the goals and purposes of instruction.
3. *Sequencing and difficulty levels.* Describe the difficulty level of the tasks, how they were sequenced, and evaluate whether they enabled the students to

progress in their cumulative understanding of the content area. Also discuss whether the sequencing facilitated the students' ability to make connections between the ideas they learned in the past to those they were expected to learn in this lesson.

Learning Environment

4. *Social and intellectual climate.* Assess to what degree the teacher established and maintained a positive rapport with and among students by showing respect for and valuing students' ideas and ways of thinking. Also discuss whether the teacher enforced classroom rules and procedures so that the students behaved appropriately.

5. *Modes of instruction and pacing.* Describe the instructional strategies used. Assess how they encouraged and supported student involvement and at the same time supported the attainment of the goals for the lesson. Also discuss whether the teacher provided and structured the time necessary for the students to express themselves and explore mathematical ideas and problems.

6. *Administrative routines.* Describe and assess the procedures used for organization and management of the classroom.

Discourse

7. *Teacher–student interaction.* Assess whether the teacher communicated with students in a nonjudgmental manner and encouraged the participation of each student. Describe whether the teacher required students to give full explanations and justifications or demonstrations orally or in writing. Also determine whether the teacher listened carefully to students' ideas and made appropriate decisions regarding when to offer information, provide clarification, model, lead, and let students grapple with difficulties.

8. *Student–student interaction.* Describe whether and how the teacher encouraged students to listen to, respond to, and question each other so that they could evaluate and, if necessary, discard or revise ideas and take full responsibility for arriving at mathematical conjectures and conclusions.

9. *Questioning.* Assess the questioning style of the teacher and determine whether she or he posed a variety of levels and types of questions using appropriate wait times that elicited, engaged, and challenged students' thinking.

Assessing Teacher Cognitions

Use the categories you have focused on all semester to make conjectures regarding the teacher's cognitions. In addition to focusing on all of the cognitions outlined in your previous observations, use the following categories to organize your report.

Preactive: Overarching Cognitions

1. *Goals.* Describe what you think the teacher's goals were for this lesson. Assess to what degree she or he wanted to help students construct their own meaning so that they would develop conceptual and procedural understanding and would value the mathematics and feel confident in their abilities.

2. *Knowledge of pupils.* Assess to what degree the teacher knew the students' prior knowledge, experiences, abilities, attitudes, and interests.

3. *Knowledge of content.* Assess to what degree the teacher had conceptual and procedural understanding of the content and whether she or he viewed the content in relation to the entire unit and past and future study.

4. *Knowledge of pedagogy.* Assess the teacher's understanding of how students learn mathematics and whether she or he anticipated specific areas of difficulty and planned suitable tasks.

5. *Beliefs about the students' role.* Assess how the teacher viewed the students' role in the classroom. To what degree did she or he view students as active participants in the lesson—students who must think, reason, discover, communicate, and take responsibility for learning?

6. *Beliefs about the content.* Assess what you believe are the teacher's beliefs about the mathematical content. To what degree did she or he view mathematics as an exciting and worthwhile area of study that is a "dynamic and expanding system of connected principles and ideas constructed through exploration and investigation" (NCTM, 1991, p. 133)?

7. *Beliefs about the role of the teacher.* Assess how the teacher viewed her or his role in the classroom. To what degree did she or he view herself or himself as a facilitator of student learning by selecting tasks and asking questions that challenge students to think for themselves and interact with one another?

Interactive Cognitions

8. *Monitoring.* Assess the thoughts you think the teacher had during the course of instruction. For example, to what degree did the teacher observe, listen to, and elicit participation of students to increase participation and assess student learning and disposition toward mathematics for the purpose of adjusting instruction?

9. *Regulating.* Assess to what degree you believe the teacher adapted instruction while teaching based on the information she or he received through monitoring student learning and interest.

Postactive Cognitions

If possible, interview the teacher at the conclusion of the lesson to obtain her or his evaluation of the lesson and how she or he might improve it if she or he were to teach it again. If you complete this interview, you can then evaluate the teacher's postactive cognitions.

10. *Self-assessing.* When the teacher spoke about the lesson, to what degree did she or he assess goal accomplishment in terms of student understanding, and to what degree was it assessed in terms of content coverage?
11. *Reflecting.* After the lesson, did the teacher give any suggestions for ways to improve the lesson? What was the nature of each suggestion? For example, did the teacher suggest ways to monitor students better or use clearer and more interesting instructional techniques?

Appendix B.11: Rubric for Grading the Observation Reports

Rating: 3

- All questions are answered carefully and insightfully, including suggestions for improvement and conjectures made for teachers' cognitions.
- Detailed explanations of the specific classroom events that support the arguments given are provided.
- If appropriate, all coding is done.

Rating: 2

- All questions are answered but only some are answered carefully and some insightfully.
- Only some explanations of the specific classroom events that support the arguments given are detailed.
- If appropriate, all coding is done.

Rating: 1

- Most questions are answered but not enough details are given.
- Very general or no descriptions of supportive classroom events are provided.
- If appropriate, most coding is done.

Rating: 0

- A description of what was observed is provided without answering guideline questions.

Note. Rating equivalencies: 3 = A, 2 = B, 1 = C, 0 = F.

Appendix C

Observation Charts Made by Preservice Teachers

Appendix C.1: Verbal Interaction Chart

Mr. G's class

FRONT OF THE CLASSROOM

F: Female
M: Male

Appendix C.2: Line Graph of On-Task Behaviors

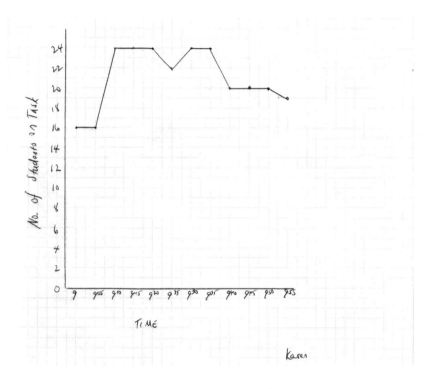

No. of Students on Task

TIME

Karen

	9:00	9:05	9:10	9:15	9:20	9:25	9:30	9:35	9:40	9:45	9:50	9:55
On task	16	16	24	24	24	22	24	24	20	20	20	19
Off task	8	8	0	0	0	2	0	0	4	4	4	5

Appendix C.3: Chart and Line Graph of On-Task Behaviors

Appendix D

Guides and Forms for Supervised Observations

Appendix D.1: Guides for Observation Written Reports and Conferences

You should consider your observation day as a wonderful opportunity for getting feedback on your teaching, sharing ideas, and learning more about yourself as a mathematics teacher. To ensure that you will maximize your learning, we suggest that you follow the following guidelines:

1. *By 5 p.m. the day before your observation.* Send your prelesson thoughts and your lesson plan by e-mail to your college supervisor (any nonelectronic materials can be given to your supervisor the day of the lesson).
2. *After the lesson share your ideas about the lesson.*
   a. Describe your general thoughts about the lesson. Use the following questions as a structure for your comments:
      i. What were your original goals for this lesson?
      ii. How did you plan to accomplish these goals?
      iii. Do you think you accomplished your goals?
      iv. How did what you planned to do compare with what you did?
      v. Explain some of the decisions you made that accounted for the differences.
   b. Give detailed explanations of what occurred during the lesson, the decisions you made while teaching, and your assessment of what you did. To be sure that you address all aspects of your instructional practice, consult Table 2.1 and address the following questions:
      i. Examine the list of suggested ideas for tasks. In terms of the given categories, assess the tasks in which you engaged your students. Discuss the strengths and weaknesses of these tasks. How might they be improved?
      ii. Examine the categories for learning environment. In terms of these categories, assess the learning environment you created in your class. Suggest ways that it might have been improved.
      iii. Examine the list of suggested ways to conduct discourse. Compare your behaviors with those recommended on the list. What accounts for any differences you detect? How might the discourse have been improved?
3. *The supervisor and cooperating teacher discuss what you have said and their ideas about the lesson.* After you have completed your analysis of the lesson, the cooperating teacher and the college supervisor will share their ideas about the lesson, request clarification of issues, and help you think about what new

knowledge you have gained or beliefs that may have changed as a result of teaching the lesson. They may also give suggestions for additional ways to improve the lesson. During this conference it is important that you do the following things:

a. Be sure to take notes so that you will have an accurate and detailed account of the complete discussion.

b. Remember that this is a professional conference about teaching mathematics. To maximize your learning, be open minded about what is discussed, do not take suggestions or criticisms personally, and, above all, *do not be defensive*. On the other hand, be sure that you express any ideas you have, ask questions, and debate interesting issues in a professional manner.

4. *Reflect on and assess the lesson again in your written postlesson activity.* Now that you have engaged in your own reflection and assessment of the lesson with the help of your supervisor and cooperating teacher, it is important that you revisit once again all the ideas that you thought about and discussed. In addition to writing your postlesson thoughts, you should use the following forms to assess the instructional practice of your lesson. (Submit all written documents to your college supervisor by e-mail *no later than 1 week after the observation.*)

a. Self-Assessment of Instructional Practice (Appendix D.4)

b. Postlesson Thoughts and Assessment (Appendix D.3)

c. Revised Lesson Plan (if required)

d. Summary Self-Assessment Form (Appendix D.5)

Appendix D.2: Written Observation Report Before the Lesson

All observations by the college supervisors will be scheduled in advance. By 5 p.m. the day before your scheduled observation, e-mail your prelesson thoughts and your lesson plan to your college supervisor.

Prelesson Thoughts

The purpose of the prelesson thoughts is twofold. First, it is written to give the supervisor the background information needed to understand better the reasons you have for creating and conducting the lesson about to be observed. Second, it is written to heighten your awareness to the variety of issues you should attend to when creating a lesson.

When writing your prelesson thoughts, please attend to the following questions. This should be done *before* you write the final version of your lesson plan.

1. Provide any personal background information that you think is important for the supervisor to be aware of (e.g., conflicts with the cooperating teacher, dilemmas you face, etc.).
2. Describe your goals for students.
3. Describe the knowledge you have of these students (e.g., ability levels, interests) and how you will use that knowledge to shape your lesson.
4. Describe the knowledge you have of the content (e.g., its place in the curriculum, its importance) and how you will use that knowledge to shape your lesson.
5. Describe the knowledge you have of different pedagogical strategies you can use for this lesson and why you are choosing one approach rather than another.
6. Describe the sources you are using to get ideas for this lesson.
7. Describe any difficulties that you are anticipating and how you intend to deal with them should they arise.

All questions are to be answered for each observation. It is expected that you add, modify, or extend the information for each observation. That is, do not simply cut and paste the same text for each observation.

Lesson Plan

Aim, objectives: State the aim of the lesson and list the specific objectives in terms of student performance.

Development: Clearly identify the motivation for the lesson, sequence the tasks logically so as to build on previous student understanding, and use appropriate instructional strategies so that the needs of all students will be addressed. Identify how the students will be actively involved in constructing ideas in the lesson.

Summary: The summary assesses the degree to which the objectives for student learning were accomplished.

Appendix D.3: Written Observation Report After the Lesson

Postlesson Thoughts and Assessment

Some of the most important learning comes from reflections about lessons already taught. It is important to use both good and bad experiences to your advantage. Write a report about what you learned from your teaching experience and from the postlesson conference. Try to address each of the following questions as well as any other issues that you would like to discuss.

1. *Goals.* Consider your original goals for the lesson. Did you accomplish these goals? How do you know?
2. *Knowledge.* Describe what new ideas you may have learned about the content, students, or best ways of teaching the lesson.
3. *Beliefs.* Describe what beliefs you had about the content, students, or best ways of teaching the lesson that changed in some way.
4. *Monitoring and regulating.* What are some of the thoughts you had during the lesson that caused you to make the decisions you made?
5. *Evaluating and suggesting*
   a. How well do you feel you evaluated the lesson at the postlesson conference?
   b. If you were to teach this lesson again, what would you do differently? Why?
   c. According to the new knowledge you have gained regarding this lesson and the feedback you have received, if you believe it is necessary, please submit a revised lesson plan.
6. *Summary Self-Assessment Form*
   a. Complete the cover sheet of the Summary Self-Assessment Form.
   b. Complete the check sheet of the Self-Assessment of Instructional Practice.
   c. Justification and explanation of the ratings on the Self-Assessment of Instructional Practice are to be included in the postlesson thoughts section of the report.

Rubric for the Postlesson Written Report and Conference Analysis

Observation Report Component (Point Value)	Target Response
Prelesson thoughts (10 points)	All questions are answered clearly and thoroughly. Each successive observation is updated, showing evidence of new information about the students and the setting.
(Revised) lesson plan (15 points)	The lesson plan reflects all of the suggested changes made at the time of the postlesson conference. The aim and objectives of the lesson are clearly stated using an appropriate format. The motivation creates a need to learn that permeates the lesson. The development is coherent so that the mathematical ideas are developed in a logical and sequential manner. The summary is structured to enable the teacher to assess whether the objectives for student learning have been accomplished. (If the original plan needed revisions, then the revised plan is what is graded; otherwise, the original plan is graded.)
Overall teaching performance (10 points)	The implementation of the lesson plan (a) reflected an environment that promoted student-centered instruction, (b) incorporated worthwhile mathematical tasks and technology that motivated students and challenged their thinking, and (c) highlighted discourse that involved students in explaining, questioning, and responding to important mathematical ideas, all of which reflected goals that addressed and contributed to students' mathematical, social, psychological, and emotional needs and development.
Postlesson Thoughts and Assessment and Self-Assessment of Instructional Practice Form (40 points)	All six items of the Postlesson Thoughts and Assessment are described clearly and thoroughly. All of the elements of the lesson that were critiqued at the postlesson conference are addressed accurately and in detail. Evidence of knowledge about and interest in continual improvement is presented.
Summary Self-Assessment Form (10 points)	The main strong points and areas for improvement are clearly and accurately summarized in keeping with the ideas discussed at the postlesson conference.
Conference analysis (15 points)	All dimensions of the lesson (i.e., tasks, learning environment, discourse) are clearly and accurately assessed with supportive evidence.

Points are deducted for each item that is either not clearly explained, inaccurate, too general, or missing completely.

Grade Equivalencies

A+: 97–100	B+: 87–89	C+: 77–79	D+: 67–69
A: 93–96	B: 83–86	C: 73–76	D: 60–66
A–: 90–92	B–: 80–82	C–: 70–72	F: 0–59

Appendix D.4: Self-Assessment of Instructional Practice

Name _____

Indicators	Evaluation				Justifications
	N/O	*1*	*2*	*3*	
Tasks					
Modes of representation					
Motivational strategies					
Sequencing/difficulty level					
Learning environment					
Social/intellectual climate					
Modes of instruction/pacing					
Administrative routines					
Discourse					
Teacher–student interactions					
Student–student interactions					
Questioning					

Evaluation Scale: Use Table 2.1 for a description of the indicators. 3 = commendable, if strong presence of indicator; 2 = satisfactory, if indicator is somewhat present; 1 = needs attention, if there is no presence of indicator; N/O = not observed or not applicable.

Appendix D.5: Summary Self-Assessment Form

Name: _____ School: _____

Observation number: _____ Co-op teacher: _____

Grade: _____ Class/group ability: _____

Lesson: _____

Date: _____

Strong points of lesson:

1. _____

_____

2. _____

_____

3. _____

_____

Areas for improvement:

1. _____

_____

2. _____

_____

3. _____

_____

Student's signature _____

Supervisor's signature _____

Appendix D.6: Evaluation of Teacher Cognitions

Name _____

Indicators	Evaluation				Comments
	N/O	1	2	3	
Preactive					
Goals					
Knowledge					
Pupils					
Content					
Pedagogy					
Lesson plan					
Aim, objectives					
Development					
Summary					
Conference analysis					
Postactive					
Written evaluation of lesson after the conference					
Suggestions for revision					

Evaluation Scale: Use Table 2.1 for a description of the indicators. 3 = commendable, if strong presence of indicator; 2 = satisfactory, if indicator is somewhat present; 1 = needs attention, if there is no presence of indicator; N/O = not observed or not applicable.

Appendix D.7: Videotaped Lesson—Final Conference

Before the end of the semester, make a final videotape of a lesson that you teach as part of your student-teaching requirements. Use this tape to

- demonstrate your ability to reflect on and assess your own lesson and your own cognitions,
- identify aspects of the tape that you can share with your supervisor that will exemplify what you have described in your written documents, and
- document areas in which you have changed based on previous videotapes.

The specific directions are listed below.

Part 1

Self-Assessment of Videotaped Lesson

1. Write your prelesson thoughts for the lesson you plan to videotape (see Appendix D.2).
2. Write your lesson plan.
3. Videotape your lesson.
4. After you view the videotape of your lesson, complete the Self-Assessment of Instructional Practice form, write your postlesson thoughts and assessment, and complete the Summary Self-Assessment Form (see Appendixes D.4, D.3, and D.5, respectively).
5. Evaluate your own cognitions by filling out the form that your supervisor usually completes: Evaluation of Teacher Cognitions (see Appendix D.6).

Part 2

Reviewing the Videotape With Your Supervisor

6. To prepare for the conference with your supervisor, locate specific points in your videotape that illustrate the most important points of your postlesson thoughts. Remember, both strong and weak points are equally important to point out. Decision-making points are essential to identify. The more organized you are, the better the conference will be. Write the time, code number, or section of the tape for each teaching episode you wish to discuss, and write your comments beside that identifying information.

Part 3

Assessing Your Professional Growth by Comparing Past and Present Videotapes

7. Select an aspect of your teaching that you believe improved over the course of the semester and that you can document by showing "before and after" video examples. Write a few paragraphs that discuss what you believe contributed to your improvement. For example, discuss how any of your beliefs or knowledge might have changed and what caused them to change.

Appendix E

Portfolio Assignment and Rubrics

Appendix E.1: Portfolio Guidelines

Using a Portfolio to Document How You Engage in Self-Assessment and Reflection

Portfolios can be used for many purposes, some more practical than others. For example, you may want to use it for professional purposes. Today it is not unusual to be asked for a portfolio when you apply for a teaching position. Furthermore, portfolios are required for National Board Certification. Or you may want to use it for personal use, as a means of documenting your professional growth and collecting the best pieces of your work for future reference.

The portfolio may be arranged in any format you like. However, it must address the following questions and include documents that clearly support your claims.

Knowledge
How has this course and the experiences you have had affected your *knowledge* of
    a. mathematics?
    b. how you and other students learn mathematics?
    c. the most effective ways to teach mathematics?

Beliefs
How has this course and the experiences you have had affected your *beliefs* about
    a. the nature of mathematics?
    b. yourself as a student of mathematics?
    c. how you or other students learn mathematics?
    d. the role of the mathematics teacher?

Goals
How has this course and the experiences you have had affected your *goals* with regard to
    a. what type of teacher you want to be?
    b. what you want your students to learn?

Please be aware that to create a portfolio that, at a minimum, addresses these questions, you must do a great deal of writing. This portfolio is far more than just a collection of all of your notes and papers. It requires careful analyses of all your work, critical arrangements of these works, and extensive written analyses of how these works address the questions above.

The portfolio will be assessed based on its organization, the written justification and rationales, the best five of your observations, the best five of your homework assignments, and other relevant written documents.

The purpose of this portfolio is to gather a representative sample of your work as a teacher. In line with the philosophy that a teacher is a professional, each piece in the portfolio must be carefully designed, implemented, critiqued, and, if appropriate, improved. In the past, student teachers have brought these portfolios to their job interviews. The idea is to prepare a portfolio that will represent you and that you will take pride in.

The portfolio will have five sections: (1) Lesson Plans, (2) Unit Plan, (3) Homework Assignments for One Week and Special Project, (4) Assessment Instruments, and (5) Peer Observation Report. Each section contains a suggested grading rubric. Specific instructions follow.

Appendix E.2: Three Sample Lesson Plans

Submit *three* lesson plans that you have used as a basis for lessons you implemented this semester. You may use lesson plans from your observations or your unit plan (see Appendix E.6), *only if* they exemplify appropriate use of state-of-the-art strategies, technology, manipulatives, or assessment tools. (One of these plans should be for the final videotape.) For each lesson plan do the following:

1. *Prelesson thoughts.* Describe what you were thinking as you constructed the plan. Explain why you constructed the plan the way you did. (As a guide, use the directions for your prelesson thoughts for the college supervisor visits.)
2. Attach the original lesson plan, in-class activity, and sample of student work.
3. *Postlesson thoughts.* Describe the implementation of your plan in the classroom. Did it proceed as you expected? Why or why not? How did you adjust this lesson plan to avoid these difficulties in the future? Explain what went particularly well or poorly in the original plan. (As a guide, use the domains of learning environment, tasks, and discourse to focus your discussion. The ideas on the sheet, Conference Guide in Appendix D.1, should help as well.)
4. When applicable include samples of student work with the lesson plans (i.e., collect student work from the class activities or tasks). A part of the reflections on these assignments will be based on the analysis of the student work. What evidence of understanding do you see in the student work? What misconceptions do these samples of student work indicate? What modifications would you make on subsequent lessons and assessments? Describe how you selected the sample of students' work.

To protect students' privacy, delete students' names from their work before including it with your work.

Rubric for Grading Lesson Plans

Rating: 3

The lesson plan, free of mathematical errors, contains the essential components (either explicitly as in the template used in the methods course or implicitly as in the required format in the student-teaching placement):

- *Aim* formulated as a focus question
- *Objectives* clearly formulated to highlight the essential components of the aim, stated with action verbs

- *Motivation* stated in the form of a problem to launch the lesson
- Logical and sequential *development* of essential concepts and skills that support the objectives; includes pivotal questions as indicators of intended discourse and plans for group work
- *Summary* stated as questions that parallel the objectives and the aim
- *Homework* that spirals past work, reinforces current work, and sets the stage for future work; reflects quality, not quantity

A state-of-the-art lesson plan contains research-based ideas, including *at least one* of the following as appropriate:

- Technology
- Manipulatives
- Real-world applications
- Attention to students with special needs

Rating: 2

The lesson plan, free of mathematical errors, contains most of the essential components as described previously, with two or three elements incomplete (e.g., objectives are not complete or stated with action verbs, the motivation is not in the form of a problem, there are no pivotal questions, the summary is not parallel to the objectives). There is nothing unique about the plan that supports research-based instruction.

Rating: 1

The lesson plan is sloppy, contains mathematical and typographical errors, is missing several essential components as described previously, and has no evidence of research-based ideas.

Note. 3 = A, 2 = B, 1 = C.

Appendix E.3: Assessment— One Quiz and One Unit Exam

Attach a Copy of the Quiz and Samples of Student Work.

1. Describe what you were thinking as you constructed the assessment instrument. That is, give a rationale for the types and number of questions you asked, time allotment, and the way you evaluated them (e.g., point values, grades, etc.). What provisions did you make for students with special needs?
2. How did the responses to the exam compare with what you expected? Explain. Cite specific examples.
3. What modifications did you make?
4. How did you use what you learned to prepare your next sets of lessons?
5. When applicable include samples of student work with the assessments (i.e., collect student work from the quiz or unit exam). A part of the reflections on these assignments will be based on the analysis of the student work. What evidence of understanding do you see in the student work? What misconceptions do these samples of student work indicate? What modifications would you make on subsequent lessons and assessments? Describe how you selected the sample of students' work.

To protect students' privacy, delete students' names from their work before including it with your work.

Rubric for Grading Quiz

Rating: 3

The quiz, employing correct mathematical language and having no mathematical errors, contains the following essential components and characteristics:

- The directions are clear.
- The point value for each item is clearly indicated.
- The presentation of the mathematical content, concepts, and procedures clearly communicates what is being tested.
- The items require students to provide explanations to access the thinking that went into their responses.
- There is at least one open-ended problem, although the entire quiz does not have to be open ended.

- The quiz items tap different levels of students' thinking.
- The layout, font size, and space for student work makes the visual presentation pleasing to the eye (i.e., the items are not too tiny, jumbled, crowded, or messy).

A state-of-the art quiz contains *at least one* of the following:

- Use of technology
- Use of student errors to assess student understanding
- Peer collaboration
- Use of real-world applications
- Attention to students with special needs

Rating: 2

The quiz, employing correct mathematical language and having no mathematical errors, contains most of the essential components as described previously, with one or two elements incomplete (e.g., point value for each item is not clearly identified, quiz items do not tap different levels of students' thinking). There is nothing unique about the quiz that supports a state-of-the-art approach to assessment.

Rating: 1

The quiz is sloppy, contains mathematical and typographical errors, is missing several essential components as described previously, and has no evidence of a state-of-the-art approach to assessment.

Note. 3 = A, 2 = B, 1 = C.

Rubric for Grading Unit Exam

Rating: 3

The unit exam, employing correct mathematical language and having no mathematical errors, contains the following essential components and characteristics:

- The directions are clear.
- The point value for each item is clearly indicated, and there is the opportunity to allot partial credit.
- The presentation of the mathematical content, concepts, and procedures clearly communicates what is being tested.
- The items require students to provide explanations and to show their work as a means to access the thinking that went into their responses.
- There are at least two open-ended problems, although the entire unit exam does not have to be open ended.

- The exam items tap different levels of students' thinking.
- The layout, font size, and space for student work makes the visual presentation pleasing to the eye (i.e., the items are not too tiny, jumbled, crowded, or messy).
- The length is reasonable and within the limits of the targeted class's ability (e.g., it should take 1 teacher minute for every 3 student minutes to answer the questions on the exam).

A state-of-the art unit exam contains *at least one* of the following:

- Use of technology
- Use of student errors to assess student understanding
- Nontraditional problem(s)
- Use of real-world applications
- Attention to students with special needs

Rating: 2

The unit exam, employing correct mathematical language and having no mathematical errors, contains most of the essential components as described previously, with one or two elements incomplete (e.g., point value for each item is not clearly identified, unit exam items do not tap different levels of students' thinking). There is nothing unique about the unit exam that supports a state-of-the-art approach to assessment.

Rating: 1

The unit exam is sloppy, contains mathematical and typographical errors, is missing several essential components as described previously, and has no evidence of a state-of-the-art approach to assessment.

Note. 3 = A, 2 = B, 1 = C.

Appendix E.4: One Week of Homework and a Project

1. Provide 1 week of homework assignments with handouts and samples of student work.
   a. Describe what you were thinking as you constructed these assignments. That is, give a rationale for the types and number of questions you asked.
   b. Describe student responses to these assignments. What proportion of the students was prepared? Describe any interesting responses to open-ended questions you may have asked. How did the language you used to phrase questions affect the types of responses you received from the students?
2. Describe the *project* you designed. Discuss why you assigned it and the quality of the student work you received. Attach the project description sheet and the grading rubric.

To protect students' privacy, delete students' names from their work before including it with your work.

Rubric for Grading 1 Week of Homework

Rating: 3

One week's worth of homework contains the following essential components and characteristics:

- There is evidence of spiraling to build in review of past topics.
- It includes a variety of questions or problems (e.g., short-answer questions, procedural questions, open-ended problems, critical thinking problems).
- The quality of the assigned problems takes precedence over the quantity of assigned problems.
- The problems represent concepts presented in the day's or week's lesson(s).
- The assignment is doable within a reasonable amount of time depending on the students' ability level (e.g., honors class, remedial class).
- The items require students to provide explanations to access the thinking that went into their responses.

- Exam-type questions are included to help prepare students for high-stakes exams.
- If appropriate, the assignment is distributed on three-hole-punched paper so students can insert separate homework sheets in their loose-leaf binders.

A state-of-the art homework assignment contains *at least one* of the following:

- Use of technology
- Use of student errors to assess student understanding
- Use of real-world applications
- Items to launch subsequent lessons
- Problems to support different ability levels, allowing for multiple entries to and multiple exits from assigned problems

Rating: 2

The homework assignment contains most of the essential components as described previously, with one or two elements incomplete (e.g., no variety of questions, compromising quality for quantity, only answers are required). There is nothing unique about the homework assignment that supports a state-of-the-art approach to assigning homework.

Rating: 1

The homework assignment is excessive, lacks coherence, lacks several essential components as described previously, and has no evidence of a state-of-the-art approach to assigning homework.

Note. 3 = A, 2 = B, 1 = C.

Rubric for Grading Project

Rating: 3

The project, employing correct mathematical language and having no mathematical errors, contains the following essential components and characteristics:

- Project description with clear directions
- Grading rubric

The project contains *at least one* of the following state-of-the-art features:

- It connects to other content (e.g., art, social studies, science).
- It is relevant to real life.

- It taps creativity.
- It taps critical thinking.
- It uses technology.
- It offers incentives (e.g., students will select projects for display in hall-way, classroom bulletin board, etc.).

Projects containing more than one of the state-of-the art features are to be rated "3+."

Rating: 2

The project, employing correct mathematical language and having no mathematical errors, contains a description or grading rubric that is not clearly stated. It employs at least one of the state-of-the-art features described previously.

Projects containing more than one of the state-of-the art features are to be rated "2+."

Rating: 1

The project does not have a description or a grading rubric and is missing a state-of-the-art feature described previously.

Note. 3 = A, 2 = B, 1 = C.

Appendix E.5: Peer Observation Report

Arrange to observe another student teacher.

1. Meet before the observation to discuss the class. Choose an area that you are working on (e.g., questioning, tasks, classroom management, motivation, summarizing the lesson) for the observer to focus on.
2. The observer should focus on this area.
3. After the observation, the observer and the teacher should meet to discuss the lesson.
4. The observer will write an observation report giving a clear and detailed description of at least three critical episodes that made an impression on you and what you learned from the experience. Be sure to back up all of your statements with specific examples from the observed lesson.

Rubric for Grading Peer Observation Report

Rating: 3

The peer observation report contains the following essential components and characteristics:

- Identification of focus of observation
- Three critical episodes with specific examples with at least one episode supporting the focus of the observation
- An explanation of what was learned from observing your peer

If supportive documentation (e.g., copy of the task, copy of the seating chart) for any critical episode is included, discussing how it applies to a critical episode, then the rating may be raised to "3+."

Rating: 2

The peer observation report contains most of the essential components as described previously, with one or two elements incomplete (e.g., a specific example missing) or one critical episode missing. An explanation of what was learned is included.

If supportive documentation (e.g., copy of the task, copy of the seating chart) for a critical episode is included, discussing how it applies to a critical episode, then the rating may be raised to "2+."

Rating: 1

The peer observation report is incomplete, with one or two critical episodes missing, specific examples missing, or an explanation of what was learned missing.

Note. 3 = A, 2 = B, 1 = C.

Appendix E.6: Unit Plan

1. As you meet with your cooperating teacher to discuss planning, determine how she or he goes about developing a unit of study.
2. Identify the big mathematical ideas (i.e., the unit objectives) before developing a sequence of lessons. These unit objectives will be part of the overview of the unit (see number 4 below).
3. Develop a sequence of at least four lesson plans that supports the big mathematical ideas.
4. Create a unit exam that is aligned with the objectives of the unit. (If this exam is a state-of-the-art exam, it may be submitted to fulfill the exam assignment.)
5. Prepare an overview of the unit describing where it fits in the sequence of the curriculum. Approximate the number of periods needed to complete each lesson and the entire unit of study.
6. Include resource materials (e.g., videotapes, computer software, Web sites) and a bibliography.

To protect students' privacy, delete students' names from their work before including it with your work.

Rubric for Unit Plan (Without Unit Exam)

Rating: 3

The unit plan, free of mathematical errors, contains an overview, a bibliography, and *at least four lesson plans* that meet the criteria for evaluating lesson plans:

- *Aim* formulated as a focus question
- *Objectives* clearly formulated to highlight the essential components of the aim, stated with action verbs
- *Motivation* stated in the form of a problem to launch the lesson
- Logical and sequential *development* of essential concepts and skills that support the objectives; includes pivotal questions as indicators of intended discourse and plans for group work
- *Summary* stated as questions that parallel the objectives and the aim
- *Homework* that spirals past work, reinforces current work, and sets the stage for future work; reflects quality, not quantity

At least two out of the four lesson plans contain research-based ideas:

- Technology
- Manipulatives
- Real-world applications
- Attention to students with special needs

The ideas contained in the progression of the lesson are cohesive, sequential, and developmental.

Each lesson contains a *homework assignment* that meets the homework assignment criteria:

- There is evidence of spiraling to build in review of past topics.
- It includes a variety of questions or problems (e.g., short-answer questions, procedural questions, open-ended problems, critical thinking problems).
- The quality of the assigned problems takes precedence over the quantity of assigned problems.
- The problems represent concepts presented in the day's or week's lesson(s).
- The assignment is doable within a reasonable amount of time depending on the students' ability level (e.g., honors class, remedial class).
- The items require students to provide explanations to access the thinking that went into their responses.
- Exam-type questions are included to help prepare students for high-stakes exams.
- If appropriate, the assignment is distributed on three-hole-punched paper so students can insert separate homework sheets in their loose-leaf binders.

A state-of-the art homework assignment contains *at least one* of the following:

- Use of technology
- Use of student errors to assess student understanding
- Use of real-world applications
- Items to launch subsequent lessons
- Problems to support different ability levels, allowing for multiple entries to and multiple exits from assigned problems

Rating: 2

The unit plan, free of mathematical errors, contains most of the essential elements as described previously, with two or three elements incomplete (e.g., only three lesson plans are in the unit; there is no overview; there is no bibliography; lesson plans have poorly stated objectives, poor motivational activities, or poor summary questions). One of the four lessons is out of sequence. There is nothing unique about the plan that supports research-based instruction.

Rating: 1

The unit plan is sloppy, contains mathematical and typographical errors, is missing several essential components as described previously, has more than one lesson out of sequence, and has no evidence of research-based ideas.

Note. 3 = A, 2 = B, 1 = C.

Appendix E.7: Portfolio Check Sheet

The portfolio grade will be a compilation of the grades listed in the following table:

Item (Percentage of Portfolio Grade)	Rating (1, 2, or 3)	Percentage of Rating Contributing to the Portfolio Grade
Lesson plan 1 (10%)		
Lesson plan 2 (10%)		
Lesson plan 3 (10%)		
One week of homework (10%)		
Project (10%)		
Quiz (10%)		
Unit plan (10%)		
Unit exam (10%)		
Peer observation report (10%)		
Other (5%)*		
Table of contents and presentation (5%)**		
Total		

* "Other" items may include notes from a professional mathematics conference, articles from newspapers with commentary, and so on.

** "Table of contents and presentation" refers to organization of items and neatness.

References

American Association of University Women. (1992). *How schools shortchange girls.* Washington, DC: American Association of University Women Education Foundation. (ERIC Document Reproduction Service No. ED339674)

Armour-Thomas, E., & Szczesiul, E. (1989). *A review of the knowledge base of the Connecticut Competency Instrument.* Hartford: Connecticut State Department of Education, Bureau of Research and Teacher Assessment.

Artzt, A. F. (1999). A structure to enable preservice teachers of mathematics to reflect on their teaching. *Journal of Mathematics Teacher Education, 2*(2), 143–166.

Artzt, A. F., & Armour-Thomas, E. (1992). Development of a cognitive–metacognitive framework for protocol analysis of mathematical problem solving in small groups. *Cognition and Instruction, 9,* 137–175.

Artzt, A. F., & Armour-Thomas, E. (1998). Mathematics teaching as problem solving: A framework for studying teacher metacognition underlying instructional practice in mathematics. *Instructional Science, 26*(1–2), 5–25.

Artzt, A. F., & Armour-Thomas, E. (1999). A cognitive model for examining teachers' instructional practice in mathematics: A guide for facilitating teacher reflection. *Educational Studies in Mathematics, 40*(3), 211–235.

Artzt, A. F., & Armour-Thomas, E. (2001). Mathematics teaching as problem solving: A framework for studying teacher metacognition underlying instructional practice in mathematics. In H. Hartman (Ed.), *Metacognition in learning and instruction: Theory, research and practice* (pp. 127–148). Dordrecht, The Netherlands: Kluwer.

Artzt, A. F., & Curcio, F. R. (with Sultan, A., & Wachter, T.). (2003). Rethinking secondary mathematics teacher preparation. In D. Kaufman, D. M. Moss, & T. Osborn (Eds.), *Beyond the boundaries: A transdisciplinary approach to learning and teaching* (pp. 69–79). Westport, CT: Praeger.

Ball, D. L. (1990). Prospective elementary and secondary teachers' understanding of division. *Journal for Research in Mathematics Education, 21,* 132–144.

Bartlett, F. C. (1932). *Remembering.* Cambridge: Cambridge University Press.

Borko, H., & Livingston, C. (1989). Cognition and improvisation: Differences in mathematics instruction by expert and novice teachers. *American Educational Research Journal, 26*(4), 473–498.

Borko, H., & Putnam, R. (1996). Learning to teach. In D. C. Berliner & R. C. Calfee (Eds.), *Handbook of educational psychology* (pp. 673–708). New York: Macmillan.

Bossert, S. (1977). Tasks, group management, and teacher control behavior: A study of classroom organization and teacher style. *School Review, 85,* 552–565.

Breyfogle, M. L., & Herbel-Eisenmann, B. A. (2004). Focusing on students' mathematical thinking. *Mathematics Teacher, 97,* 244–247.

Brown, A. L. (1978). Knowing when, where, and how to remember: A problem of metacognition. In R. Glaser (Ed.), *Advances in instructional psychology* (Vol. 1, pp. 77–165). Hillsdale, NJ: Lawrence Erlbaum.

Brown, C. A., & Baird, J. (1993). Inside the teacher: Knowledge, beliefs, and attitudes. In P. S. Wilson (Ed.), *Research ideas for the classroom: High school mathematics* (pp. 245–259). New York: Macmillan.

Brown, C. A., & Borko, H. (1992). Becoming a mathematics teacher. In D. A. Grouws (Ed.), *Handbook of research on mathematics teaching and learning* (pp. 209–239). New York: Macmillan.

Brown, J. S., Collins, A., & Duguid, P. (1989). Situated cognitions and the culture of learning. *Educational Researcher, 18*(1), 32–42.

Campbell, P. B. (1995). Redefining the "girl problem in mathematics." In W. G. Secada, E. Fennema, & L. B. Adajian (Eds.), *New directions for equity in mathematics education* (pp. 225–241). New York: Cambridge University.

Carpenter, T. P., Fennema, E., Franke, M. L., Levi, L., & Empson, S. B. (1999). *Children's mathematics: Cognitively guided instruction*. Portsmouth, NH: Heinemann.

Cazden, C. B. (1986). Classroom discourse. In M. C. Wittrock (Ed.), *Handbook of research on teaching* (pp. 432–463). New York: Macmillan.

Cobb, P. (1986). Contexts, goals, beliefs, and learning mathematics. *For the Learning of Mathematics, 6*(2), 2–9.

Cohen, D. (1990). A revolution in one classroom: The case of Mrs. Oublier. *Education Evaluation and Policy Analysis, 12*(3), 311–329.

Confrey, J. (1990). What constructivism implies for teaching. In R. Davis, C. Maher, & N. Noddings (Eds.), *Journal for Research in Mathematics Education Monograph Number 4: Constructivist views on the teaching and learning of mathematics* (pp. 107–122). Reston, VA: National Council of Teachers of Mathematics.

Cooney, T. J. (1985). A beginning teacher's view of problem solving. *Journal for Research in Mathematics Education, 16*, 324–336.

Cooney, T. J. (1993). On the notion of authority applied to teacher education. In J. R. Becker & B. J. Pence (Eds.), *Proceedings of the fifteenth annual meeting of the North American chapter of the International Group for the Psychology of Mathematics Education* (Vol. 1, pp. 40–46). San Jose, CA: San Jose State University.

Cooney, T. J., & Shealy, B. (1997). On understanding the structure of teachers' beliefs and their relationship to change. In E. Fennema & B. S. Nelson (Eds.), *Mathematics teachers in transition* (pp. 87–110). Mahwah, NJ: Lawrence Erlbaum.

Cooney, T. J., Shealy, B., & Arvold, B. (1998). Conceptualizing belief structures of preservice secondary mathematics teachers. *Journal for Research in Mathematics Education, 29*, 306–333.

Dewey, J. (1933). *How we think: A restatement of the relation of reflective thinking to the educative process*. Boston: D.C. Heath.

Ernest, P. (1989). The knowledge beliefs and attitudes of the mathematics teacher: A model. *Journal of Education for Teaching, 15*(1), 13–33.

Fendel, D., & Resek, D. (with Alper, L., & Fraser, S.). (1997). *Interactive mathematics program: The overland trail*. Berkeley, CA: Key Curriculum Press.

Fennema, E., Carpenter, T. P., Franke, M. L., Levi, L., Jacobs, V. R., & Empson, S. B. (1996). A longitudinal study of learning to use children's thinking in mathematics instruction. *Journal for Research in Mathematics Education, 27*, 403–434.

Fennema, E., Carpenter, T. P., & Peterson, P. L. (1989). Teachers' decision making and cognitively guided instruction: A new paradigm for curriculum development. In N. F. Ellerton & M. A. (Ken) Clements (Eds.), *School mathematics: The challenge to change* (pp. 174–187). Geelong, Victoria, Australia: Deakin University Press.

Fennema, E., & Franke, M.L. (1992). Teachers' knowledge and its impact. In D. Grouws (Ed.), *Handbook of research on mathematics teaching and learning* (pp. 147–164). New York: Macmillan.

Fernandez, C., & Yoshida, M. (2004). *Lesson study: A Japanese approach to improving teaching and learning*. Mahwah, NJ: Lawrence Erlbaum.

Flavell, J. H. (1981). Cognitive monitoring. In W.P. Dickson (Ed.), *Children's oral communication skills* (pp. 35–60). New York: Academic Press.

Fosnot, C. T., & Dolk, M. (2001a). *Young mathematicians at work: Constructing multiplication and division*. Portsmouth, NH: Heinemann.

Fosnot, C. T., & Dolk, M. (2001b). *Young mathematicians at work: Constructing number sense, addition, and subtraction*. Portsmouth, NH: Heinemann.

Franke, M., Fennema, E., & Carpenter, T. P. (1997). Changing teachers: Interactions between beliefs and classroom practice. In E. Fennema & B. S. Nelson (Eds.), *Mathematics teachers in transition* (pp. 255–282). Mahwah, NJ: Lawrence Erlbaum.

Garofalo, J., & Lester, F. K. (1985). Metacognition, cognitive monitoring, and mathematical performance. *Journal for Research in Mathematics Education, 16,* 163–176.

Goldsmith, L., & Schifter, D. (1997). Understanding teachers in transition: Characteristics of a model for developing teachers. In E. Fennema & B. S. Nelson (Eds.), *Mathematics teachers in transition* (pp. 19–54). Mahwah, NJ: Lawrence Erlbaum.

Good, T. L., & Brophy, J. (1995). *Contemporary educational psychology*. New York: Longman.

Greeno, J. G. (1989). A perspective on thinking. *American Psychologist, 44,* 134–141.

Grossman, P., Schoenfeld, A., & Lee, C. (2005). Teaching subject matter. In L. Darling-Hammond & J. Bransford (Eds.), *Preparing teachers for a changing world* (pp. 201–231). San Francisco: Jossey-Bass.

Harris, K. R. (1979). Developing self-regulated learners: The role of private speech and self-instructions. *Educational Psychologist, 25*(1), 35–49.

Hiebert, J. (Ed.). (1986). *Conceptual and procedural knowledge: The case of mathematics.* Hillsdale, NJ: Lawrence Erlbaum.

Hiebert, J., & Carpenter, T. P. (1992). Learning and teaching with understanding. In D. Grouws (Ed.), *Handbook of research on mathematics teaching and learning* (pp. 65–97). New York: Macmillan.

Hill, J., Yinger, R. J., & Robbins, D. (1981, April). *Instructional planning in a developmental preschool*. Paper presented at the annual meeting of the American Educational Research Association, Los Angeles.

Hinsley, D. A., Hayes, J. R., & Simon, H. A. (1977). From words to equation: Meaning and representation in algebra word problems. In M. A. Just & P. A. Carpenter (Eds.), *Cognitive processes in comprehension* (pp. 89–106). Hillsdale, NJ: Lawrence Erlbaum.

Interstate New Teacher Assessment and Support Consortium. (1990). *INTASC standards.* Washington, DC: Council of Chief State School Officers.

Jackson, P. W. (1968). *Life in classrooms.* New York: Holt, Rinehart & Winston.

Jaworski, B. (1994). *Investigating mathematics teaching: A constructivist enquiry.* London: Falmer Press.

Jones, B. F., Palincsar, A. S., Ogle, D. S., & Carr, E. G. (1987). Strategic teaching: A cognitive focus. In B. F. Jones, A. S. Palincsar, D. S. Ogle, & E. G. Carr (Eds.), *Strategic teaching and learning: Cognitive instruction in the content areas* (pp. 33–63). Alexandria, VA: ASCD.

Kemmis, S. (1985). Action research and the politics of reflection. In D. Boud, R. Keogh, & D. Walker (Eds.), *Reflection: Turning experience into learning.* London: Kogan Page.

Klinzing, G., Klinzing-Eurich, G., & Tisher, R. (1985). Higher cognitive behaviors in classroom discourse: Congruencies between questions and pupils' responses. *Australian Journal of Education, 29,* 63–75.

Kounin, J., & Gump, P. (1974). Signal systems of lesson settings and the task-related behavior of pre-school children. *Journal of Educational Psychology, 66,* 554–562.

Lampert, M. L. (1985). How teachers teach. *Harvard Educational Review, 55,* 229–246.

Lampert, M. L. (1986). Knowing, doing, and teaching multiplication. *Cognition and Instruction, 3,* 305–342.

Lappan, G., Fey, J. T., Fitzgerald, W. M., Friel, S.N., & Phillips, E. D. (1998). *Connected Mathematics Project: Stretching and shrinking.* Palo Alto, CA: Dale Seymour.

Leinhardt, G., & Greeno, J. G. (1986). The cognitive skill of teaching. *Journal of Educational Psychology, 78,* 75–95.

Leiva, M. A. (1995). Empowering teachers through the evaluation process. *Mathematics Teacher, 88,* 44–47.

Livingston, C., & Borko, H. (1990). High school mathematics review lessons: Expert–novice distinction. *Journal for Research in Mathematics Education, 21,* 372–387.

Mathematical Sciences Education Board & National Research Council. (1991). *Counting on you: Actions supporting mathematics teaching standards.* Washington, DC: National Academy Press.

National Council of Teachers of Mathematics. (1989). *Curriculum and evaluation standards for school mathematics.* Reston, VA: The Council.

National Council of Teachers of Mathematics. (1991). *Professional standards for teaching mathematics.* Reston, VA: The Council.

National Council of Teachers of Mathematics. (2000). *Principles and standards for school mathematics.* Reston, VA: The Council.

Newell, A. (1980). Physical symbol systems. *Cognitive Science, 4,* 135–183.

Noddings, N. (1990). Constructivism in mathematics education. In R. Davis, C. Maher, & N. Noddings (Eds.), *Journal for Research in Mathematics Education Monograph Number 4: Constructivist views on the teaching and learning of mathematics* (pp. 7–18). Reston, VA: National Council of Teachers of Mathematics.

Oakes, J. (1990). Opportunities, achievement, and choice: Women and minority students in science and mathematics. *Review of Educational Research, 16,* 153–222.

Paris, S. G., & Newman, R. S. (1990). Developing aspects of self-regulated learning. *Educational Psychologist, 25*(1), 87–102.

Perkins, D. N., & Salomon, G. (1989). Are cognitive skills context bound? *Educational Researcher, 18*(1), 16–25.

Peterson, P. L. (1988). Teachers' and students' cognitional knowledge for classroom teaching and learning. *Educational Researcher, 17*(5), 5–14.

Peterson, P. L., Fennema, E., Carpenter, T. P., & Loef, M. (1989). Teachers' pedagogical content beliefs in mathematics. *Cognition and Instruction, 6,* 1–40.

Peterson, P. L., Marx, R. W., & Clark, C. M. (1978). Teacher planning, teacher behavior, and student achievement. *American Educational Research Journal, 15,* 417–432.

Pólya, G. (1945). *How to solve it.* Garden City, NY: Doubleday.

Posamentier, A. S., Smith, B. S., & Stepelman, J. (2006). *Teaching secondary mathematics: Techniques and enrichment units* (7th ed.). Upper Saddle River, NJ: Pearson, Merrill, Prentice Hall.

Richards, J. (1991). Mathematical discussions. In E. von Glasersfeld (Ed.), *Radical constructivism in mathematics education* (pp. 13–51). Dordrecht, the Netherlands: Kluwer.

Rogers, C. (1983). *Freedom to learn: For the 80's.* Columbus, OH: Merrill.

Rogoff, B., & Lave, J. (1984). *Everyday cognition: Its development in social context.* Cambridge, MA: Harvard University Press.

Rowe, M. (1974). Wait-time and rewards as instructional variables. *Journal of Research in Science Teaching, 11,* 81–94.

Rowe, M. (1986). Wait time: Slowing down may be a way of speeding up! *Journal of Teacher Education, 37,* 43–50.

Rumelhart, D. E. (1975). Notes on a schema for stories. In D. B. Bobrow & A. M. Collins (Eds.), *Representation and understanding* (pp. 211–236). New York: Academic Press.

Samson, G., Strykowski, B., Weinstein, T., & Walberg, H. (1987). The effects of teacher questioning levels on student achievement: A quantitative synthesis. *Journal of Educational Research, 80,* 290–295.

Saphier, J., & Gower, R. (1987). *The skillful teacher: Building your teaching skills.* Acton, MA: Better Teaching.

Schifter, D., & Simon, M. A. (1992). Assessing teachers' development of a constructivist view of mathematics learning. *Teaching and Teacher Education, 8*(2), 187–197.

Schoenfeld, A. H. (1987). What's all the fuss about metacognition? In A. H. Schoenfeld (Ed.), *Cognitive science and mathematics education* (pp. 189–215). Hillsdale, NJ: Lawrence Erlbaum.

Schoenfeld, A. H. (1998). Toward a theory of teaching-in-context. *Issues in Education, 4*(1), 1–94.

Schoenfeld, A. H. (2002). A highly interactive discourse structure. In J. Brophy (Ed.), *Social constructivist teaching: Its affordances and constraints* (Vol. 9 of the series Advances in Research on Teaching, pp. 131–170). New York: Elsevier.

Schon, D. A. (1983). *The reflective practitioner: How professionals think in action.* New York: Basic Books.

Schram, P., Wilcox, S., Lappan, G., & Lanier, P. (1989). Changing preservice beliefs about mathematics education. In C. A. Maher, G. A. Goldin, & R. B. Davis (Eds.), *Proceedings of the eleventh annual meeting of the North American chapter of the International Group for the Psychology of Mathematics Education* (pp. 296–302). New Brunswick, NJ: Rutgers University, Center for Mathematics, Science and Computer Education.

Secada, W. G. (1992). Race, equity, social class, language, and achievement in mathematics. In D. Grouws (Ed.), *Handbook of research on mathematics teaching and learning* (pp. 623–660). New York: Macmillan.

Shulman, L. S. (1986). Those who understand: Knowledge growth in teaching. *Educational Researcher, 15,* 4–14.

Silver, E. A. (1985). Research on teaching mathematical problem solving: Some underrepresented themes and needed directions. In E. A. Silver (Ed.), *Teaching and learning mathematical problem solving: Multiple research perspectives* (pp. 247–266). Hillsdale, NJ: Lawrence Erlbaum.

Silver, E. A. (1986). Using conceptual and procedural knowledge: A focus on relationships. In J. Hiebert (Ed.), *Conceptual and procedural knowledge: The case of mathematics* (pp. 181–198). Hillsdale, NJ: Lawrence Erlbaum.

Silver, E. A., & Smith, M. S. (1996). Building discourse communities in mathematics classrooms. In P. C. Elliott (Ed.), *1996 yearbook: Communication in mathematics K-12 and beyond* (pp. 20–28). Reston, VA: National Council of Teachers of Mathematics.

Simon, M. A. (1997). Developing new models of mathematics teaching: An imperative for research on mathematics teacher development. In E. Fennema & B. S. Nelson (Eds.), *Mathematics teachers in transition* (pp. 55–86). Mahwah, NJ: Lawrence Erlbaum.

Sternberg, R. J. (1986). *Intelligence applied: Understanding and increasing your intellectual skills.* New York: Harcourt, Brace, Jovanovich.

Swafford, J. O. (1995). Teacher preparation. In I. M. Carl (Ed.), *Prospects for school mathematics* (pp. 157–174). Reston, VA: National Council of Teachers of Mathematics.

Thompson, A. G. (1991). The development of teachers' conceptions of mathematics teaching. In R. G. Underhill (Ed.), *Proceedings of the thirteenth annual meeting of the North American Chapter of the International Group for the Psychology of Mathematics Education* (Vol. 2, pp. 8–14). Blacksburgh, VA: Virginia Polytechnic Institute.

Thompson, A. G. (1992). Teachers' beliefs and conceptions: A synthesis of the research. In D. Grouws (Ed.), *Handbook of research on mathematics teaching and learning* (pp. 127–146). New York: Macmillan.

Tobin, K. (1983). The influence of wait-time on classroom learning. *European Journal of Science Education, 5*(1), 35–48.

Van de Walle, J. A. (2007). *Elementary and middle school mathematics: Teaching developmentally* (6th ed.). Boston: Pearson Education.

Van Manen, M. (1977). Linking ways of knowing with ways of being practical. *Curriculum Inquiry, 6,* 205–228.

von Glasersfeld, E. (1987). Learning as a constructive activity. In C. Janvier (Ed.), *Problems of representation in the teaching and learning of mathematics* (pp. 3–17). Hillsdale, NJ: Lawrence Erlbaum.

von Glasersfeld, E. (1991). Abstraction, re-presentation, and reflection: An interpretation of experience and Piaget's approach. In L. P. Steffe (Ed.), *Epistemological foundations of mathematical experience* (pp. 45–67). New York: Springer-Verlag.

Vygotsky, L. S. (1978). *Mind in society: The development of higher psychological processes.* Cambridge, MA: Harvard University Press.

Wood, P., Bruner, J., & Ross, G. (1976). The role of tutoring in problem solving. *Journal of Child Psychology and Psychiatry, 17,* 89–100.

Wood, T., Cobb, P., & Yackel, E. (1995). Reflections on learning and teaching mathematics in elementary school. In L. Steffe & J. Gale (Eds.), *Constructivism in education* (pp. 401–422). Hillsdale, NJ: Lawrence Erlbaum.

Zimmerman, B. J. (1990). Self-regulated learning and academic achievement. *Educational Psychologist, 25*(1), 3–17.

Author Index

Subject Index